About the Author

David Levy is an International Chess Master and a prolific chess writer. He became famous in the computer world as a result of a bet, started in 1968, that he would not lose a chess match against a computer program within 10 years – in 1978 he won the bet which then stood at £1,250.

His computing career began at Glasgow University, where he taught Algol programming and Artificial Intelligence during the early 1970s. He is widely regarded as one of the world's leading authorities on computer chess, and is Chairman of a London-based software house which specialises in programming intelligent games.

Available in Century's Science & Technology series

Dictionary of New Information Technology
A. J. MEADOWS, M. GORDON and A. SINGLETON

What to Buy for Business: A Handbook of New Office Technology
JOHN DERRICK and PHILLIP OPPENHEIM

The Electronic Mail Handbook
STEPHEN CONNELL and IAN A. GALBRAITH

The Way the New Technology Works
KEN MARSH

Mind
DAVID A. TAYLOR

Computers and Your Child
RAY HAMMOND

In association with 'Personal Computer World'

Microcomputing for Business: A User's Guide
edited by DICK OLNEY

The Microcomputer Handbook: A Buyer's Guide
edited by DICK OLNEY

The Spectrum Handbook
TIM LANGDELL

35 Programs for the Dragon 32
TIM LANGDELL

The Intimate Machine
NEIL FRUDE

35 Educational Programs for the BBC Micro
IAN MURRAY

Century Computer Programming Course
PETER MORSE and IAN ADAMSON

Information Technology Yearbook
edited by PHILIP HILLS

50 New Programs for the Spectrum
PETER MORSE and IAN ADAMSON

The Word Processing Handbook
SIMON DISMORE

The BASIC into BASIC Handbook
edited by PERSONAL COMPUTER WORLD

Computer Gamesmanship

THE COMPLETE GUIDE TO CREATING AND STRUCTURING GAMES PROGRAMS

DAVID LEVY

CENTURY PUBLISHING
LONDON

First published mostly as articles in 1980, 1981
by *Personal Computer World*

This edition published in Great Britain in 1983
by Century Publishing Co. Ltd,
76 Old Compton Street, London W1V 5PA
in association with *Personal Computer World*

Reprinted 1983

ISBN 0 7126 0015 5

Cover illustration
by Angel Matica/Design by Deadman Stone

Printed in Great Britain by
Butler & Tanner Ltd, Frome, Somerset

Contents

Introduction

Ever since the advent of the electronic computer, man has been fascinated by the idea that a computer can play games of skill. The very word 'skill' implies some form of intelligence, and it is widely assumed that only we humans can exhibit the type of intelligence needed to play games of skill, such as chess, bridge and poker. But it so happens that the type of person who enjoys programming computers is very often the type of person who enjoys playing games of skill, and for this reason there has always been a widespread interest amongst the computing fraternity in the task of programming games of skill.

One might argue that, during the first 30 years or so in the history of computers, when the beasts cost hundreds of thousands or even millions of pounds, it was somewhat frivolous of programmers to squander expensive computer time on tasks such as playing chess. Against this is the scientific aspect of chess programming, namely that in creating a computer program which can perform a task usually associated with human intelligence, one is somehow creating an artificial intellect, and the science of Artificial Intelligence is one which has blossomed during the past decade or two. Another argument in support of those who devoted their efforts to writing chess programs and programs for other games is that, in successfully programming a game in which long-term planning is involved, one would devise techniques which could later be used in programming other aspects of long-term planning, such as economic forecasting.

Now that we are in the 1980s, we fortunately do not need

any more justification for programming games than to say that we do it because it, the programming, and they, the games, are fun! Computing is now so cheap that for £50 (or $100) one can buy one's very own computer, and program it to play almost any game of skill. There is an enormous amount of pleasure and satisfaction to be derived from writing one's own game playing programs, and there is also the more natural pleasure which comes from playing the games themselves – after all, you may like to play gin rummy, but if you have no one at home to play with, your computer can act as a surrogate opponent.

This book, which stems from a series of articles published in various personal computing magazines (*Personal Computer World* – England and Australia; *Creative Computing* – USA; *Data* – Denmark; *Databus* – Netherlands; *L'Ordinateur Individuel* – France), is aimed at those who would like to know how computers play games. The reader may be a programming enthusiast, who would like to write his or her own games playing programs; or a games enthusiast who would like to know how computers can be taught to 'think' like people; or someone who uses a home computer to play games and has a general interest in the subject. I begin by discussing the most elementary principles of programming a computer to play games, and I have placed special emphasis on the particular problems posed by running these programs on a micro-computer. My main aim has been to acquaint the reader with the techniques of games programming so that (s)he will have the confidence and ability to program any intellectual game for a personal computer. Although I have used most of the more popular games of skill as my examples, the same general principles found in this book can be applied to any game of skill in which the computer competes against the user. In the early chapters, I set the reader seven programming tasks, and the serious student will find the implementation of these tasks rewarding.

There should be something in this book for anyone who is

interested in computer games. I have expanded the section on chess, to include a discussion of some unresolved problems in the realm of chess programming, and I have made one or two minor corrections. I very much hope that my readers will enjoy this book, and that many of them will put it to good use and write their own game playing programs.

DAVID LEVY
London, December 1982

CHAPTER 1
First Principles and One-Person Games

Input/output

I/O on a personal computer is often largely a matter of taste, though certain points are worth bearing in mind when writing a game playing program:

1 The output should be easy to follow. You may not think this important, and many programmers take the attitude that if they can understand their output nothing else matters; but how about someone else? If you want to show your program off to a friend it will be so much better received if the output is clear, concise and unambiguous. Remember to output any information that may be helpful, for example in a chess program you should always announce check, checkmate and stalemate. These little touches take hardly any extra effort, and they make your program that much more attractive to another user.

2 If you want to use neat graphics or printout, plan the layout carefully, taking into consideration all possibilities. It's not much use having your bridge program display pretty pictures of the cards if one day you discover that when you are dealt ten cards in a suit only nine of them will fit on to one line and your whole display is messed up.

3 Ensure that the user can easily see whose turn it is to play, and what the last 'move' was. It can be infuriating to leave the computer for a minute or two and then return to find that the program has moved but you do not know what it has done.

4 Make it easy for the user to enter a move and to clear an incorrect move entry.

5 Ensure that the program will reject an illegal, impossible or ambiguous move, or any entry that does not conform to your simple input rules.

One-person games: The 8-puzzle

A one-person game does not involve an opponent. You play against a microcosm of the forces of nature and if you make a mistake it may be possible to recover, and then go on to win. Solving a problem or a puzzle is a good example of a one-person game – when you get near to a solution there is no one to oppose you by suddenly making the problem more difficult. It may seem at first glance that patience games are one-person games, but in fact many patience games do not permit the player any freedom of choice, so the 'game' has no real interest. Once the cards are cut the player either will or will not finish the game, and all of his decisions are made for him by the rules.

A well-known one-person game is the 8-puzzle, in which a 3×3 array of tiles contains the numbers 1 to 8 and an empty space. (The numbers are sometimes replaced by letters.) The player shuffles the tiles and then tries to reach some target position by successively moving tiles into the empty space (see Figure 1).

Here the task is simple, and one way in which the target can be reached from the starting configuration is by moving the tiles in the following order: 3,2,1,4,6,7,8,3,2,1,4,6,7,8,5. With other starting and target configurations the task may be more difficult, and for those who find the 8-puzzle too simple there is always the 15-puzzle, in which a 4×4 array has fifteen tiles and an empty space; then there's the 24-puzzle, the 35-puzzle and the $(n^2 - 1)$-puzzle. In fact there is no

STARTING CONFIGURATION

3		8
2	5	7
1	4	6

TARGET CONFIGURATION

1	2	3
4		5
6	7	8

FIGURE 1

reason, other than tradition, why the puzzles need to be square.

Heuristics and algorithms: Nim

The 8-puzzle is an excellent example of the type of problem that lends itself to solution by heuristic means. Before describing how we should set about programming games of this type, it would be as well to distinguish between the terms 'heuristic' and 'algorithm', which are often misunderstood.

An *algorithm* is a technique for solving a problem (the problem may be finding the best move in some game) if a solution exists. If there is no solution to the problem the algorithm should determine this fact. Thus, an algorithm always works, otherwise it is not an algorithm.

Most interesting games do not have an algorithm solution, at least in the practical sense. Of course there is an algorithm for finding the perfect move in a game of chess – simply examine every possible move for both sides until one player is mated or a draw is established – but since the total number of chess games is greater than the number of atoms in the universe, this algorithm would be somewhat slow in practice. In contrast, however, there does exist a useful algorithm for the interesting game of Nim. Nim is played with a number of piles of objects, often matches, and with various numbers of objects in each pile. The players move alternately, and to make a move a player must remove, from one and only one pile, any number of objects he chooses – from one object to the whole pile. The player who removes the last object loses the game. (In another version of the game the player who takes the last object is the winner.)

In order to win at Nim one need only know the following algorithm, and a few exceptional cases: *If the number of objects in each pile is expressed in binary, and each binary column of numbers is added in decimal (without carrying numbers), then if the decimal totals are all even or zero then the person who is next to move is in a losing position* (see Figure 2).

			binary
Pile A:	1111111	= 7 matches =	111
Pile B:	11111	= 5 matches =	101
Pile C:	111	= 3 matches =	11
Pile D:	1	= 1 match =	1
		totals:	224

FIGURE 2

All three totals are even so whoever moves next will lose, provided that his opponent plays correctly.

There are some obvious exceptions to the rule. For example if piles A, B, C and D each have one match then the player who moves next will win, and the same is true of a position in which there's only one pile of matches, provided that there are at least two matches in this pile.

The existence of this algorithm does not detract from the interest of the game since its implementation is somewhat difficult for a human being, unless the number of piles and the number of matches in each pile is small. But for a computer program the task is trivial. The program considers each move that it can make, taking one match from pile A, two matches from pile A, and so on, and it evaluates each of the resulting positions until it finds one where the decimal totals of the binary columns are all even or zero, whereupon it makes the move leading to that particular solution. Once a candidate move has been rejected it may be thrown away, so RAM is required only for the current situation, the move or decision currently under consideration, and workspace for the binary/decimal calculations. The program tries each move from the current position, and if a move is found to be unsuccessful it is 'unmade', and the next move tried. In this way it is not even necessary to store both the current position and the candidate position – the program can switch to and fro between them by making and unmaking moves, a technique which is useful for saving RAM in a highly restricted memory environment.

One trick to remember for Nim, or any other game with an algorithmic method of play, is this. Should the program find itself in a theoretically losing position, as might happen at the start of the game, it should make the move that leaves its opponent with the most complex decision. In this way the opponent is more likely to make a mistake. In Nim I would suggest that if your program is in a losing position it should remove one match from the largest pile.

A *heuristic* method of solving a problem relies on commonsense techniques for getting closer and closer to the solution, until the solution is actually within sight. A heuristic is therefore a rule of thumb – it will usually help us to find a solution to the problem, but it is not guaranteed to do so. In situations where a heuristic does work, it will often find the solution much faster than any algorithmic method, though some heuristics, for best results, are often employed in conjunction with an algorithm. A frequently used device which makes use of heuristics is the *tree*, and we shall now examine a method of solving the 8-puzzle by use of a tree and a simple heuristic.

Let us return to the starting configuration in Figure 1. We

always refer to the starting configuration, or the point from which the program must move, as the *root* of our tree. Before we can decide which move might be best we must know which moves are possible, i.e. in accordance with the rules of the game. A list of these moves is usually supplied by a subroutine called a *legal move generator*, which may be extremely complex, as in chess, or very simple, as in the 8-puzzle. It is not difficult to see that in our starting configuration there are three tiles which may be moved, 3, 5 and 8. Our legal move generator would determine these moves by examining the elements of the 3 × 3 array which are horizontally or vertically adjacent to the empty space, and there are many simple methods for doing so. We might, for example, store all the legal moves in a table (see Figure 3).

If we number the elements of the array table thus:
123
456
789
our table of moves might look like this:

vacant	*moves*
1	2,4
2	1,3,5
3	2,6
4	1,5,7
etcetera	

FIGURE 3

By knowing which element in the array was vacant the program could immediately list the legal moves. This type of approach is called *table-driven move generation*. It is often the fastest way to generate the moves but for some games it consumes too much program memory for it to be a feasible proposition.

Having generated the moves 3, 5 and 8 from our starting configuration, we can now begin to see the tree grow.

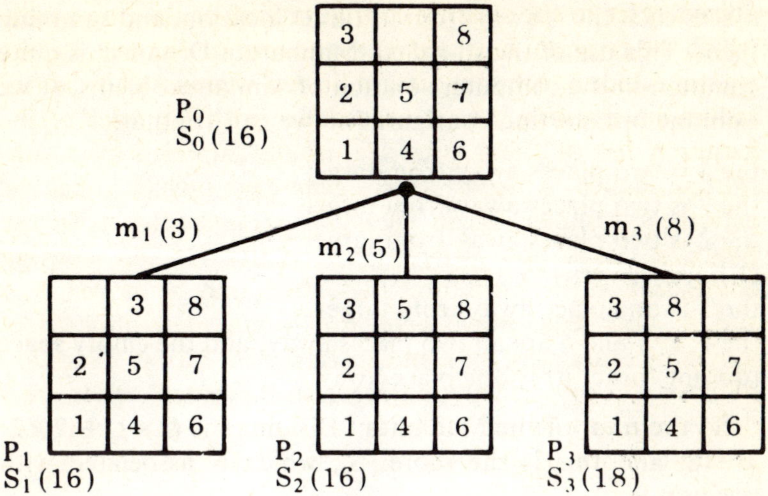

FIGURE 4

The *branches* of the tree are the moves (m_1 m_2 m_3) that can be made from the root of the tree. We may denote the root position by P_0, the position arising after making the move m_1 is P_1; after making the move m_2 it is P_2, and after m_3 it is P_3. These positions are represented on the tree by *nodes*.

The program now looks to see if it has solved the problem, and if it has done so it will output the move leading to the solution, followed by a statement to the effect that the game is over and it has found a solution in however many moves, which are then listed. If it has not solved the problem the program might then like to know how close each of its moves has come to providing a solution, in which case it must evaluate each of the resulting positions. This is done with a device known as an *evaluation function* (or scoring function), which supplies a numerical score that represents nearness to or distance from a solution.

A simple evaluation function for the 8-puzzle can be programmed by counting how many vertical and horizontal places each tile is away from its target location, and summing them. This use of the so-called 'Manhattan Distance' is quite common in the computer solution of similar problems. If we examine our starting configuration we can see that:

the 3 is two places away from target
the 8 is two places away from target
the 2 is two places away from target
(1 horiz. 1 vert.)
the 5 is one place away from target
the 7, 1, 4 and 6 are all two places away, and the empty space (do not forget it) is one place away.

So the total of the Manhattan Distances is $(2\times 1)+(7\times 2) = 16$, and this is the score, S_0, which is associated with position P_0.

Counting the Manhattan Distances in P_1, P_2, and P_3 we get:

$S_1 = 16$
$S_2 = 16$
$S_3 = 18$

(Note that when a solution is found, S will be zero.)

So on the basis of our evaluation function it looks as though moves m_1 and m_2 are likely to lead to a faster solution than m_3, since positions P_1 and P_2 seem nearer the target position than does P_3. And this is where the story really begins.

An obvious, though tedious, algorithmic solution to this problem is to look at each of the positions P_1, P_2 and P_3, then generate all the legal moves from each of these positions – look at the newly resulting positions, then generate all the moves from these positions, and so on, until one of the positions is found to be the target (i.e. its score S, the sum of the Manhattan Distances, will be zero). Eventually, this method (which is called *exhaustive search*) will find a solution, that is so long as the program does not run out of RAM. But by using a simple heuristic we can head the program in the right direction, and hopefully a solution will be found sooner than if the exhaustive search algorithm were used.

We have seen that when we expand the node P_0, of the three new positions that appear on the tree, P_1 and P_2 appear to be more promising than P_3. It is clearly logical to expand the more promising nodes before the less promising ones, so at first we should neglect P_3 and concentrate on P_1 or P_2. Since they are of equal apparent merit, the program may choose between them at random. Let us assume that it chooses to expand P_1, from which it will generate the moves of the 2 tile and the 3 tile. Since the 3 tile was moved on the previous turn, and the program is intelligent enough to know that it does not want to go back to where it has just come from, the only move (m_{11}) that the program needs to consider seriously is the move of the 2 tile, which would lead to the position (shown in Figure 5) which we denote by P_{11}, and which has a score (S_{11}) of 14.

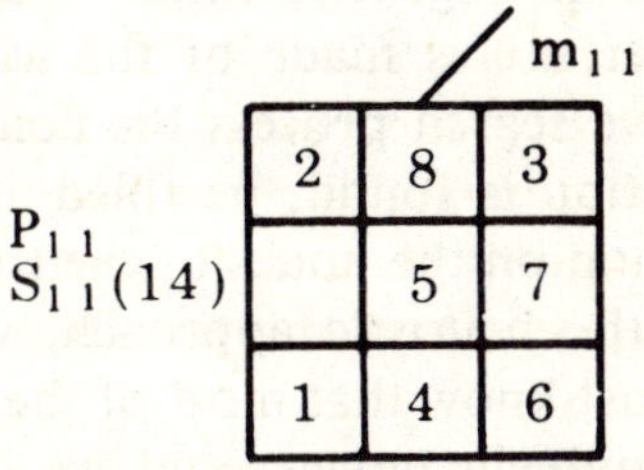

FIGURE 5

The best position now on the tree, i.e. the position closest to the target configuration, is P_{11}, since its score of 14 is lower than the scores of all the other nodes. So remembering not to allow the retrograde move of the 2 tile, the program now expands position P_{11}, and the choice is to move the 1 tile or the 5 tile, giving rise to the position shown in Figure 6.

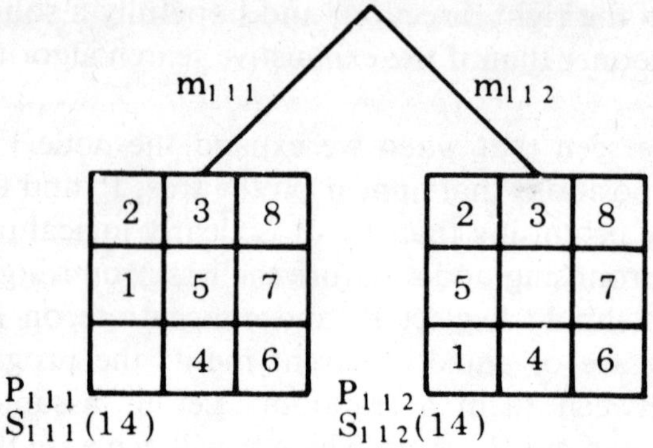

FIGURE 6

Once again we have a tie, two 'best' positions with scores of 14, and so the program again makes an arbitrary choice.

This process continues until a solution is found. It is easy to see that the method can hardly fail to be substantially faster than the exhaustive search process described earlier. The tree is grown intelligently, rather than in a dumb-ox manner, and better use is made of the available memory. With the exhaustive search process the computer's memory will, unless a solution is found, be filled at a stage when a very large proportion on the nodes of the tree are not of any real merit. With the heuristic approach, when memory is exhausted we at least know that most of the memory has not been wasted on unlikely moves, and we can use the best sequence of moves found so far.

What to do when memory is exhausted

Working with a personal computer inevitably poses memory constraints on a different scale from those encountered when writing for a large machine. How can the programmer combat this problem when examining large trees in an attempt to solve a one-person game? I shall describe two approaches to this particular problem:

(1) Follow a path through the tree to the best position found so far and output the moves on this path. Then make this 'best position' into the root of a new tree and start again.

(2) More intelligently, when memory becomes full, delete the currently 'worst position found so far' and use the newly scrubbed bytes to store the next position that the program generates. If this process is continued for long enough, either a solution will be found or the tree will eventually have two paths, each path having no offshoots. When that happens the program must choose the best of the paths, and make the terminal position on this path into the root of the new tree, remembering to output all the moves on the path leading to this position.

For example, our tree generated for the 8-puzzle is now as in Figure 7.

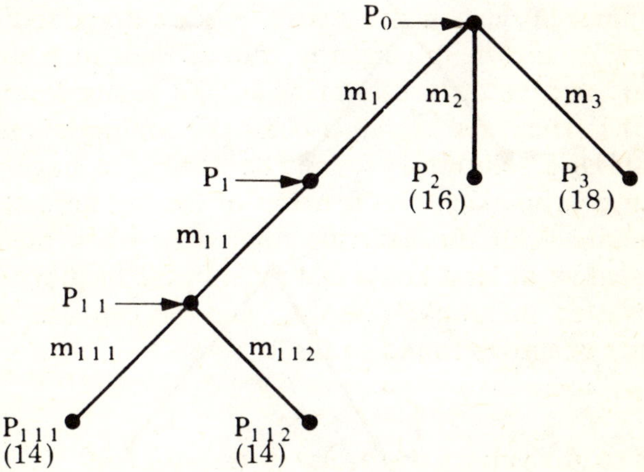

FIGURE 7

If memory is now full the program would delete m_3 (and P_3), to make room for the successor position produced when it expands P_{111}, or P_{112}. Let us assume that both m_2 (P_2) and m_3

(P_3) are deleted, to make way for P_{111} and P_{112}. We then have the tree in Figure 8 and the program can now output the moves m_1 and m_{11}, making position P_{11} the root of a new tree (see Figure 9).

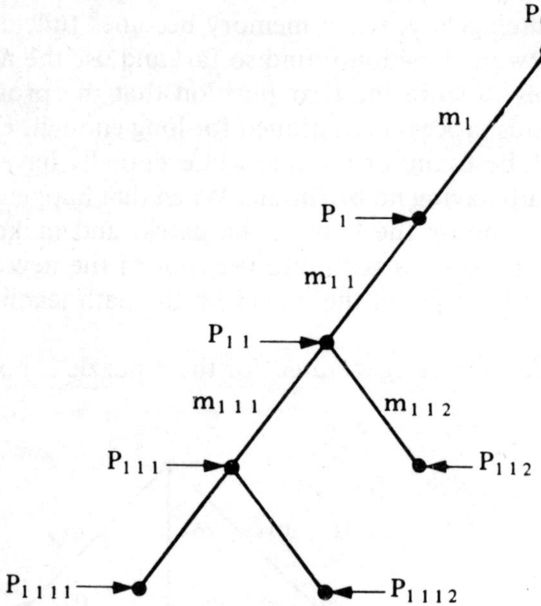

FIGURE 8

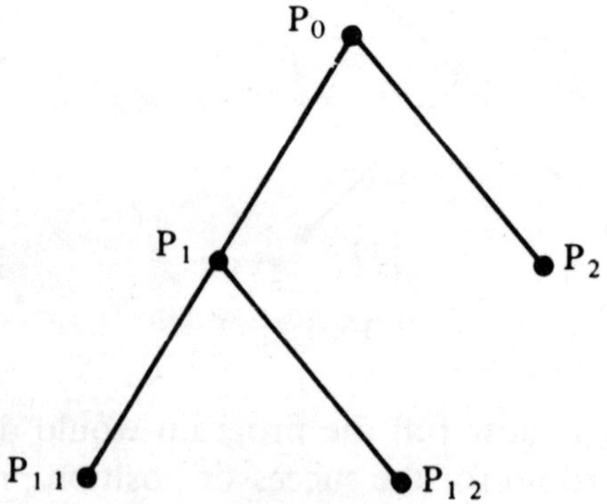

FIGURE 9

The new P_0 is the old P_{11}
The new P_1 is the old P_{111}
The new P_2 is the old P_{112}
The new P_{11} is the old P_{1111}
The new P_{12} is the old P_{1112}

And thus the search for a solution continues.

The shortest solution

In most games it is sufficient to win, but there may be reasons why one wishes to win as quickly as possible. For one-person games there exist various refinements on this method of tree searching which are likely to produce such a result.

The underlying philosophy in the search for a speedy solution is the notion that it is not only important how near (or far) you are from victory, it also matters how many moves it took you to get there. With the 8-puzzle, for example, a ten move sequence leading to a position with score 12, may not be so likely to lead to a short solution as a two move sequence leading to a score of 13 – perhaps in the next eight moves it will be possible to improve on the 13 by more than 1, thereby finding a shorter route to the solution.

This notion might be expressed numerically in the following evaluation function:

score = sum of Manhattan Distances + M

where M is the number of moves needed to reach this position. Whether or not this expression is the best method of relating the score to effort invested and achievement realised, can only be determined by trial and error. Perhaps M should be replaced by ½M or by 2M, or some other function of M. Playing around with the evaluation function in this way, changing the terms in the function, is one of the delights of game playing programming. When you hit upon a really good evaluation function and you see the program's performance improve dramatically as a result, there is a feeling of exhilaration, rather like watching your child crawl for the first time. Later we shall see how evaluation functions can be modified in the light of experience gained with the program, and it will be shown that it is even possible for the program itself to learn from its mistakes and modify its own evaluation routine.

Flow chart

A generalised global flow chart for the search of a one-person game tree is given in Figure 10. Remember that the most creative part of the work lies in finding a good evaluation function, and the performance of your function can be

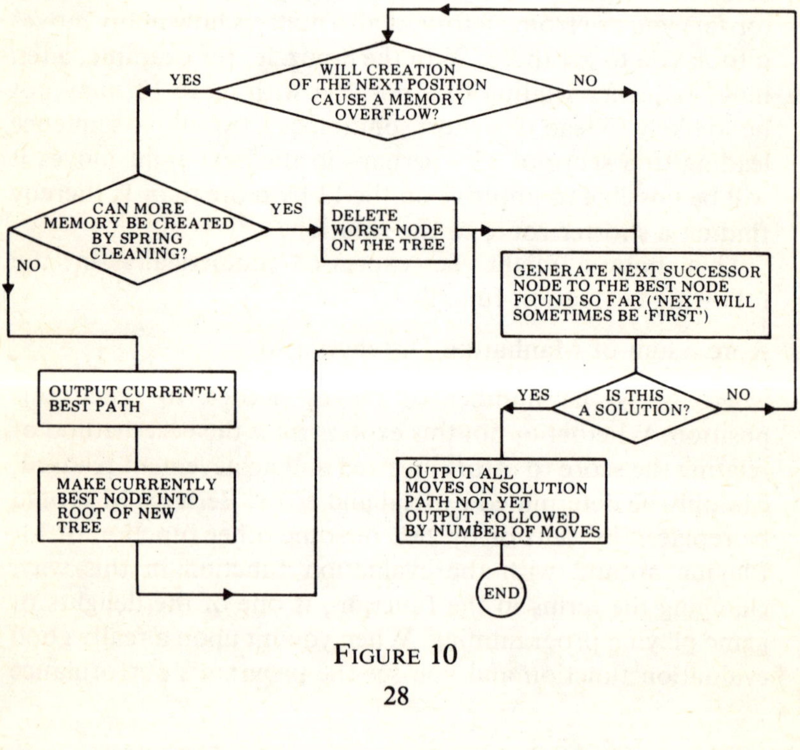

FIGURE 10

measured by the number of spurious nodes that are expanded *en route* to a solution. A perfect evaluation function will never expand a spurious node. The very worst function will expand each node at one level in the tree before looking ahead to the next level (this is exhaustive search).

Task 1

Write a program to solve the 8-puzzle in the shortest number of steps it can. Test the program by setting up various starting and target configurations, and see if your program solves the problems in fewer steps than you do. (Probably neither you, nor your program, will be as fast as Bobby Fischer, who can solve these puzzles with phenomenal rapidity.) When trying the problems yourself remember not to cheat – if you move a tile and then change your mind and move it back, add two to your count.

Bibliography

Nilsson, N. J.: *Searching Problem-Solving and Game-Playing Trees for Minimal Cost Solutions*. Proceedings IFIP Conference 1968, vol. 2, pp. 1556–1562.

Schofield, P. D. A.: *Complete Solution of the 'Eight-Puzzle'*. Machine Intelligence 1 (Ed. Collins, N. L. and Michie, D.), Oliver & Boyd, 1967, pp. 125–133.

Slagle, J. and Bursky, P.: *Experiments with a Multipurpose, Theorem-Proving Heuristic Program*. Journal Association Computing Machinery, Vol. 15, no. 1, pp. 85–99, January 1968.

CHAPTER 2
Two-Person Games

Two-person games, such as chess, backgammon and draughts, are usually more interesting and challenging than one-person games, and it is to these that we shall be devoting most of our studies. The introduction of a second player creates manifold difficulties that do not exist in a one-person game, but fortunately for today's programmers these difficulties have been extensively analysed in the computing literature and the problems are now rather well understood.

The two-person game tree

Game trees become more complex structures when an opponent appears on the scene. Let us consider a relatively simple game, noughts and crosses (tic-tac-toe to our American cousins), and examine how its tree will look after a move or two of look-ahead. We shall assume that 'cross' moves first (see Figure 11).

From the initial position there are three essentially different moves:

(1) e (the centre)
(2) a, c, g and i (the corners)
(3) b, d, f and h (middle of the edges)

On the first move, any of group (2) is equivalent to any other, since all four moves are merely reflections or rotations of each other. Similarly, within group (3) all moves are equivalent. This technique of utilising symmetry to reduce the magnitude of the problem is well worthwhile when programming a game that lends itself to a symmetrical analysis. By reducing the number of moves that need to be examined at any point in the tree you will be cutting execution time dramatically, because the combinatorial effects of tree growth are enormous. The savings in time that can be achieved through using symmetry can be extremely valuable when improving the performance of the program by making its evaluation function more sophisticated (and slower).

If we so decide, our program can terminate its search of the tree after looking at each of its possible moves from the root. This is called a 1-ply search because the program only looks one 'ply' deep. (The term 'ply' is used to denote a single move by one player.) In order to decide which move to make, out of m_1, m_2 and m_3, the program will then apply its evaluation function to the three positions at the lower end of the tree (these are called the terminal positions). Whichever position had the best score would then be assumed to be the most desirable position for the program, and the program would make the move leading to that position.

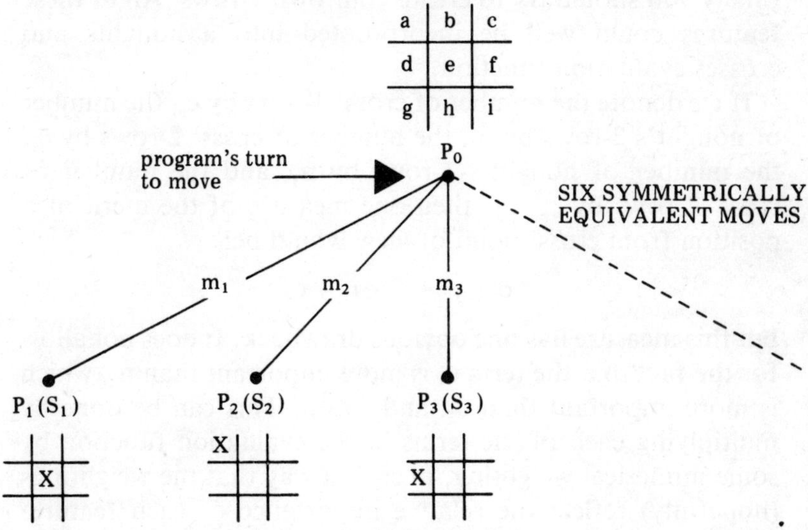

FIGURE 11

How should we set about designing our evaluation function? This is one of the fundamental problems in game playing programming because a good evaluation function will help the program to make good judgements, and hence to play well, even though the depth of look-ahead may be shallow. A poor function, on the other hand, might well result in poor play even with a deep and time consuming search of the game tree. It is therefore very much worthwhile putting some careful thought into the design of the evaluation function, and the following example should illustrate the type of thinking that is necessary.

The object of the game is to create a row of three of your own symbols. We shall call this a '3-row'. The next most important thing is to prevent your opponent from making a 3-row, which means that he should not have a 2-row after you move (a 2-row has two symbols of one player and one empty space). Next most important is the creation of your own 2-rows; then it is important not to leave your opponent with 1-rows (one of his symbols and two empty spaces); and finally you should try to create your own 1-rows. All of these features could well be incorporated into a noughts and crosses evaluation function.

If we denote the number of cross' 3-rows by c_3, the number of nought's 2-rows by n_2, the number of cross' 2-rows by c_2, the number of nought's 1-rows by n_1, and the number of cross' 1-rows by c_1 . . . then one measure of the merit of a position from cross' point of view would be:

$$c_3 - n_2 + c_2 - n_1 + c_1$$

but this measure has one obvious drawback. It does not allow for the fact that the term c_3 is more important than n_2, which is more important than c_2, and so on. This can be done by multiplying each of the terms in the evaluation function by some numerical weighting, in such a way that the weightings (hopefully) reflect the relative importance of each feature. The evaluation function then becomes

$$(k_3 \times c_3) - (k_2' \times n_2) + (k_2 \times c_2) - (k_1' \times n_1) + (k_1 \times c_1)$$

where k_3, k_2', k_2, k_1' and k_1 are the numerical weightings. Since one c_3 is worth more than all the n_2s in the world, i.e. a winning row is more important than any number of 2-rows, we can set k_3 to be some arbitrarily high number, say 128. By studying the game for a few minutes it is possible to see that if one side has a 3-row, the other side may have at most two 2-rows, so to reflect the relative importance of one's own 3-rows and enemy 2-rows it is necessary to ensure that $k_3 > 2 \times k_2'$. We can therefore try $k_2' = 63$. (If one side has a 3-row and his opponent two 2-rows, the opponent will not have any 1-rows to upset this scoring mechanism.)

If there are no 3-rows, but one side only has a 2-row, his opponent cannot have more than three 1-rows, as in Figure 12.

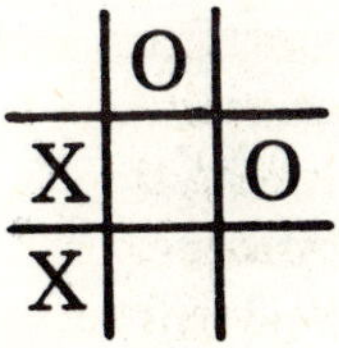

FIGURE 12

So $k_2' > 2 \times k_1$ and $k_2 > 2 \times k_1'$

and we can try $k_2 = 31$, $k_1' = 15$ and $k_1 = 7$. Remember that we can modify these values in the light of experience with the program, the values 128, 63, 31, 15 and 7 are merely our first estimates. Having made these estimates we should then ensure that the score for a noughts and crosses position will never cause an overflow, and we do this by setting up positions which will have the largest and smallest possible scores, and counting the number of 3-rows etc. in each. This is a very important part of evaluation function design, and I remember a chess programmer who could not understand why his program crashed whenever it was winning or losing by a great margin – he had forgotten to allow for the possibility of one side being two queens ahead and when that happened his evaluation calculations created an overflow.

If we return to Figure 11 we can see that each of the three possible first moves results in the creation of a different number of 1-rows. Applying the evaluation function

$$128 \times c_3 - 63 \times n_2 + 31 \times c_2 - 15 \times n_1 + 7 \times c_1$$

to the three positions P_1, P_2 and P_3 we find that in each case $c_3 = n_2 = c_2 = n_1 = 0$, and therefore:

$$S_1 = 128 \times 0 - 63 \times 0 + 31 \times 0 - 15 \times 0 + 7 \times 4 = 28$$
$$S_2 = 128 \times 0 - 63 \times 0 + 31 \times 0 - 15 \times 0 + 7 \times 3 = 21$$
$$S_3 = 128 \times 0 - 63 \times 0 + 31 \times 0 - 15 \times 0 + 7 \times 2 = 14$$

and S_1 is the most desirable of these scores so the program would make the move m_1 to reach position P_1 (i.e. it would play in the centre).

The 2-ply search

The 1-ply search is the simplest form of tree search in a two-person game, but it does not take into account the fact that once the program has made its move there is an opponent waiting to reply. It may be the case that a move which, superficially, looks strong, is seen to be an error when we look a little bit further into what may happen. The 2-ply search will 'see' more than the 1-ply search and so moves made on the basis of a 2-ply search will be more accurate (provided that the evaluation function is not a disaster area). How can we take into account this extra dimension of the opponent's move?

Let us look at the same tree, grown one ply deeper, i.e. to a total depth of two ply – one move by the program and one move by its opponent (Figure 13).

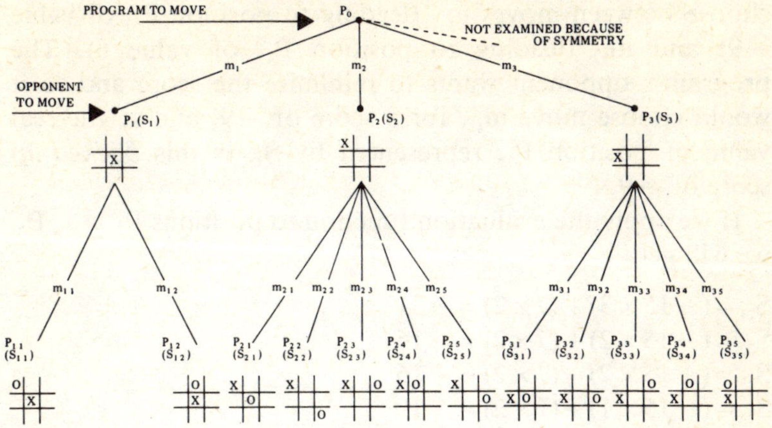

FIGURE 13

If 'cross' plays in the centre, 'nought' has two essentially different replies, in a corner or on the middle of an edge (represented by positions P_{11} and P_{12} respectively). If 'cross' makes his first move in a corner (P_2), 'nought' will have five different reply moves (m_{21} m_{22} m_{23} m_{24} and m_{25}) leading to positions P_{21} P_{22} P_{23} P_{24} and P_{25}. After 'cross' plays move m_3, 'nought' again has five replies. It is easy to see how the tree grows. In the last example, the 8-puzzle, the branching factor (number of branches from each position on the tree) was never more than three. Here it is more, even allowing for symmetry.

Let us consider how the program might analyse the situation. It uses its evaluation function to assign scores to the terminal nodes P_{11} and P_{12}. In each case $c_3 = n_2 = c_2 = 0$. In position P_{11}, $c_1 = 3$ and $n_1 = 2$. In position P_{12}, $c_1 = 3$ and $n_1 = 1$. We now have:

$$S_{11} = (-15 \times 2) + (7 \times 3) = -9$$
$$S_{12} = (-15 \times 1) + (7 \times 3) = 6$$

This information indicates that if the program is sitting in position P_1, with its opponent to move, its opponent may choose between moves m_{11} (leading to position P_{11} of value -9) and m_{12} (leading to position P_{12} of value 6). The program's opponent wants to minimise the score and so it would choose move m_{11}, for a score of -9, and so the real value of position P_1, represented by S_1, is this *backed-up* score of -9.

If we apply the evaluation function to positions $P_{21} \ldots P_{25}$ we will get:

$$S_{21} = (-15 \times 3) + (7 \times 2) = -31$$
$$S_{22} = (-15 \times 2) + (7 \times 2) = -16$$
$$S_{23} = (-15 \times 2) + (7 \times 2) = -16$$
$$S_{24} = (-15 \times 1) + (7 \times 2) = -1$$
$$S_{25} = (-15 \times 2) + (7 \times 3) = -9$$

Wishing to minimise the score when making its move from P_2, the program's opponent would choose move m_{21}, leading to position P_{21} and a score of -31.

Similarly, when applying the evaluation function to positions $P_{31} \ldots P_{35}$, we get:

$$S_{31} = -38$$
$$S_{32} = -8$$
$$S_{33} = -31$$
$$S_{34} = -16$$
$$S_{35} = -23$$

so the program's opponent, when making its move from P_3, would choose move m_{31} for a score of -38.

We now have the following situation. If the program makes move m_1, its opponent, with best play, can achieve a score of -9. If the program plays m_2 then its opponent can achieve a score of -31. If the program plays m_3 then its opponent can score -38.

Just as the program's opponent wishes to minimise the score, so the program wishes to maximise the score. The program must now choose between m_1 (for -9), m_2 (for -31) and m_3 (for -38). Since the maximum of these three values is -9, the program will play move m_1, and the backed-up score at the root of the tree will be -9. This represents the score that will be achieved with best play from both sides.

This procedure of choosing the maximum of the minimums . . . etc. is known, not surprisingly, as the minimax method of tree searching. It is an algorithm that finds the move which will be best, assuming correct play for both sides, provided that the evaluation function is reasonably accurate.

Memory requirements for a minimax search

One of the great advantages of the minimax type of search is that it is not necessary to retain the whole tree in memory. In fact it is necessary to keep only one position at each level of look ahead, together with a certain amount of information about the moves from each of these positions. Let us see how this works for our 2-ply tree (see Figure 13).

From the initial position P_0, the program generates the first move for cross, to position P_1. Before proceeding to the other moves that cross can make, the program generates the first reply move by nought, m_{11}, reaches position P_{11} and assigns it the score S_{11} (-9). This is the first terminal node to be evaluated, so the score of -9 represents the best score found so far and this is the score that is assigned to S_1. Since P_1 is the first move at 1-ply to be examined, this score of -9 also represents the best score found so far at the 1-level, and this is the score assigned to S_0.

The program now looks at P_{12}, which we sometimes refer to as the brother of P_{11} (and P_1 is father to both of them). The program determines the score S_{12}, compares this value (6) with the best score found so far at this level (-9) and finds the -9 preferable, so the scores S_1 and S_0 need not be adjusted at this stage. The program next looks for a brother to P_{11}, but finding none it goes back up the tree and looks for a brother to P_1, which leads it to position P_2 and then to P_{21}.

On the way down this part of the tree the program assigns to P_2 a score of -9, since this is the best that can be achieved so far. When looking at P_{21} the program finds a score of -31, which is better for the program's opponent than -9 and so S_2 is now set to -31.

Note that as this process continues, the brother nodes that have been examined in the past no longer serve any useful purpose and so they can be discarded. At the present point in our search we no longer need the brother of P_2 that has already been examined (P_1), so P_1 and its successor nodes are not kept in the tree at this time. The tree, at this moment, comprises only P_0, P_2 and P_{21}.

Having evaluated P_{21} we throw it away and look at P_{22}, which has a score of -16. The program's opponent would not prefer this to the -31 already discovered, and so no change is made to S_2. The program discards P_{22} and replaces it with P_{23} for a score of -16, also of no value to the program's opponent, and this is replaced in turn with P_{24} and P_{25} which also produce no change in S_2.

Since S_2 (-31) is less attractive for the program than the best score found so far (-9 at S_0), the score at P_2 is not backed-up. P_2 itself is discarded to make way for P_3, and the same process continues, with the program looking in turn at the scores of $P_{31} \ldots P_{35}$.

Task 2

The evaluation function for noughts and crosses which we have been using in this example has five features. Try to devise evaluation functions with as few features as possible, for playing noughts and crosses with (a) a 2-ply search; and (b) a 3-ply search, and test your functions by writing a program to play the game using a minimax search. The fact that deeper search will sometimes compensate for a less powerful evaluation function may make it possible for you to reduce the number of features while still writing a program that can play perfectly. If you complete this task, or even if you do not, you might like to think of a way to make the search much faster. This will be the subject of the next chapter.

CHAPTER 3
Games With Big Trees

In Chapter 2 we discussed the use of the minimax method to search game trees, using noughts and crosses as our example. This is a game with sufficient symmetry to reduce the number of essentially different moves at the start to three: the centre, a corner and the middle of an edge. At the second ply there are a total of 12 essentially different positions, so with only seven spaces then remaining there will be an upper bound of $12 \times 7!$ on the total number of terminal positions in the whole of the game tree. In practice the total will be somewhat less than this figure, since a number of paths will lead to a win for one side or the other, or a draw (i.e. a position in which every row, column and diagonal has at least one 'O' and one 'X' in it), before all nine elements of the 3×3 array have been filled. In order to play a perfect game of noughts and crosses with the crudest of evaluation functions, we could search the game tree exhaustively, using a score of $+1$ for a variation won by the program, -1 for a variation won by the opponent, and 0 for a draw.

Most interesting two-person games have much larger trees than this: in chess there are roughly one million terminal positions in an average 4-ply search, in Go the figure would be ten thousand million for a 4-ply search at the start of the game. How can we cope with such gigantic combinatorial growth in our game trees? The answer lies in a refinement of the minimax method known as the alpha-beta algorithm.

The alpha-beta algorithm

The alpha-beta algorithm owes its power to the argument that if a player can choose from a number of moves, once he finds one move which serves his purpose he need not examine the remainder of the moves in that group. Let us look at a simple two-person game tree to illustrate this point (Figure 14).

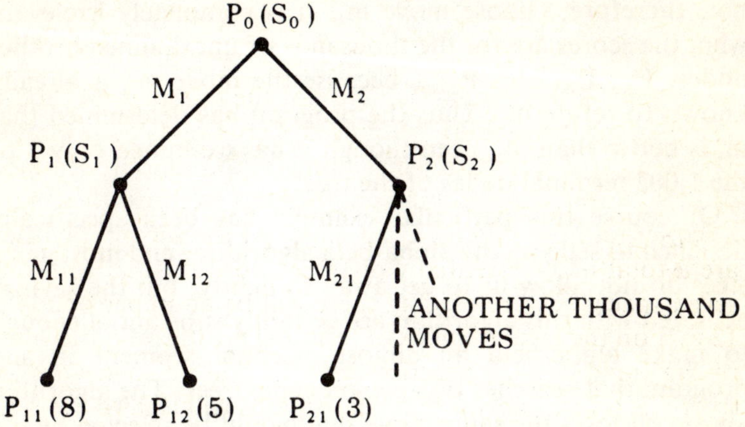

FIGURE 14

We shall assume that a program searches the tree from left to right, and that the evaluation function assigns scores of 8, 5 and 3 respectively to the terminal nodes P_{11}, P_{12} and P_{21}. If the program is to move from position P_0, it first considers move m_1 and then tries to decide what its opponent will do from position P_1. The opponent may choose between scores of 8 and 5, and since we have adopted the convention that the opponent's target is a low score, the opponent will choose position P_{12} with a score of 5.

The program now knows that if it chooses m_1, its opponent can prevent it from achieving a score of more than 5. This value of 5 is therefore the value of positon P_1, assuming correct play by the opponent, and so the value 5 is assigned to S_1. We call this process of assigning values as the program back-tracks up the tree 'backing-up'.

The score at S_1 is now backed up to S_0 and the program then considers position P_2, to determine whether it will prefer to play move m_1 or m_2. It sees that from position P_2 its opponent can, if he wishes, move to P_{21} for a score of 3, and since 3 is better than 5 from the opponent's point of view, the program will wish to deny its opponent this option and it will not, therefore, choose move m_2. It is completely irrelevant what the scores are for the thousands of unexamined brother nodes, P_{22}, P_{23}, . . . P_{21001}, because the move m_{21} is already known to refute m_2. Thus the program has determined that m_1 is better than m_2, even though it has examined only 3 of the 1,002 terminal nodes of the tree!

Of course this particular example has been specifically designed to sell you the alpha-beta algorithm, and most game trees do not allow us to get away so lightly, but the savings achieved with this algorithm are certainly substantial enough to make alpha-beta an almost essential segment in any program that searches two-person game trees. The algorithm always chooses the same move that would be selected by the minimax algorithm, but usually in a fraction of the time.

Since alpha-beta is so very important in game playing, I make no apologies for including another, more complex example (Figure 15). This will show how the method works for a 3-ply tree and will illustrate why it has been given its strange name.

Initially, all non-terminal nodes at even ply are assigned the value $-\infty$ (α). All non-terminal nodes at odd ply are assigned the value $+\infty$ (β). As usual it is the program's turn to move from the root position P_0, and the program is trying to maximise the value of α. The opponent moves from positions P_1 and P_2, trying to minimise the value of β. The program moves from the positions at ply$-$2 (P_{11}, P_{12}, P_{21} and P_{22}), trying to maximise α.

The tree search now proceeds as follows:

1 Examine P_{111}. The score of 8 is greater than $-\infty$ so α at S_{11} is set to 8. This score is then compared with β at S_1 and found

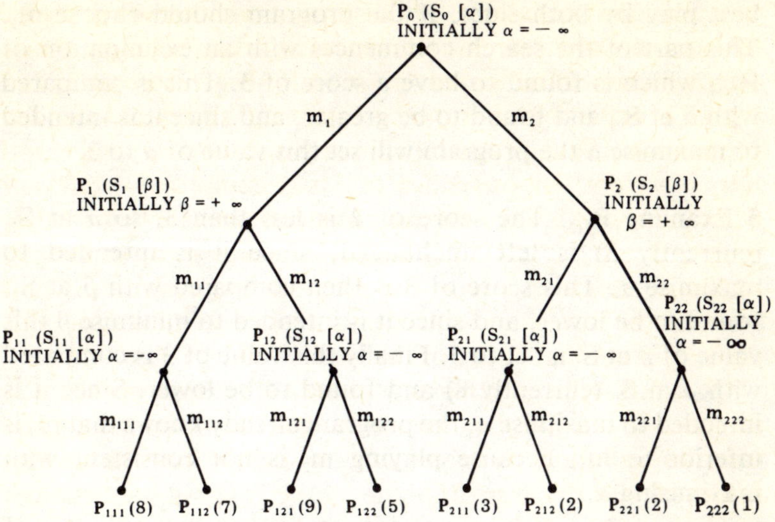

FIGURE 15

to be less than $+\infty$, so this value of β is also set to 8. In order to decide whether the program might be willing to play m_1, this score of 8 at S_1 is compared with $-\infty$ at S_0 and found to be greater, so α at S_0 is set to 8.

2 Examine P_{112}. The score of 7 is less than α at S_{11}, which is now 8, and since it is intended to maximise α, the value of α at S_{11} is not adjusted, and therefore the value of β at S_1 and that of α at S_0 also remain unchanged.

3 Examine P_{121}. The score of 9 is greater than $-\infty$, so α at S_{12} is set to 9. This score is then compared with β at S_1 and found to be greater, and since it is intended to minimise β the program can reject move m_{12}, knowing that its opponent can do better with move m_{11}.

4 The left hand side of the tree has now been examined and the search proceeds to the comparison of the best score achieved so far (8) with whatever can be reached, assuming best play by both sides, if the program should choose m_2. This part of the search commences with an examination of P_{211}, which is found to have a score of 3. This is compared with α at S_{21} and found to be greater, and since it is intended to maximise α the program will set this value of α to 3.

5 Examine P_{212}. The score of 2 is less than 3, so α at S_{21} (currently 3) is left unchanged, since it is intended to maximise α. This score of 3 is then compared with β at S_2, found to be lower, and since it is intended to minimise β this value of β at S_2 is set to 3. Finally this value of 3 is compared with α at S_0 (currently 8) and found to be lower. Since it is intended to maximise α, the program already knows that m_2 is inferior to m_1, because playing m_2 is not consistent with maximising α.

The search is now over and it can be seen that only five of the eight terminal nodes needed to be examined. If you wish to verify the validity of this process by practical means, try assigning sets of values to positions P_{122}, P_{221} and P_{222}, and you will always find that the program prefers move m_1 to move m_2.

How powerful is the alpha-beta algorithm?

During the past few years there has been considerable research into the question of just how big are the savings achieved using this algorithm rather than simple minimax. A full discussion of the theoretical and practical results of this research is well beyond the scope of this book, but the studious reader will find this work well documented in the bibliographic references found at the conclusion of this chapter. What follows is a summary of the most important results, and a brief discussion of their significance.

Monroe Newborn has investigated the power of the alpha-beta algorithm when searching game trees in which the moves within any group are examined in a random order. Figure 16 shows, for various branching factors (b), the number of terminal nodes which we would expect a program to examine, using alpha-beta, in searches of 2- and 3-ply.

	2-ply search		3-ply search	
b	total terminal nodes	expectation	total terminal nodes	expectation
2	4	3.67	8	6.84
4	16	12.14	64	40.11
8	64	38.65	512	220.37
16	256	122.11	4096	1214.45

FIGURE 16

It will be seen that as the branching factor increases, so the proportion of nodes that can be ignored thanks to the alpha-beta algorithm also increases. And as the depth of search increases the effect of the algorithm is again increased. So the bigger the tree becomes, the greater will be the savings using the alpha-beta method.

The savings become even more dramatic when the branches of the tree are examined in an intelligent order. In general it is true to say that within any group of moves the best one should be examined first, so that if the best one is not good enough we need not waste time in examining the second best, third best and inferior moves. If the tree is searched in such a way that the moves are examined in their optimal order, then the number of terminal nodes examined will be approximately $2 \times \sqrt{N}$, where N is the total number of terminal nodes on the tree. Thus, for a game of chess in which the branching factor is typically 36, the number of terminal nodes on the tree is 36^4 for a 4-ply tree. Yet by using the alpha-beta algorithm, if the tree is optimally ordered we need examine only 2×36^2 terminal nodes before we find the best move from the root of the tree, a saving of well over 99% when compared with the simple minimax method.

Taking the figures from Newborn's results quoted above, we can compare the expected number of nodes examined with random ordering and the number of nodes examined with optimal ordering (Figure 17).

	2-ply search		3-ply search	
b	random	optimal*	random	optimal*
2	3.67	3	6.84	5.66
4	12.14	7	40.11	15
8	38.65	15	220.37	44.248
16	122.11	31	1214.45	127

FIGURE 17

*The approximation $2\times\sqrt{N}$ referred to above is made slightly more accurate by subtracting 1. This is not important for very large trees but it has been done here for the sake of accuracy.

I hope that the reader is now convinced that for all two-person game trees, except the smallest of the small, alpha-beta is a must. The most important implication of these results is that if it is at all possible, you should generate and/or examine the moves within any group or family in such a way as to take maximum advantage of the savings that can be achieved, and this means ordering the search in some way. We shall discuss various techniques for speeding up the alpha-beta search in the following chapter, but one obvious method can be mentioned here. First, generate all the moves at the root of the tree, m_1 m_2 . . . etc., and evaluate the resulting positions with the evaluation function. Sort the moves so that the move with the highest score will be examined first, then the move with the next highest, and so on.

Next, look at the first position on the list and generate its successor positions. These are assigned scores using the evaluation function and they are then sorted, this time with the lowest scored position coming at the top of the list and the highest scored position at the bottom. (This is because the program's opponent is trying to minimise the score.)

This process is repeated all the way down the tree, except for the terminal nodes, which are not sorted. Now, when searching the tree with the alpha-beta algorithm, the tree will be found to be much nearer an optimally sorted tree than if this process had not been applied. One disadvantage of this method, however, is that it requires us to keep in memory all the successor nodes to each node on the principal variation, apart from the terminal nodes. So in a search of a chess tree, with 36 moves at each node, this method would require us to keep in memory:

(a) the root node
(b) 36 nodes at each level of look-ahead apart from the terminal node.

In order to combat this problem we might try to find an extremely compact method of representing a position, but if this compactness results in a slowing down of the search process while each position is unravelled or created, much of the effect of the fast alpha-beta algorithm will be lost. Such problems require careful thought and it is often necessary to experiment before the best balance is achieved between representation and optimality of search.

Other useful techniques for examining the moves in a sensible order can often be found by thinking a little about the nature of the game. Let us consider once again the game of noughts and crosses. The elements of the 3 × 3 array might be numbered as in Figure 18a.

1	2	3
4	5	6
7	8	9

FIGURE 18a

A simple way to generate all the legal moves from any position is to look at the elements, starting with 1 and working up to 9, and putting any empty space on the move list. But with a basic knowledge of the strategy of the game we can speed up the search process by looking first at element 5, then 1, 3, 7 and 9, and finally at 2, 4, 6 and 8. This method of move generation takes no longer than 1, 2, 3, 4, . . . 9, yet it enables the alpha-beta algorithm to examine the moves in a more sensible order, thereby taking us closer to an optimal search process.

Task 3

Write a program to play noughts and crosses, taking advantage of symmetry and employing the alpha-beta algorithm. Search the whole game tree using the primitive evaluation function described above (+1 is a win for the program, −1 a win for the opponent and 0 a draw).

Test the program (a) when the moves are generated in a random order; and (b) when the moves are generated in the order: centre, corners, middle of edges. The results should indicate a useful improvement with ordered search over random search.

Bibliography

Knuth, D. E. and Moore, R. W.: *An Analysis of Alpha-Beta Pruning*. Artificial Intelligence, vol. 6, pp. 293–326, 1975.

Newborn, M. M.: *The Efficiency of the Alpha-Beta Search on Trees with Branch-dependent Terminal Node Scores*. Artificial Intelligence, vol. 8, pp. 137–153, 1977.

CHAPTER 4
Speeding up the Search

In the last chapter we introduced the extremely powerful alpha-beta algorithm for searching two-person game trees, and we saw how dramatic the effects of alpha-beta pruning can be when the branches of the tree are searched in their optimal order. Although optimal ordering is impossible to achieve (if we knew what the best move was, there would be no need to search the game tree to find it), there are a number of useful techniques which form the subject of this chapter.

Ordering by short look-ahead

Consider a program which searches a game tree to a depth of 10-ply. If the average branching factor is 36, as in chess, the tree will be enormous and any saving that can be achieved by optimising the order of the search will be well worthwhile. One way in which this might be done is to carry out a much shorter look-ahead search, to a depth of 3-ply for example, and then order the moves on the basis of this shallower search. Once this has been done, the search routine moves down the tree and performs its full search of the tree, the first 3-ply of which have already been put into an approximate order. As a result of the approximate ordering, the full look-ahead search is conducted in a more efficient manner, with considerable savings in time. The following example should help the reader convince himself of the value of conducting a preliminary search.

Let us suppose that in a chess position there are 36 moves. On the basis of a shallow search it appears that move m_1 wins the opponent's queen, move m_2 wins only a pawn, and no other moves force the win of any material. At the other end of the scale, move m_{35} appears to lose a pawn while m_{36} looks as though it loses a bishop. The program now orders these 36 moves on the basis of its preliminary look-ahead, and it first carries out a full 10-ply search on the move that appears to win the queen, m_3. Unless there is some deep reason why this move does not win the queen, the program's alpha-beta search will return a score to the root of the tree that indicates its opinion that move m_1 wins a queen, and so the number of branches which are pruned off during the search process will be high. The same thing happens when the full search process examines m_3, m_4, . . . m_{35}, m_{36}. The reason why we need to order all 36 moves is that our ordering will not be absolutely correct, but the effect of an error in one or more value judgements will be minimised if we make the preliminary ordering as accurate as possible. For example, if move m_{36} actually turned out to win a bishop instead of losing a bishop, the move would still be inferior to m_1 (winning a queen) so we would still wish to examine m_{36} after examining m_1.

Some interesting results on preliminary ordering were discovered by Richard Russell who wrote a Kalah program in 1964. Kalah (or Owari) is one of a family of games that go under the generic name Mancala. These games are played in Asia and Africa, and the rules vary slightly from one region to another. The game in Figure 18b presents an ideal programming exercise because the rules are simple, the branching factor is typically no more than 6, and it is relatively simple to devise a satisfactory evaluation function.

Each player controls a number of pits or bowls (often pits in the sand) and one large pit or bowl called his Kalah. In the above diagram the pits labelled 'a' and the Kalah labelled 'A'

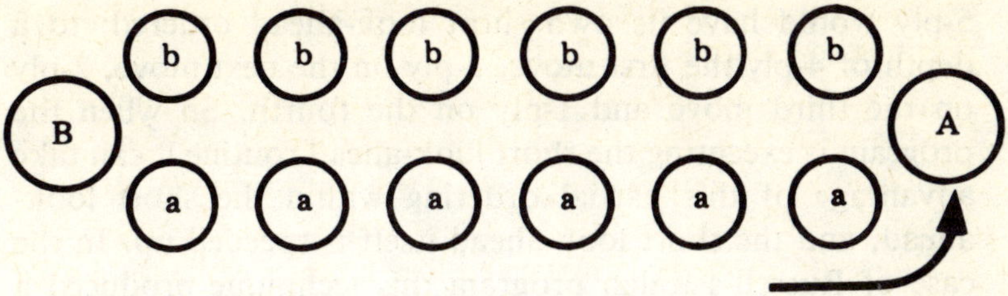

FIGURE 18b

all belong to one player, pits 'b' and Kalah 'B' belong to his opponent. At the start of the game each pit contains an equal number of stones, say 5, and each Kalah is empty.

The players move alternately. To make a move a player picks up all the stones in one of his pits and, moving his hand in an anti-clockwise direction, drops one stone into each pit and into his own Kalah, but not into his opponent's Kalah. When his hand holds no more stones the player has had his turn, and it is then his opponent's turn to play; but if the last stone lands in a player's Kalah he has another turn, so it is advantageous to plan the game so that you will have two or more turns in succession. The other important rule is that if a player's last stone lands in an empty pit on his own side, he captures all of the stones in the opposite pit and places them, together with the stone making the capture, in his own Kalah.

At the end of the game the player with the most stones in his Kalah is the winner.

Russell experimented with preliminary searches of various depths. With a full look-ahead of 10-ply he discovered that the program consumed the minimum CPU time when 90% of its total search time was spent in the short look-ahead of 5-ply. He then found a method for improving the search speed still further. Rather than begin a new 5-ply search at each ply, he used the fact that the short look-ahead searches overlap – the 5-ply search conducted at one position in the tree could be used as a 4-ply search of a position at the next level down in the tree. This means that a short look-ahead of

5-ply would have its own short look-ahead ordered: to a depth of 4-ply the first move, 3-ply on the next move, 2-ply on the third move and 1-ply on the fourth. So when the program is executing the short look-ahead routine it can take advantage of this partial ordering within the short look-ahead, and the short look-ahead itself is speeded up. In the case of Russell's Kalah program this technique produced a reduction in total search time of approximately 65%.

One of the problems of implementing this short look-ahead method on a personal computer is the need to store the whole of the short look-ahead tree. For most games this will be impossible without a floppy disk system, and even then there will be games for which there is insufficient memory to cope with anything more than a 2-ply or 3-ply short look-ahead search. Nevertheless, the idea is worth remembering, either for games with relatively small branching factors, or for the day when you upgrade your micro by adding a hard disk. But with even the smallest memory configuration you can utilise this method to some extent, simply by restricting your short look-ahead to a 1-ply search! Let us see how this might work in practice, using noughts and crosses (tic-tac-toe) as in our example (Figure 19).

The program generates the three, essentially different first moves: the central move (location 5), a corner move (location 1) and a move in the middle of an edge (location 2). Those of you who have followed the earlier chapters will know that the moves may actually be generated in that order by the application of an elementary understanding of the game.

The program evaluates the resulting positions, i.e. the positions it has found from a 1-ply search, and sorts them so that the best move is examined first. We shall assume that our evaluation function retains the order in which the moves were generated, in which case the program next produces the moves from position P_1, the position arising after making the central move (location 5). In reply to this move there are two, essentially different moves, a corner (location 1) and the

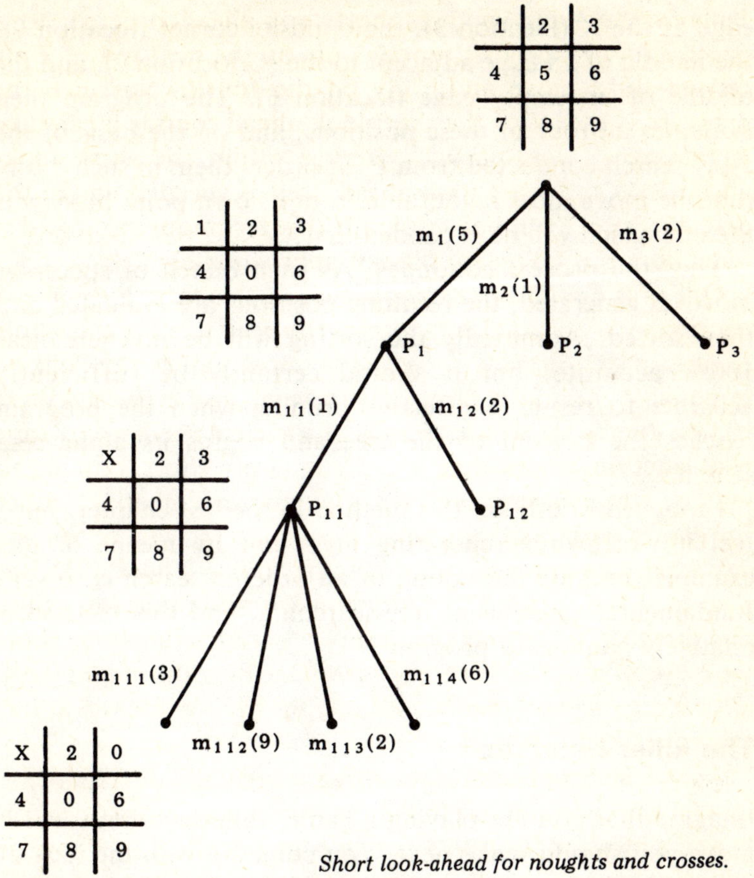

Short look-ahead for noughts and crosses.

FIGURE 19

middle of an edge (location 2). We generate these moves in exactly that order, and then we evaluate the resulting positions (P_{11} and P_{12}) using our evaluation function. Let us assume that the scores for P_{11} and P_{12} indicate that P_{11} is a better position than P_{12} from our opponent's point of view. Then on the basis of the 1-ply search conducted from position P_1 we can say that the next set of moves to be generated should be the successors of position P_{11}. Here there are four, essentially different moves: a corner on the same edge as the X (location 3), the opposite corner (location 9), the middle of an edge adjacent to the X (location 2), and the middle of an empty edge (location 6). The program then evaluates all four of these positions, and on the basis of the 1-ply search conducted from P_{11} it orders them in such a way that the move most favourable from its own point of view is the one which will be expanded first.

Thus the process continues. As each bunch of successor moves is generated, the resulting positions are evaluated and then sorted. Admittedly the sorting will be nowhere near 100% accurate, but it should certainly be sufficiently accurate to result in effective pruning when the program reaches the bottom of the tree and begins its alpha-beta search.

I touched briefly on this method in the last chapter, but I feel it worthwhile reiterating my point by means of this example, because the notion of an ordered search is so very fundamental to efficient tree-searching, and this method is relatively painless to program.

The killer heuristic

Imagine that you are playing a game, thinking about which move you should make next. You come up with the idea of making move m_1, but then you notice that if you do play this move your opponent has the very strong reply ZAP at his disposal, completely wrecking your position. You therefore stop thinking about m_1 and start to think about another move, m_2, but now you have been forewarned because you have already spent some of your thinking time on the discovery of the refutation move ZAP. You therefore look to see whether m_2 can be met by ZAP, and if so, with what result.

The logic behind this approach is not difficult to understand. If ZAP killed your prospects of victory after you make the move m_1, it is quite possible, even likely, that ZAP will ruin you after you make the move m_2. In chess and many other games there is the concept of the threat, and ZAP moves often fall into this category. If your queen is threatened and you play a random move, the chances are that your opponent will be able to capture your queen on his next turn. Each time you think of a move you should first look to see if it loses your queen in the same way, and if it does so then you will have pruned off large chunks of the game tree simply by finding the refutation move (sometimes called the 'killer' move) early in the search.

The implementation of the killer heuristic is not difficult, but it does require the use of extra RAM. At each level in the tree, keep a note of which move produced the last cutoff (this is the killer move) and try that move first when examining the next group of positions at the same level. This method becomes clearer from an examination of the example in Figure 20.

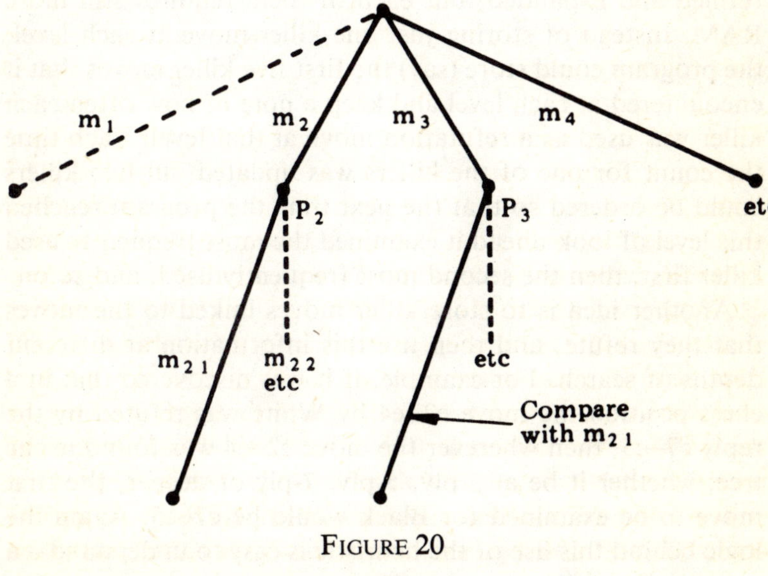

FIGURE 20

The program has already looked at the first move from the root of the tree, and returned a score to the root position. It now examines move m_2, leading to position P_2, and soon discovers that in reply to m_2 if its opponent chooses m_{21} then the opponent will have improved on his score which is currently at the root of the tree. In other words, move m_{21} refutes move m_2, and the program need not look at m_{22}, m_{23}, . . . , etc.

Next the program examines move m_3. It knows that m_{21} refuted m_2 so it first looks at its list of legal moves from position P_3 to see if the same move as m_{21} can be found in this list – if so it examines that move first, in the hope of finding that here too the same move provides a refutation, thereby terminating the search from m_3 after examining the minimum number of branches. If it turns out that m_3 is refuted by a different move, then this new killer move replaces the original one and it is this new killer which is looked for first when examining the successors to m_4.

There are various ways in which this heuristic may be refined and expanded, but each of them requires still more RAM. Instead of storing just one killer move at each level, the program could store (say) the first five killer moves that it encountered at each level and keep a note of how often each killer was used as a refutation move at that level. Each time the count for one of the killers was updated, all five killers could be ordered so that the next time the program reached this level of look-ahead it examined the most frequently used killer first, then the second most frequently used, and so on.

Another idea is to store killer moves linked to the moves that they refute, and then use this information at different depths of search. For example, if it was discovered that in a chess position the move e2–e4 by White was refuted by the reply c7–c5, then wherever the move e2–e4 was found in the tree, whether it be at 3-ply, 5-ply, 7-ply or deeper, the first move to be examined for Black would be c7–c5. Again the logic behind this use of the heuristic is easy to understand – a decision which is bad today will probably be bad in a similar situation tomorrow.

The principal continuation

When a program has finished its search of the game tree, and has decided on its move, it will have in its memory the path through the tree which it considers to represent the best play by both sides. Its own best move will be at the top of the tree, then the move which it expects its opponent to make in reply, then the move which it thinks is the most likely reply to its opponent's expected move, and so on. It seems a pity to waste this information when so much effort has been put into its acquisition, and no more memory is required to take advantage of the information than one needs for the killer heuristic. Simply use the 3rd ply move from the current search as the first move to be examined when the program next begins to compute a move. The 4th ply move in the current search can serve as the 'killer' at ply-2 in the next search; the 5th ply move now can be the first killer at ply-3 next time, and so on. Very little computation time will be taken up with this method, and it is as well to start your search looking at vaguely sensible moves.

The alpha-beta window

This is another trick, inexpensive in terms of code, which will often speed up the search process. Under certain circumstances it may actually slow down the speed of search but if the parameters are carefully chosen the overall effect will be beneficial.

In most games it is true to say that in general it will not be possible to force a substantial gain within the next ply, nor will it be likely that the player whose turn it is to move must concede a substantial loss. In view of this it seems unreasonable to set the values of alpha and beta to $-\infty$ and $+\infty$ respectively at the start of the search. Let us take chess as our example. We can start our search by assuming that White (whose turn it is to move) cannot force the win of more than two pawns, and that White is not faced with the inevitable loss of more than two pawns. We can therefore set the 'window' to be four pawns wide, by assigning to alpha and beta the values of minus two pawns and plus two pawns respectively. This means that when searching for a move for White the program will only examine moves which, at worst, lose two pawns for White, and when looking for Black moves the program will ignore all moves which permit White to win more than two pawns. This process will speed up the tree search provided that the true value of the root position does lie within the window. Occasionally though, it will be possible for White to win more than two pawns or impossible for White to avoid conceding more than two pawns. Under these circumstances the search will terminate without the values of alpha and beta undergoing any change, and the program must then think again, widening its window.

The flow chart

The flow chart in Figure 21 illustrates how the alpha-beta algorithm works when backing-up in the tree search. This diagram is an abbreviated form of Figure 4 from Whaland's excellent article (see Bibliography).

(i) is the ply number currently under investigation.
L(i) is a pointer to the list of moves possible at level i (all sharing the same parent move at level i–1).
m(i) is the move, at level i, currently being processed.
E(i) is the evaluation of this move.

The left hand part of the tree assigns values to the nodes as

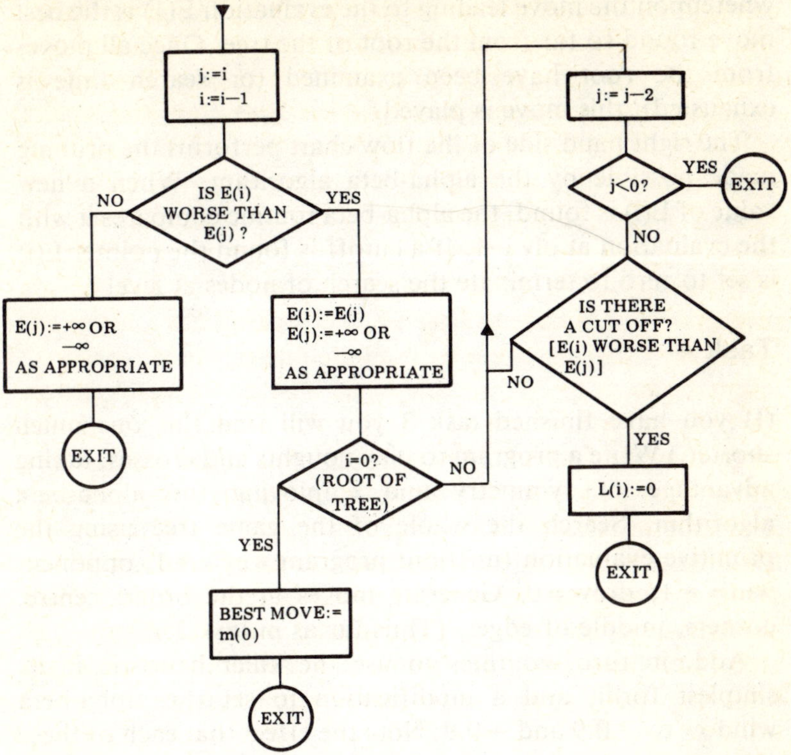

FIGURE 21

the search proceeds. A value of + ∞ is assigned as initial values to nodes at odd depths, and – ∞ as initial values to nodes at even depths. These are the values which are to be bettered if a candidate node is to be acceptable. The program compares the value of E(i) with E(i–1) and replaces E(i–1) with E(i) if E(i–1) is 'worse than' E(i). To be worse than E(i), it is necessary for either: E(i–1) to be greater than E(i) and i to be even; or E(i–1) to be less than E(i) and i to be odd.

When there are no more moves to consider from a particular node, the value of E(i–1) is compared with E(i–2), and so on, back up through the tree, until E(1) replaces E(0) whereupon the move leading to the evaluation E(1) is the best move found so far from the root of the tree. Once all moves from the root have been examined (or search time is exhausted), this move is played.

The right hand side of the flow chart performs the pruning made possible by the alpha-beta algorithm. When a new value of E(i) is found, the alpha-beta routine compares it with the evaluation at ply i–1. If a cutoff is found the pointer L(i) is set to zero to terminate the search of nodes at level i.

Task 4

(If you have finished task 3 you will find this one much shorter.) Write a program to play noughts and crosses, taking advantage of symmetry and employing the alpha-beta algorithm. Search the whole of the game tree using the primitive evaluation function: program win = + 1, opponent win = – 1, draw = 0. Generate moves in the order: centre, corners, middle of edges. (Thus far as in task 3.)

Add, in turn, routines to use the killer heuristic in its simplest form, and a modification to set the alpha-beta window to – 0.9 and + 0.9. Note the effect that each of these changes has on the time taken to search the whole of the game tree from the initial position. Add a routine to make use of the principal continuation, and test this by timing the program's computation, with and without this routine, after one move has been made by each side (remember to use symmetry here also).

The results should bear out the assertions contained in this chapter.

Bibliography

Frey, P. W.: *Chess Skill in Man and Machine.* Springer Verlag, 1977.

Russell, R.: *Kalah – The Game and the Program.* Stanford Artificial Intelligence Project, Memo No. 22, September 3rd 1964.

Russell, R.: *Improvements to the Kalah Program.* Stanford Artificial Intelligence Project, Memo No. 23, September 3rd 1964.

Whaland, N. D.: *A Computer Chess Tutorial.* Byte, vol. 3, pp. 168–181, October 1978.

CHAPTER 5
More Complex Evaluation Functions

How good is good?

Show a chess master a position from a game of chess and he will most likely make some comment about which side has the advantage. He might say: 'White is slightly better', or 'Black has a clear advantage', or 'White is winning'. Press him further and he will tell you why it is that White is slightly better: perhaps the reason will be simple, such as White has an extra knight . . . or maybe it will be more subtle, such as Black having the inferior pawn structure (or, even more specifically, a pair of 'doubled pawns').

In the language of chess players all of the master's comments will mean something. But when we write a chess program we have to put some numerical value on advantages such as an extra knight or a superior pawn structure, and the accuracy with which we can do this is one of the principal factors in determining the strength of our program. The result of our efforts to quantify various forms of advantage is a device called an evaluation function, and for all interesting games the evaluation function is part of the key to successful programming.

In an earlier chapter I suggested a simple evaluation function for noughts and crosses, the justification for which lies in the fact that only rows, columns or diagonals with moves by one player only (and not his opponent) are of any real interest. Once a row has one move by each player, that row is of no further use to either of them. I did not get this evaluation function from a World Champion noughts and crosses player, I made it up by taking a brief look at the underlying structure of the game. Alas, chess, checkers, backgammon, etc., etc., are all far too complex for such a simple approach to be possible. We must therefore rely, for our evaluation function, on the advice of experts, either spoken or in books.

There are three stages in building a useful evaluation function for a complex game, and I shall illustrate these stages by using chess as my example.

Identifying the important features

In order to be able to tell a good position from a bad one, it is first necessary to know what features to look for. If you know nothing about chess, and you and I both look at the same position, I will be able to make a fairly accurate assessment of which side has the advantage and by how much, simply because I know what to look for. You will be looking at the same thing but will not understand what you see. But suppose I were to tell you that the most important thing in chess is material – how many pieces each player has on the board, and that the player with the most pieces usually wins. Then you can count the pieces, and if White has 16 pieces but Black has only 8 you will hazard a guess that White is doing quite well, and in general you will be correct. I could further advise you that the pieces have different values: that a queen is worth 9 pawns, a rook 5, a bishop or knight 3, and that the king was beyond normal values. Then you could look at a position and fairly easily tell which side, if any, was ahead on material. You may know nothing else about chess but at least you can make a meaningful, first order estimate of which side is ahead and by how much.

If it were possible for a chess program to search a tree 200-ply deep, an evaluation function with material as its only feature would almost certainly be sufficient to enable the program to play better than Bobby Fischer. But such is the nature of the game that a 20-ply search is not yet realistic, let alone 200-ply, so our evaluation function must have more features.

In order to discover which features of the game are important, you may do one or both of two things. You may read some books on the subject, in the search for general advice (heuristics), and you may ask someone who is expert at the game. In answer to your question 'What else is important in chess, apart from material?', you may well receive the reply 'Control of the central squares'. On investigating further you discover that pieces in the centre can move to, or attack, more squares than pieces on an edge or in a corner. And pieces that attack central squares may eventually be able to move to a central square, so attacking central squares is a useful thing to do.

Further questioning, and/or reading, will reveal that if your pieces are getting in each other's way they will not be able to do very much, whereas if they have plenty of scope to move they will be more likely to help you improve your position; thus it is important for your pieces to have as many moves as possible.

Everyone knows that the king is the most important piece in chess, so obviously one should look after one's own king. Expert advice will tell you to keep it away from the centre of the board until the final stage of the game has been reached; castle during the opening stage so as to put your king nearer a corner, where it will be safer than on its original square; and don't rashly advance the pawns in front of it once you have castled. You can learn all this from any decent book on the game.

A fifth feature, whose importance is often underestimated is pawn-structure. Good chess players know that 'isolated pawns', that is pawns which do not have any supporting pawns on adjacent columns, are weak, because if the opponent attacks them they can only be defended with something more valuable than a pawn, and it is always best to use your less valuable pieces for defence. Also, it is usually a disadvantage to have 'doubled' pawns, i.e. two of your own pawns, one in front of the other, since they will not be able to defend each other and the front one will block its colleague's path.

To summarise this stage of function building: read some good books on the game and try to get advice from a strong player. You need to know which features in a position are important, and you need to understand why they are important so that you can measure roughly how much of each feature is present in a position.

Quantifying the features

I have already explained how to measure the material situation in a chess position. The scale of values: queen = 9, rook = 5, bishop = knight = 3, pawn = 1 is a very useful guide. Some programmers find that giving the bishop a value between 3 and 3½ leads to a more accurate assessment, but it is useful to work with integer values since integer arithmetic is faster than decimal. So if you decide to use non-integer values, scale everything up so that the final calculations are all integer.

These values of 9, 5, 3 and 1 are known to work well, though there is no logical explanation as to why they are better than some other set of values. It has simply been shown, throughout the modern history of chess, that a knight is worth roughly three pawns, but that a player with four pawns is better off than a player with a knight, while the man with only two pawns will probably lose to the man with the knight.

Features other than material are not so easy to quantify. This is probably because the material count is something that can be performed quickly by anyone who can add, while a count of (say) the number of squares that your pieces attack is not an easy matter for a human player to accomplish when thinking ahead. Because human players do not use any method of quantifying centre control, mobility, etc., when playing games against each other, there exists no well-tested set of values for these features. We must therefore devise our own.

In an earlier chapter I gave a simple evaluation function, for solving the 8-puzzle. Since the object of the exercise is to move tiles from their present location to some target location, it seems logical to measure the merit of a configuration by summing the straight line distances that the tiles need to be moved before they will all be on target. Similarly, for any feature in any other game, we look for a logical explanation of why that feature is important, and this will often lead us to a possible method of quantifying the feature. In chess, as we have discovered, control of central squares is important because from the centre of the board a piece exerts more influence (i.e. it attacks more squares) than it does from an edge or corner square. So to determine the relative values of the squares, from the point of view of centre control, we should, perhaps, count how many moves can be made by each piece, on each square, when the remainder of the board is empty. Of course the remainder of the board is never empty, and sometimes it is very cluttered, but this approach does have a logical foundation and provides us with a first order measure of central square values. A detailed discussion of this method can be found in Jack Good's paper, to which I refer in the Bibliography.

Let us assume that we decide to assign square values as follows (see Figure 22): each of the four central squares counts 4, those next nearest the centre count 3, the next group 2 and those on the edge of the board count 1. We might then count the total centre control for a player by summing the square values on which his pieces stand, or by summing the values of all the squares that his pieces attack. This may sound like a rather ad hoc statement, but the quantification of features is something of a trial and error process. Since you are interested in computers you must have a logical mind, so apply some logic to the feature in question and you will come up with a quantification that will serve as a useful model.

1	1	1	1	1	1	1	1
1	2	2	2	2	2	2	1
1	2	3	3	3	3	2	1
1	2	3	4	4	3	2	1
1	2	3	4	4	3	2	1
1	2	3	3	3	3	2	1
1	2	2	2	2	2	2	1
1	1	1	1	1	1	1	1

FIGURE 22

How easy or difficult it is to quantify a feature varies enormously. To take some more examples from chess: mobility (the freedom of movement of the pieces) may be measured simply by counting how many moves each player has at his disposal. In fact mobility is the second most important feature in chess, and if you plot (White's mobility – Black's mobility) throughout a master game, you will almost certainly discover that whoever wins the game has a lead in mobility throughout much of its duration. The two key elements of pawn-structure, isolated pawns and doubled pawns, are also easy to measure – we can simply count them.

But what about king safety? This is not so easy because there are so many aspects of the position to take into consideration. The king is usually safest when it hides behind a few of its own pawns, but when these pawns advance they offer considerably less protection. A king is normally much safer near a corner of the board, but not if the opponent has many of his pieces trained on that particular corner. It is usually advisable to castle early in chess, to put the king into safety, but if queens are exchanged during the first few moves it may be better to leave the king nearer the centre, since it will be relatively safe during the middlegame and better placed for the endgame. With so many factors to take into consideration, the quantification of a feature such as king safety can be rather prone to error, but some attempt to do so is essential, so don't be put off if you encounter difficulties of this sort.

Weighting the features

Having decided which features to include in your evaluation function, and worked out a suitable method of quantifying each of them, you must then decide which of them are the most important, and assign some numerical weighting to each, to indicate its importance relative to the other features.

Let us suppose that we are writing a chess program and that we have decided to employ only two features in our evaluation function, material and mobility. We quantify material using the scale of values given above (9, 5, 3, 3, 1) and we measure mobility by counting how many moves each side can make from a given position. Let us denote the material difference (program's material – opponent's material) by Ma, and the mobility difference (program's mobility – opponent's mobility) by Mo. If we were to compute a score for a chess position simply by adding Ma and Mo, the result would be unrealistic. The reason for this is that one unit of material (in our case one pawn) is not of equal value to one unit of mobility (a move). A pawn is more valuable than a move (other things being equal) and so we must weight the material feature accordingly, multiplying Ma by some numerical weighting WMa. If we set WMa at 3, we are telling the program that one pawn is equivalent to three extra moves, so if it sees an opportunity to increase its mobility scores by 4, the program would be willing to sacrifice a pawn to do so.

The best method of arriving at a good set of weightings for an evaluation function is to start with values that seem to be in the right range, and then improve these values in the light of the program's performance. With our two featured chess functions, if we were to play a number of games we would almost certainly discover that with WMa set at 3, the program would not be sufficiently careful about its own pieces, and that as WMa was increased to 5 or 6 the program's performance would also improve. The task becomes more difficult and more time consuming when using a multi-feature function. I would recommend building up your function slowly, starting with two features and getting their weightings adjusted satisfactorily, then adding a third feature and adjusting its weighting while keeping the other two constant, then add your fourth feature, and then add new ones in descending order of importance. As you add each new feature you should carry out some experiments, if you have sufficient memory, by playing the new version of the program against the previous one. You may discover that the addition of a particular feature, while giving a more accurate position assessment, results in such an increase in computation that the program can search only a much smaller tree and the end result is weaker play.

Making your program learn

You will have gathered from the previous paragraph that it is often a very time consuming and difficult matter to reach an optimal set of weightings for your evaluation function. One way to help overcome this is to make the program learn from its experience and improve its own evaluation function!

A simple example is the case of our two featured chess function:

$$WMa \times Ma + Mo$$

We could modify our program so that it was able to play against itself, using two different values of WMa in each of the two 'versions' of the program. If we start out in total ignorance, we could make WMa = 1 in version 1, and WMa = 100 in version 2. We then set the program to play a large number of games against itself, in half of which version 1 would be White and in the other half it would be Black. At the end of the series we would discover that version 1 had lost almost all, if not all, of the games. (I have already explained that one pawn is worth much more than one move.) We then set WMa to be 2 in version 1 (or we could reduce WMa in version 2) and keep the other value constant. After another series of games we would find that version 1 still lost very heavily, but possibly not quite so heavily as in the first series. If WMa was kept at 100 in version 2, we would discover that as the value of WMa reached 3 in version 1, version 1 would start to win a few games; when it reached 4 or 5 its results would improve considerably, and by the time WMa was 6 it would possibly be outscoring the version with WMa = 100, because although material is more important than mobility there are situations in which the sacrifice of a pawn or two can advantageously increase a player's mobility, and WMa = 100 will never recognise those situations.

This process of adjusting the weighting in accordance with the program's results can, of course, be fully automated, so you could switch on at night, go to sleep for a week, and when you woke up your program would be playing like a Grandmaster. But with more than two features in the evaluation function this type of learning process can be difficult to operate – the self-learning reaches a local peak in the n-dimensional surface representing the various possible weightings and their results (n is the number of features), and it becomes difficult to climb out of the local peak in the search for a global peak. A method of overcoming this problem was discovered by Arthur Samuel, author of a famous draughts (checkers) program, but more about that in a moment. First I would like to describe a simple method of learning called 'Boxes', which can be applied to equally simple games with surprisingly effective results.

Boxes

Boxes is a method of decision taking that allows for a certain amount of program learning. A task (such as making the best move in a game) is split up into a number of sub-tasks (such as making a move in a particular game position) and a box assigned to each sub-task. Inside the box is the information that is used by the program to guide its decision, and this information can be updated in the light of the program's experience.

Boxes was originally tested on the game of noughts and crosses. Donald Michie has calculated that there are 288 essentially different positions with which the player moving first may at some time be confronted. To each of these 288 positions is assigned one box (matchboxes were used) and inside each box there are a number of beads. The beads each have a number on them, the numbers indicating vacant elements in the noughts and crosses array (i.e. places in which the box 'program' can make its next move). If one box corresponds to a situation in which elements 1, 2 and 3 are vacant, then that box will start out life with an equal number of '1 beads', '2 beads' and '3 beads'.

When this box is opened (i.e. when the 'program' has to make a move from the configuration corresponding to that box), a bead is drawn out at random, and the move is made according to the number on that bead. The bead is then replaced but the 'program' makes a note of the fact that this box was used, and that the bead chosen was (say) numbered 2. When the game is over, the boxes which were opened during the game are referred to again. If the 'program' won the game, then each box used during the game has one bead added to it, the number on the new bead corresponding to the move made from that box. If the game was a draw the contents of the box remain unchanged, but if the game was lost then one bead is removed from each box in order to reduce the probability that the same move will be played again should that situation ever arise in a future game.

The interested reader is referred to the paper (1968) by Michie and Chambers, which is mentioned in the Bibliography. The authors describe how the boxes method, with some modification, learned so well that it could win at noughts and crosses between 75% and 87% of the time when it had played a series of 1,000 games against a program which played first in every game and always moved at random. Of course methods such as this are far too simple to be able to cope with games of the complexity of chess or bridge, but it is interesting to see how effective a learning mechanism can be in a simple environment.

Samuel's draughts (checkers) program

Probably the most famous game playing program up to the late 1960s was the draughts (checkers) program written by Arthur Samuel of IBM. I shall be discussing Samuel's work in some detail in a future chapter so here I shall restrict myself to a description of two methods of learning which the program employed.

The simpler of the two methods is called rote learning. Each time the program conducts a tree search from a position (the root of the tree), it provides an evaluation of this position based on the results of the look-ahead search. This evaluation is therefore more accurate than the evaluation which would be achieved by applying the evaluation function directly to the root position. Thus the evaluation of the root position is stored, together with the position itself, and when the program next encounters the same position, but as a terminal node, instead of applying the evaluation function to the terminal node it looks up the stored evaluation. The process is relatively fast, since the positions can be hash coded and stored in such a way as to make retrieval easy; it results in more accurate play because the evaluation taken from the store is more reliable than a superficial evaluation. The obvious disadvantage of this method, from the micro-user's point of view, is the large memory required to make effective use of the rote learning process. (By the time that the program reached the peak of its playing ability, quite a high proportion of all reasonable draughts positions were in its store, and the program played at or near championship level.)

A more generalised approach to learning was Samuel's method for the self-modification of the weightings in the evaluation function. Samuel used the argument that if an evaluation function was ideal, the score obtained by applying the function directly to a position would be the same as the score obtained as a result of a look-ahead search *from* that position. The fact that the two scores are often different was employed in the following way.

Let us assume that our evaluation function has three features, A, B and C, and that the features are weighted with WA, WB, and WC respectively, so that the whole function is expressed as:

$$(A \times WA) + (B \times WB) + (C \times WC) = \text{score}$$

where A, B and C are the quantities present of each feature. We shall denote the backed-up score for a root position by S_b, and the score which was backed-up to that same position during the previous tree search (two-ply ago) as S_p. Note that if the tree search is normally n-ply, the score S_b will be the result of an n-ply search, whereas the score S_p, although arrived at during an n-ply search, is only the result of a search to depth n-2. S_b is therefore a more reliable score than S_p.

Samuel computed, for each such pair of values, the difference, which he called delta. If $S_b - S_p$ (i.e. delta) was positive, then he argued that S_p was in error and terms in the evaluation function which contributed positively should have been given more weight, while features which contributed negatively should have been given less weight. Whenever delta was negative he used the converse argument that features which contributed negatively should have been given more weight, and those which contributed positively should have been weighted less.

Samuel kept note of the correlation existing between the signs of the individual feature contributions (i.e. the signs of A, B and C) and the sign of delta, and he updated these correlation coefficients after every move of the game. He then selected the feature with the largest correlation coefficient (other than material advantage, which is always the most important feature), and he set the weighting for this feature at a prescribed maximum value, with the weightings of the other features adjusted in accordance with their correlation coefficients. In fact Samuel set all the weightings to be integer powers of 2, so that if the ratio of two correlation coefficients lay between n and $n+1$ then the ratio of their feature weightings would be 2^n. (If a correlation calculation gave rise to a negative sign, the sign associated with the weighting itself would be reversed.)

The obvious advantage of Samuel's generalised learning method is that it can be implemented on a microcomputer with little difficulty, because it is not necessary to store an enormous number of board positions. When your program makes a move from the root of the tree, you need only store all the 2-ply positions in the relevant part of the tree together with their backed-up scores. (In chess this would normally be in the region of 36 positions, in checkers probably less than 10.) A problem arises when the alpha-beta algorithm prunes off the branch actually selected by the program's opponent, since the relevant 2-ply position will not have been stored, but it is reasonable to argue that this will only happen when the opponent makes a mistake (or a move which the program thinks is a mistake), so such instances could be ignored. More accurately, if the program's opponent makes an unexpected move, before computing its reply move the program could first re-examine the relevant part of the tree from the previous root position, searching along the path represented by the opponent's move. This refinement would permit the program to take into consideration the S_b and S_p comparison for positions which, in the first instance, had been pruned away.

Task 5

Write a noughts and crosses program, using an evaluation function in which the features are:

c_3: The number of cross' '3-rows' (i.e. the number of rows containing 3 crosses).
c_2: The number of cross' 2-rows (2 crosses and an empty space).
c_1: The number of cross' 1-rows (1 cross and two empty spaces).
n_3, n_2 and n_1: Corresponding features for noughts.

Your program should perform a 3-ply exhaustive search (without alpha-beta pruning) and the evaluation function should start with all weightings equal. Modify your exhaustive search noughts and crosses program (Task 3) so that it can act as a sparring partner for the present program, and set the two programs playing each other. After every move of every game, the 3-ply search program should modify its weightings using Samuel's method. After each game, print out (or display, if you have no printer) the result of the game and the new weightings in the valuation function. Observe how the 3-ply program improves its performance.

Bibliography

Chambers, R. A. and Michie, D.: *Boxes: An Experiment in Adaptive Control.* Machine Intelligence 2 (Ed. Dale, E. and Michie, D.), Oliver & Boyd, 1968, pp. 137–152.

Good, I. J.: *A Five-Year Plan for Automatic Chess.* Machine Intelligence 2 (Ed. Dale, E. and Michie, D.), Oliver & Boyd, 1968, pp. 89–118.

Samuel, A. L.: *Some Studies in Machine Learning Using the Game of Checkers.* IBM Journal of Research and Development, vol. 3, 1959, pp. 211–229 (reprinted, with minor additions and corrections, in Computers and Thought, edited by Feigenbaum and Feldman, McGraw-Hill, 1963).

CHAPTER 6
Card Games – Guessing the Odds

Deduced probabilities

When playing a game of cards you usually know which cards you have been given, but normally you will not see the cards that have been dealt to your opponent(s). You may be able to deduce certain things about an opponent's card holding from the way in which he bids or plays, but it is unlikely that you will know exactly what he holds until very near the end of the hand. Decisions made in this sort of environment must be made on a probabilistic basis; in other words, you play with the odds and hope for the best. If you have calculated the odds correctly you will win more often than you lose.

Shuffling

Before proceeding to the main point of this chapter I should perhaps interpose a brief section on how to shuffle the cards in your program. The simplest way of creating a randomly sorted deck is as follows. Starting with the deck in any order you wish (even perfectly sorted), interchange the first card in the deck with the Rth card, where R is a pseudo-randomly chosen integer on the range 1 to n (n is the total number of cards in the deck). Then interchange the second card with another randomly chosen card, then the third, and so on to the end of the pack. The manner in which you generate your random numbers is of some consequence – I would recommend that while developing your program you use one of the seeding methods in which the i + 1 th random number is generated from the i th number, and the series is started with a 'seed' which may be chosen by the user. This approach has the advantage that if you spot a bug in your program you can recreate the hand simply by starting with the same seed. Once your program is debugged you may use the computer's internal clock to supply the seed, for example by using the time elapsed between the pressing of two keys.

One seeded random number generator which will suffice is:

$R_i = a^i \times \text{seed} \pmod{m}$

where R_i = i th pseudo-random number
$a = 8t + 3$ (for any positive integer t)
$m = 2^b$ where b is the number of bits per word in your computer.

Deducing information from the play of the cards

For the purpose of creating a simple example I have invented the following card game. The game is played by three players who are each dealt 17 cards at the start of a hand. The 52nd card in the deck is turned face up and that suit is trumps.

Starting with the player on the dealer's left, the player leads a card and the other players must follow suit if they can, or they may trump if they wish (provided that they are unable to follow suit). The player who wins one trick leads to the next, and the player who wins most tricks wins the hand.

Let us assume that we are dealt the following hand:

SPADES (trumps): A K 4 2
HEARTS: Q 10 7 5
DIAMONDS: K 10 9 6 2
CLUBS: J 8 6 4

and that the 7 of Spades is the card turned up. It is our turn to lead first.

At the start of the hand we know absolutely nothing about which cards our opponents hold, except for the fact that between them they hold all 34 of the unseen cards. But we do not have any indication as to how these 34 cards are distributed between the unseen hands, so the probability of each of the cards being in a particular hand is 0.5. We can therefore begin to construct, for each of our opponents (Bill and John) probability estimates for each card in the deck. At the start of the hand the estimates for each of them will be as shown in Figure 23.

	A	K	Q	J	10	9	8	7	6	5	4	3	2
SPADES:	0.0	0.0	0.5	0.5	0.5	0.5	0.5	0.0	0.5	0.5	0.0	0.5	0.0
HEARTS:	0.5	0.5	0.0	0.5	0.0	0.5	0.5	0.0	0.5	0.0	0.5	0.5	0.5
DIAMONDS:	0.5	0.0	0.5	0.5	0.0	0.0	0.5	0.5	0.0	0.5	0.5	0.5	0.0
CLUBS:	0.5	0.5	0.5	0.0	0.5	0.5	0.0	0.5	0.0	0.5	0.0	0.5	0.5

FIGURE 23

Assume that we lead the 4 of Spades, and that the next player (Bill) plays the 9 of Spades and the third player (John) takes the trick with the Q. What have we learned about the probabilities of the other cards, if anything?

Before answering this question I must explain an important theorem from probability theory, called Bayes' theorem.

Bayes' theorem

Let us suppose that there are two bags, each containing five balls. Bag A contains 1 white and 4 black balls, bag B contains 3 white and 2 black balls. I take a ball at random from one of the bags, and the ball is white. What is the probability that I took the ball from bag A?

The probability that a ball selected at random from bag A will be white is 1/5.

The probability that a ball selected at random from bag B will be white is 3/5.

Bayes' theorem shows that the probability that a randomly selected white ball actually came from:

$$\text{bag A} = \frac{1/5}{(1/5 + 3/5)} = 1/4$$

The reader will be able to generalise from this example, and the application to our game of cards will soon become apparent.

What have we learned?

Let us now return to the question of what, if anything, we have learned about Bill and John's hands from the cards they played to trick one? We probably cannot say very much at all about Bill's hand at the moment, but we already know something about John's cards.

John took the first trick with the Q of spades. The A and K are in our own hand and so the only cards that John could possibly have used to take the trick were the Q, J and 10. If John had held the Q and 10 but been missing the J, he would have played the 10, so from the fact that he played the Q we know that his original Spade holding included:

Q, J and 10 *or* Q and J *or* Q (without J or 10).

Now we can use the tables of probabilities for the individual cards to determine the *a priori* probability that John held each of these three holdings.

Probability that he held the Q, J and $10 = 0.5 \times 0.5 \times 0.5 = 0.125$

Probability that he held the Q and J but not the $10 = 0.5 \times 0.5 \times 0.5 = 0.125$ (Note that since the probability of his holding the 10 is 0.5, the probability of his not holding it is $1 - 0.5 = 0.5$)

Probability that he held the Q but not the J or $10 = 0.5 \times 0.5 \times 0.5 = 0.125$

And from Bayes' theorem we can show that the probability that the Q came from each of these three holdings is:

Q,J,10: $0.125/(0.125+0.125+0.125)=1/3$
Q,J: $0.125/(0.125+0.125+0.125)=1/3$
Q: $0.125/(0.125+0.125+0.125)=1/3$

Note that had the calculations been performed later in the hand, when the probabilities were not all equal (0.5), the final values would not all have been 1/3.

From these last calculations we can see that the probability that John holds the 10 of Spades is 1/3 (in which case he also holds the J), and the probability that he holds the J is 2/3. We can therefore adjust the probabilities for the individual cards in John's hand as follows:

For the 10 of Spades: probability = 0.333
For the J of Spades: probability = 0.667
For all other unseen cards the probabilities are equal, and these are:

$$\frac{16-0.333-0.667}{32-1-1}=\frac{15}{30}=0.5$$

Since there are 16 unseen cards in John's hand, and 32 unseen cards in total (the probabilities of the J and 10 of Spades being in John's hand are subtracted from the number of cards in his hand, and one is subtracted for each of them from the total number of unseen cards).

If the probability of the J of Spades being in John's hand is 0.667, then the probability of it being in Bill's hand is 0.333, and by the same argument the probability of Bill holding the 10 of Spades is 0.667. So we have been able to make some adjustments in the probabilities simply on the basis of John having played the Q of Spades at trick one. We can also make note of the fact that if John ever shows the 10 of Spades, we will know that he holds the J.

At trick two, John must lead because he won trick one. He leads the A of hearts, we play the 5, and Bill trumps with the 8 of Spades. What have we learned from trick two? First of all, Bill would obviously use his lowest trump or one of his lowest contiguous group of trumps. The 7 was the original face up card, we played the 4 on trick one and Bill played the 9. We hold the 2 of Spades and so Bill's 8 of Spades must have been played from one of the following holdings:

J,10,8,6,5,3:
J,10,8,6,5:
J,10,8,6:
J,10,8:
10,8,6,5,3:
10,8,6,5:
10,8,6:
10,8:
8,6,5,3:
8,6,5:
8,6:
8:

and by using Bayes' theorem we can determine the probabilities of each of the above holdings being in Bill's hand, and from these probability estimates we can determine estimates for the cards being in John's hand. We can also adjust the probabilities for all the Hearts: those which are not in our own hand must all be in John's hand.

Deducing information from the bidding

In many card games there is a bidding phase between the deal and the play of the cards. The best known of such games is bridge, but the popular German game of Skat is another widespread example (it is said that Skat can be played by more than 50% of the entire population of Germany). Since each bid has a meaning, it should be possible for the card playing program to learn something about its opponents' hands from the way that they bid, and it can then adjust its probability estimates for each card in their hand. How this is done will obviously vary from one game to another. Let us take a brief look at Bridge, to see how we might modify the probability estimates of the unseen cards in the light of the bidding.

We are sitting South and hold 10 high card points. We look at the 13 cards in our hand and assign a probability of 1/3 to each of the remaining 39 cards in each of the other three hands. West opens the bidding and bids one Spade, indicating that he has a stronger than average hand and that Spades is his best suit. (Of course, this bid can mean other things, but we shall assume for this example that the above meaning is correct in the particular bidding system that West and his partner employ.) We may now adjust the probabilities of the Spades, so that each Spade in West's probability array has a slightly higher probability (say 0.45 instead of 0.33), and we may also adjust the probabilities of the high valued cards (Aces, Kings, Queens and Jacks) so that they give an expected high card holding which corresponds to a typical one Spade opening bid. (If this bid is made with an average of 13 points, the Ace counting 4 points, King 3, Queen 2 and Jack 1, then by making each of the high card probabilities 0.4333 we give West an expectation of 13 out of the remaining high card points: there are 40 high card points in total and we hold 10 of them, leaving 30, and 13/30 = 0.433.) We should, in fact, give a slightly higher probability to a card which is both a Spade and a high card.

Having assigned new probabilities to the Spades and the high cards, we can then adjust the probabilities for the remaining cards in West's hand, so that the sum total of his probabilities is 13 (the total number of cards in his hand), and we can adjust the probabilities for each card in North's and East's hands by subtracting West's probability from 1 and dividing the result by 2, remembering to ignore all cards in our own hand.

So from his first bid we can make quite a lot of probabilistic estimates about West's cards, and hence about those in the North and East hands.

The bidding then passes to North, and depending on his bid we make adjustments to his probabilities using similar, logical arguments, and then we adjust the probabilities for West and East. This process continues until the end of the bidding – each time we acquire some information that increases the likelihood of a card being in a particular place, we increase the probability for that place and reduce it accordingly in the other hands. When there is some negative information about the position of a card we use it in a similar way.

By the end of the bidding phase a good bridge program should have a fairly accurate estimate of how each of the other three hands is made up. By summing up the probability values for all the Spades in a hand the program can get an estimate of how many Spades that player holds. By summing the products (high card probability × high card point value), the program can estimate the number of high card points in each suit in each hand. It will then be better able to plan its play of the hand, and of course the probabilities will be adjusted all through the playing phase.

How to use deduced information

The most obvious use of our deduced probabilities arises when the probability estimates for all unseen cards are all either 1 or 0, i.e. we know where all the remaining cards lie. We then have a case of a perfect information game, and we can solve this game by performing a tree search to the end of the game. Even though there may be three or more players, the tree approach should still work, though we must make certain assumptions about the way that the other players are going to make their decisions. For example, let us assume that we are two tricks from the end of a hand of our three-player card game.

We hold: A of Spades, 10 of Diamonds.
Bill holds: J of Diamonds, 5 of Clubs.
John holds: 3 and 2 of Clubs.
It is our turn to lead (remember that Spades are trumps).

The program now constructs a game tree, of depth 6-ply. Part of the tree will look like Figure 24. We assign to the terminal nodes of the tree, scores corresponding to the number of tricks won by each player, and we back-up

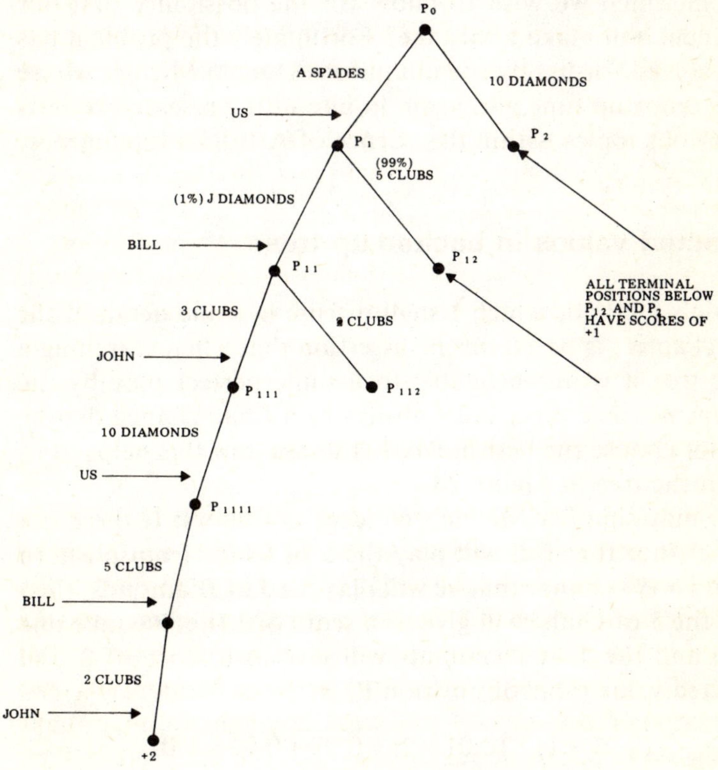

FIGURE 24

through the tree until we can determine which card should be played next. In this example the situation is simple because if we lead the A of Spades first we *may* take two tricks, whereas if we lead the 10 of Diamonds we can only make one trick. Note the use of the word 'may'. In order to make two tricks we need some help from Bill, who must make a mistake and discard the J of Diamonds in the hope that our second card is the 2 or 3 of Clubs and he will make his 5. But since we lose nothing by playing the A of Spades first, that is clearly the best way to continue. How can we modify our traditional methods of tree-searching to cater for situations such as this one, in which we wish to allow for the possibility that our opponent will make a mistake? Fortunately the problem has been solved for us, by the ubiquitous Donald Michie, whose name crops up time and again in interesting research reports on various topics within the science of Artificial Intelligence.

Expected values in backed-up trees

Michie's method, which I shall discuss in some detail in the next chapter, is based on the assertion that when searching a game tree it is unreasonable to assume perfect play by the opponent, since there must always be a finite chance that he will not choose the best move. Let us see how this helps us to search the tree in Figure 24.

We may simplify Michie's concept as follows: If there is a 99% chance that Bill will play the 5 of Clubs from position P_1, and a 1% chance that he will play the J of Diamonds, then since the 5 of Clubs will give us a score of 1 (i.e. we take one trick) and the J of Diamonds will give us a score of 2, the expected value to us of position P_1 is

$$(0.99 \times 1) + (0.01 \times 2) = 0.99 + 0.02 = 1.01$$

whereas if we play the 10 of Diamonds from position P_0, the expected (in fact the certain) value of position P_2 will be 1 (i.e.

we will take one trick no matter how Bill and John play). Since 1.01 is greater than 1, we should play the A of Spades from P_0 because it maximises our expected score. The reader will probably have realised by now that not only does Michie's method allow us to optimise our practical chances when we *know* exactly where all the unseen cards lie, it also enables us to use our probability estimates of the locations of the unseen cards, to build game trees which will help in the play of the hand. In other words, Michie has shown us how to play with the odds!

Task 6

Find or invent a simple card game in which information may be deduced from the play of the cards. (Avoid bidding games, unless you are extremely confident and have many free hours.) Write a program to play this game, modifying the probability estimates of the unseen cards in the light of the user's play. Experiment with various methods of adjusting these estimates until the program plays at least moderately sensibly. At the point in the game where exhaustive search will not be too time consuming, set up a probabilistic game tree à la Michie to search to the end of the game.

Bibliography

Michie, D.: *A Theory of Evaluative Comments in Chess.* Memorandum MIP-R-105, Department of Machine Intelligence and Perception, University of Edinburgh, July 1974.

Mirhram, G. A.: *Pseudo-Random Number Generators are Really Card Shufflers.* Personal Computer Proceedings, National Computer Conference, New York, 1979, pp. 318–326.

(For more information on Bayes' theorem see any good book on statistics or probability theory.)

CHAPTER 7
Bluffing and Psychology

It may sound strange to suggest that a deterministic animal such as a computer is capable of performing in a psychologically motivated manner, but those of us who believe that Artificial Intelligence is here to stay will argue that if *you* can do it, so can a computer (or microcomputer) program. This chapter is devoted to a discussion of the ways in which the 'thought' processes of a game playing program may be modified to perform in a manner that takes advantage of its opponent's psychological makeup.

Michie's work

I have referred earlier to Donald Michie's paper *A Theory of Evaluative Comments in Chess*. In this paper Michie makes use of the fact that in a two-person game tree, it is not absolutely accurate to assume that the opponent will always make the best move at his disposal. Players are liable to make mistakes, and Michie's paper is centred around this fallibility. A strong player, in chess or any other game, will often encounter a situation in which the best move, based purely on deterministic considerations, is not the move most likely to maximise a player's chance of success. Let us consider a concrete example which I witnessed in an international chess tournament (Figure 25).

The position was something like this. Both players had been very short of time and had been making their moves at great speed. White is clearly losing, and had his opponent not been in time trouble he would probably have resigned. But

FIGURE 25

White tried one last chance. He played 1 Qa2–h2, giving check. The first thing that I should mention is that these two players were using a very large chess board and set. This had a bearing on White's plan, because he hoped that his opponent's gaze would be attracted to the black king, and that he would not notice the fact that the queen, way over on the other side of the board, was attacked by and attacking the white queen. Had Black not noticed this fact, he would have moved his king and allowed White to capture his queen on the next move, whereupon White would have won. In fact Black did notice, and knowing his opponent rather well he had been half expecting this surprising queen check on h2, so without a moment's pause Black captured the white queen and our hero resigned. He had not lost anything by trying the ludicrous queen check, because his position was totally lost; he was merely hoping for a one in ten thousand chance.

Moving into the realm of tree searching, we shall now consider a similar example in terms more familiar to the reader.

A player has two moves at his disposal, M_1 and M_2. He is good enough to see that if he makes move M_1 the result of the game will inevitably be a draw. So the expected result from making move M_1 is 0.5.

If he makes move M_2 the player sees that his opponent can defeat him, but only by finding a 15-ply deep continuation that is very difficult to spot. Otherwise, our player will win. He assesses the probability of his opponent finding this 15-ply win as being 0.1. The expected result from making move M_2 is therefore

$$(0.1 \times 0) + (0.9 \times 1) = 0.9$$

So even though, with correct play, M_1 is theoretically better than M_2, our player will be better off making move M_2.

Michie analyses his tree in the following manner. (I am using a simpler example: see Figure 26.)

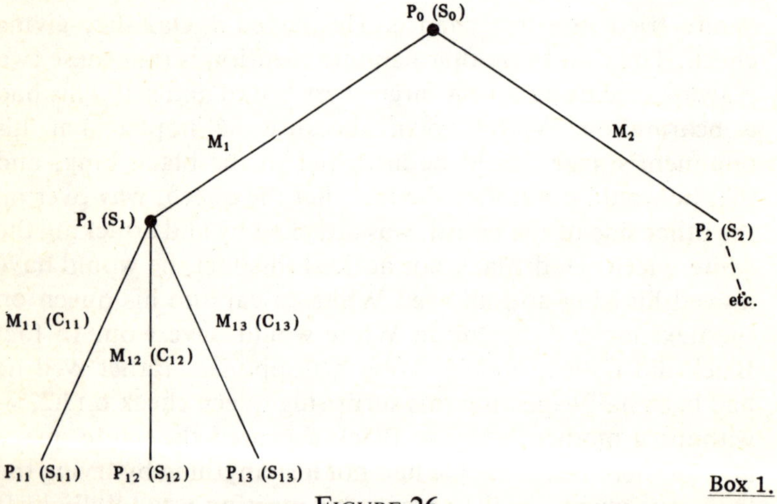

FIGURE 26

Let us assume that we are growing a 2-ply tree, with terminal positions P_{11} P_{12} and P_{13} . . . etc., and terminal scores S_{11} S_{12} S_{13} . . . etc., respectively. The program considers its possible move from the root position P_0 to P_1, and notes that its opponent will then have the choice of making the moves M_{11} M_{12} and M_{13}. Let us say that the program estimates the chance (or probability) of its opponent making move M_{11} to be C_{11}, the chance of its opponent choosing M_{12} to be C_{12}, and the chance of move M_{13} to be C_{13}. Then instead of assigning to position P_1 a score of S_1 which is the *minimum* of S_{11} S_{12} and S_{13}, the program assigns a value of

$$S_1 = (C_{11} \times S_{11}) + (C_{12} \times S_{12}) + (C_{13} \times S_{13})$$

and it is this score which is backed-up to P_0 (remember that the program, which 'thinks' at even depths, will always make the move with highest expected score). This part of Michie's method will work perfectly well for a normal minimax search, but in an alpha-beta search there is the problem that a large number of branches are pruned from the tree so an accurate, backed-up expected score is impossible to achieve. Possibly one could attempt an approximation for alpha-beta searching, but this could lead to extremely unreliable results.

Discernibility

Consider the plight of an imperfect player trying to decide which move to make in a game. There are three aspects of his situation that may affect his decision:

(1) How strong a player is he? If he is very strong then he will nearly always make the best move. If he is very weak then he will often make the wrong one.

(2) How obvious is the right move? If you and I are playing chess, and you capture my queen, it is fairly obvious, even to a weak player, that I must recapture your queen unless there is something special about the position. In a 'quiet' position, in which neither side has any direct threats or simple captures, the correct move is far more difficult to perceive, because there may be a number of moves of roughly equal merit.

(3) What extraneous (psychological!?) factors affect the decision? If the correct move is a queen move and our player suffers from some peculiar sexual fantasy that precludes certain types of queen move, it is likely that he will fail to play the correct move.

These three factors combine to affect discernibility – the ease of finding the right move. Michie has devised the following model for discernibility in chess:

$$d = (M + 1)^{\frac{3(r+3)}{r+e}}$$

where M is the player's rating in kilo-points on the international rating scale (Bobby Fischer's M is roughly 2.8, David Levy's is 2.3, the average of all those who can play chess is 0.8).

r is the number of ply that a terminal evaluation has been backed up.

e is a small number chosen to avoid the expression becoming infinite for $r = 0$.

Michie's formula is derived from the fact that discernibility is directly related to playing strength and inversely related to the number of plausible or possible moves ('plausible' being a function of playing strength). He further argues that the probability of a player whose discernibility is d, making a move leading to an expected score of u, will be given by:

$$p \propto d^u$$

Using these expressions, it would be possible for a strong chess program to plan its play according to the rating of its opponent, taking greater risks against weaker opponents and being cautious against strong ones. At the start of a game it would need to be told its opponent's rating, or if it were extremely sophisticated it could estimate its opponent's strength by performing regression analysis on the moves he made as the game progressed, thereby enabling it to update its estimate of his rating on a move-by-move basis.

How to psych your opponent

A good player will sometimes use psychology to help him win games. He will make moves that are probably not the very best, but which will be difficult or unpleasant for his particular opponent to meet. In chess, for example, a player who is equally at home in quiet, clear positions or in sharp, tactical skirmishes, will himself choose quiet play against a tactical genius but sharp moves against a quiet player. How can this be achieved by a computer program, particularly when employing an alpha-beta search?

Let us assume that the program examines every 1-ply position with a search that analyses only captures and checks. If the program counts the number of moves examined in each of these capture searches, it can compute a measure for the complexity or 'turbulence' of the 1-ply position. This measure might be some fraction of the logarithm of the number of positions in the capture search. The program can then add this turbulence score to the 1-ply position so that when conducting the full tree search the program assigns greater scores to the moves that lead to more complex positions, which in turn will encourage the program to head for this type of position. If the program's opponent dislikes 'quiet' positions, the program should subtract the turbulence measure, thereby encouraging it to play into quiet positions. It would even be possible for the program to psycho-analyse its opponent during a game, by measuring his tendency to head for quiet or complex situations. It could then act accordingly, avoiding positions that suited its opponent's style of play, and aiming for positions that would be less pleasant for the opponent to face.

Bluffing

In some card games it is important to try to mislead your

opponent(s) some of the time. In others it is absolutely essential. The human player does this by bluffing, which in reality is little more than creating extra opportunities for the opponent to make a mistake. When you bluff at the card table you are not, in one sense, making the objectively best play, because your opponent may catch you out and punish you. So from a strict minimax point of view, a bluff is not a valid notion, because minimax depends on the assumption that each player will make the best move at his disposal, thereby indicating that all bluffs will be called.

On the other hand, everyone knows that in order to be a successful poker player it is essential to bluff from time to time. This is done for various reasons, one of which is that if your opponent believes you he will pass with the winning hand, thereby allowing you to win the money despite holding inferior cards. There is also the point that if you are caught bluffing once or twice in a session, your opponents will be more inclined to call your big bets when you really do have a powerhouse, thus increasing your overall profits from good hands. The big question, of course, is how often and when should a player bluff? The human will plan his bluff on an intuitive basis, the computer program must do so in a more scientific manner. Let us now consider how a program might determine whether a bluff is likely to prove profitable.

Rummy

In one form or another, rummy is one of the most popular card games in the world. Let us assume that our program is playing a game of Compu-Rummy, which has the following rules: Each player is dealt 12 cards and tries to form 'melds' – groups of three or more cards of the same denomination (three Queens, four Aces, etc.), or three or more cards of the same suit in sequence (4, 5, and 6 of Hearts). Each player in turn may pick up a card from the face-up pile or from the face-down pile, and must then discard a card on to the face-up pile. When a player has melded all of his cards he wins the hand.

To play this game well it is important to remember which cards have been thrown by your opponent, as these give an idea of which cards he is collecting (or rather which cards he is not collecting, which information can be used by subtraction to estimate which cards he *is* collecting). There are many ways in which a Compu-Rummy program might work; a simple idea is for the program to use an evaluation function to decide which card to discard after it has made a pick-up. The most important feature in this evaluation function will almost certainly be the number of melds or part melds remaining in his hand after a discard. The program might score n points for an n-card meld, and 1 point for a 2-card part meld that might later become a 3-card meld. In order to decide which card to throw on the face-up pile, the program computes a score for the cards remaining in its hand after each of the 13 possible discards, and it then makes the discard leading to the position (or holding) with the highest score. If two or more discards appear to be of equal value, the program can employ additional features in its evaluation function to discriminate between these discards. Since the loser in a hand of Compu-Rummy is penalised by the number of points contained in his unmelded cards, it would be advisable for the program to throw high point cards rather than low point cards.

These two heuristics are the most obvious features of a Compu-Rummy evaluation function. But there is another important aspect of rummy, which is known in the trade as 'advertising'. If you are hoping to make a meld that runs from the 3 of Clubs to the 7 of Clubs, but you are missing the 5 of Clubs, you might be able to entice your opponent into discarding the 5 of Clubs by making the discard of another 5, if you hold one. Your opponent, seeing (for example) the discard of the 5 of Diamonds, will immediately assume that you are not collecting fives, and unless he has seen you pick up the other Clubs in your potential meld he will be quite likely to consider the 5 of Clubs a safe discard, should he hold this card in his hand or pick it up at a later stage. This type of play is made by all skilled rummy players, and should be included in a Compu-Rummy program. The simplest way to implement a bluff of this type is to give a small bonus for discarding a card that is close to a card that you hope to pick up. You might score 0.5 points for discarding a card of the same denomination as the card you need, or a card of the same suit but one pip removed, and it would then be sensible to score 0.25 for a discard that was of the same suit but two pips removed from a desired card. One problem with an algorithm of this type is that your opponent will, if he is intelligent, soon learn what is going on, and will modify his play accordingly. So the frequency with which advertising is encouraged should vary, and in a sophisticated program it may even be adjusted dynamically as the game progresses, to take into account the manner in which the opponent is playing. An intelligent computer program can monitor its opponent's play and modify its own strategy accordingly. I have touched briefly on the subject of learning programs in an earlier chapter and later I will discuss learning techniques in more detail.

Poker

In my opinion, poker is the most skilful card game of all. I have played poker for many years and I enjoy it even more than chess. Part of the reason for my enjoyment comes from the psychological struggle that takes place at the poker table, and most of this struggle emanates from the bluffing aspect of the game. Bluffing in poker must be handled in a scientific manner, because each situation will depend on how much money the program stands to win or lose by its attempted bluff. Let us first look at a simple situation in a hand of 5-card stud poker.

Joe: ? 5 7 A K (all Hearts)
Ben: ? 6 6 8 9

$100 currently in the pot.

To understand this example it is not really necessary for the reader to know the rules of poker. A brief description of the implications of this situation will suffice.

The game is played by dealing each player one card face down and one face up. A round of betting takes place, and all those who remain in the hand then receive another face-up card, and indulge in another round of betting. This continues until the fourth face-up card and its round of betting, and once everyone has put the same amount of money in the pot, the player with the best cards wins.

In the above hand, Joe and Ben are the only players remaining in the pot when the final cards are dealt. It is Joe's turn to bet, and he can either 'check' (putting no money into the pot and allowing Ben the option of betting), or he can bet the limit of $100. Joe's hidden card is the Queen of Clubs which gives him a useless hand, but Ben does not know this. So far as Ben is concerned, Joe might have another Heart, in which case he has a hand known as a flush, which will win irrespective of whether or not Ben has more than a pair of sixes. What thoughts will pass through Joe's mind when he thinks about whether or not to try a bluff?

Reducing the hand to its simplest terms, Joe may put in $100 *knowing* that if Ben calls the bet Ben will win. But if Ben is bluffed into thinking that Joe has that fifth Heart, Ben will pass the $100 bet and Joe will pick up the $100 currently in the pot. If Joe is human he will use inborn intuition to make his decision. He has been playing poker with Ben for some time so he knows how Ben usually reacts in situations of this type. The intelligent computer program must simulate this intuitive process in some way.

The following simple algorithm should prove rather effective in some situations, but it is by no means intended to be exhaustive. Anyone intending to write a poker program will need to think of a very large number of typical situations – here I am dealing with only one. (See Figure 27.)

SITUATION: Open pair facing a possible flush.

PLAYER:	Ben	Joe	Fred	Tim	Dave	Henry	Mike
PROB OF CALLING:	0.3	0.6	0.7	0.4	0.3	0.5	0.2

FIGURE 27

By monitoring the players, the program builds up a picture of what each of them has done when having an open pair (such as Ben's pair of sixes) against a possible flush, and the player with the possible flush has bet the limit. The program has noted that Fred likes to live dangerously and call 70% of such bets while at the other end of the scale Mike is very conservative and will be less likely to call. When the program reaches this particular situation, and holds four face-up cards of the same suit, it can decide whether or not to bluff in a probabilistic manner. (See Figure 28.)

Investment = 100 Amount currently in the pot = 100
Probability of opponent calling the bet = p
Probability of opponent not calling the bet = 1 – p
Expected income = Expected gain – Expected loss
= (1 – p) × 100 – p × 100

FIGURE 28

For Ben the probability of his calling the bet is 0.3, so the expected income is 70 – 30 = 40. For Joe the probability is 0.6, so the expected income is 40 – 60 = – 20. So the program would not try to bluff in this situation against Joe, but it would against Ben, and it would determine whether or not to try a bluff against the other players in a similar manner. If you are writing a poker program and your computer system supports a cassette or disk, it will be possible for you to retain the information learned during one playing session for use in the next. Of course it is quite possible for one or more of the program's opponents to change his style from one session to another, but it is always useful to have some reference point at the start of a game. For players with unknown characteristics, the program will employ fixed estimates, stored in a table, which can be updated during a playing session as the program learns how each player acts at the poker table. It will also be possible for an intelligent program to make certain generalisations: for example, Joe is quite likely to call a possible bluff in a parallel but as yet unrecorded situation (the probability of the bettor having a cast iron cinch being roughly the same as his having a flush when showing four cards of the same suit). Again this is largely a matter of learning.

Task 7

Those of you who completed the earlier tasks involving noughts and crosses programs, will find this exercise somewhat trivial, but nonetheless instructive.

Write a noughts and crosses program to play a perfect game by means of exhaustive tree search. Test this version of the program against a program that moves at random, playing a number of games and noting the percentage score.

Modify the program to use Michie's method of backing up expected values, based on the assumption that the opponent will be moving at random, and play this version of the program against the random version. The results should indicate that slightly imperfect play can result in a better score than perfect play!

CHAPTER 8
Draughts (Checkers)

Up to now this book has been devoted entirely to the general principles involved in writing programs to play intelligent games. Now we start on a new tack, with chapters that describe specific games in some detail and comment on the most notable work in each field.

The subject of the present chapter is the game of draughts (known as checkers in North America and dames throughout much of continental Europe). I have already described one of the learning techniques employed in Arthur Samuel's checker program; now we shall be making a closer inspection of other aspects of this famous project. The chapter will conclude with some additional comments on computer learning, as applied to games.

Samuel's checker program

Arthur Samuel began to program checkers in 1952, using an IBM 701 computer. It was rewritten for the IBM 704 in 1954 and the following year the first learning mechanism was introduced.

The fundamental program structure employed a minimax tree search, since the alpha-beta algorithm had not yet been invented. All moves were examined to a depth of 3-ply, and the program would look selectively at moves at the next ply, provided that:

(i) The move was a capture;
(ii) The previous move was a capture; or

(iii) The move offered the opponent the chance to exchange men.

At the next ply the program ignored all moves for which the previous move was not a capture, and at the sixth ply and deeper levels in the tree only capture moves were examined. By the time the program reached this depth the number of moves being examined from any position was small, but it was still possible for the program to find itself getting involved in ridiculous capture sequences, and so at a depth of 11-ply the search would terminate if either side was more than two kings ahead (an overwhelming advantage). At 20-ply the search terminated under all circumstances so that the program did not run out of memory for storing the tree.

Samuel's criteria for pruning the tree were chosen in such a way as to encourage the evaluation of positions that were quiescent, and to discourage evaluation in turbulent positions. The concepts of quiescence and turbulence are perhaps better understood when related to the two different aspects of game playing: strategy and tactics. Strategy involves planning and manoeuvring. Tactics (e.g. capturing) are used to punish blunders and to convert a strategic advantage into something more concrete, such as material. The argument in favour of Samuel's approach is that the three-ply of exhaustive search gives the program some strategic grasp of what is happening, while the deeper tactical search ensures that it does not perform erroneous evaluations in turbulent positions. The necessity to restrict the deeper search in this way is clearly dependent on the nature of the game and the number of branches at each node of the tree (the branching factor). The number of positions evaluated in a minimax is roughly proportional to b^d where b is the average branching factor and d is the depth of search, and anything that can be done to reduce the 'b' will produce a combinatorial improvement in playing speed.

The evaluation function used in the early version of

Samuel's program employed 39 terms or features, only 17 of which were in use at any one time. The features were temporarily suspended from duty if and when it was found that they did not contribute significantly to the evaluation process. Correlation measurements indicated which of the 17 features currently in use were the least effective, and once the effectiveness dropped below some threshold value they were replaced by the features at the top of the reserve list, while the rejects were added to the bottom of the reserve list. Material was the dominant feature, and Samuel recognised the need to encourage the program to trade off pieces when it was ahead but to avoid exchanges when behind. This may be accomplished in various ways but the most reliable is probably to determine the value of:

$$\begin{matrix}\text{(program material –} \\ \text{opponent's material)}\end{matrix} \times \frac{\text{(greater side's material)}}{\text{(lesser side's material)}}$$

A full list of the other features in the linear part of the evaluation function is given below. There were, in addition, some non-linear terms in the function. In the following list the board notation is as used in the draughts (checkers) literature (see Figure 29):

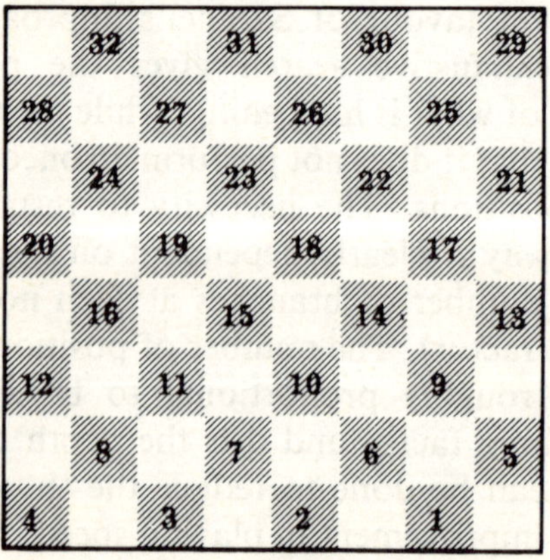

FIGURE 29

ADV (Advancement)
The parameter is credited with 1 for each passive man in the 5th and 6th rows (counting in passive's direction) and debited with 1 for each passive man in the 3rd and 4th rows.

APEX (Apex)
The parameter is debited with 1 if there are no kings on the board, if either square 7 or 26 is occupied by an active man, and if neither of these squares is occupied by a passive man.

BACK (Back Row Bridge)
The parameter is credited with 1 if there are no active kings on the board and if the two bridge squares (1 and 3, or 30 and 32) in the back row are occupied by passive pieces.

CENT (Centre Control I)
The parameter is credited with 1 for each of the following squares: 11, 12, 15, 16, 20, 21, 24 and 25, which is occupied by a passive man.

CNTR (Centre Control II)
The parameter is credited with 1 for each of the following squares: 11, 12, 15, 16, 20, 21, 24 and 25, that is either currently occupied by an active piece or to which an active piece can move.

CORN (Double-Corner Credit)
The parameter is credited with 1 if the material credit value for the active side is 6 or less, if the passive side is ahead in material credit, and if the active side can move into one of the double-corner squares.

CRAMP (Cramp)
The parameter is credited with 2 if the passive side occupies the cramping square (13 for Black, and 20 for White) and at least one other nearby square (9 or 14 for Black, and 19 or 20

for White), while certain squares (17, 21, 22 and 25 for Black, and 8, 11, 12 and 16 for White) are occupied by the active side.

DENY (Denial of Occupancy)
The parameter is credited with 1 for each square defined in MOB if on the next move a piece occupying this square could be captured without an exchange.

DYKE (Dyke)
The parameter is credited with 1 for each string of passive pieces that occupy three adjacent diagonal squares.

EXCH (Exchange)
The parameter is credited with 1 for each square to which the active side may advance a piece and, in so doing, force an exchange.

EXPOS (Exposure)
The parameter is credited with 1 for each passive piece that is flanked along one or the other diagonal by two empty squares.

FORK (Threat of Fork)
The parameter is credited with 1 for each situation in which passive pieces occupy two adjacent squares in one row and in which there are three empty squares so disposed that the active side could, by occupying one of them threaten a sure capture of one or the other of the two pieces.

GAP (Gap)
The parameter is credited with 1 for each single empty square that separates two passive pieces along a diagonal, or that separates a passive piece from the edge of the board.

GUARD (Back Row Control)
The parameter is credited with 1 if there are no active kings and if either the Bridge or the Triangle of the Oreo is occupied by a passive piece.

HOLE (Hole)
The parameter is credited with 1 for each empty square that is surrounded by three or more passive pieces.

KCENT (King Centre Control)
The parameter is credited with 1 for each of the following squares: 11, 12, 15, 16, 20, 21, 24 and 25, which is occupied by a passive king.

MOB (Total Mobility)
The parameter is credited with 1 for each square to which the active side could move one or more pieces in the normal fashion, disregarding the fact that jump moves may or may not be available.

DIA (Double Diagonal File)
The parameter is credited with 1 for each passive piece located in the diagonal files terminating in the double-corner squares.

DIAV (Diagonal Moment Value)
The parameter is credited with 1/2 for each passive piece located on squares 2 removed from the double-corner diagonal files and with 3/2 for each passive piece in the double-corner files.

MOVE (Move)
The parameter is credited with 1 if pieces are even with a total piece count (2 for men, and 3 for kings) of less than 24, and if

an odd number of pieces are in the move system, defined as those vertical files starting with squares 1, 2, 3 and 4.

NODE (Node)
The parameter is credited with 1 for each passive piece that is surrounded by at least three empty squares.

OREO (Triangle of Oreo)
The parameter is credited with 1 if there are no passive kings and if the Triangle of Oreo (squares 2, 3 and 7 for Black, and squares 26, 30 and 31 for White) is occupied by passive pieces.

POLE (Pole)
The parameter is credited with 1 for each passive man that is completely surrounded by empty squares.

RECAP (Recapture)
This parameter is identical with Exchange, as defined above. (It was introduced to test the effects produced by the random times at which parameters are introduced and deleted from the evaluation polynomial.)

THRET (Threat)
The parameter is credited with 1 for each square to which an active piece may be moved and in so doing threaten the capture of a passive piece on a subsequent move.

Different sets of weightings were tried in the evaluation function and an initial set was chosen by playing through a series of checker games from a book and computing the correlation coefficient of the moves chosen by the program and those chosen by the original (human) player.

Rote learning

The most elementary type of learning worth programming is

the storing of a large number of game positions together with their scores as determined by the evaluation function. Samuel pointed out that if a score for a position was arrived at as a result of a 3-ply search, the next time this position is encountered as a terminal node in the tree (say at depth 3) the evaluation of the root position will be made on the basis of a search which has, in one variation, been examined to a depth of 6-ply. In this manner a program with a large storage capability could learn to play a game such as checkers rather well. The problem facing personal computer users is clearly one of space, and without a floppy disk system the task will be impossible for any moderately interesting game. Even with a floppy, games such as checkers will very soon use up all available memory.

Move-phase-tables

Another method of learning, described in 1974 by Arnold Griffith, is quite unusual. Griffith discovered that in each particular phase of the game a certain move would, fairly consistently, either be a good move or a bad move. This is an oversimplification of his thesis, but it will suffice for the purpose of this chapter.

Griffith analysed a number of games from draughts books. Whenever an expert player made a move, Griffith noted the move and defined the position arising after that move as a 'strong' position. A position which would have arisen after an alternative move was assumed to be less desirable, and hence termed a 'weak' position. He then tabulated all the possible forward moves, of which there are 49, and for each forward move he noted the proportion of occasions in which this move led to a strong position in each phase of the game (1st ten moves, 2nd ten, 3rd ten, 4th ten, 5th ten and move 50 onwards). The first rows of his table are shown in Figure 30.

When the program came to evaluate a move it could simply

MOVE	PHASE 1	PHASE 2	PHASE 3	PHASE 4	PHASE 5	PHASE 6
1 − 5	0.07	0.09	0.12	0.06	0.05	0.05
1 − 6	0.11	0.18	0.15	0.06	0.07	0.02
etc.	....	....	....	....	....	....

FIGURE 30

look up the table entry corresponding to the particular move and the appropriate phase of the game. One way of utilising such a method would be to employ Michie's probabilistic approach described in the last chapter, since this would provide a more global view of whether a particular path in the tree was heading in a desirable direction.

I must confess that I find Griffith's method somewhat curious, but it appears to work to a certain extent in draughts, and presumably the same will be true in other games which (a) have a fairly restricted move set, and (b) have a dependence relationship between the various phases of the game and the moves themselves. In chess, for example, the move of the king towards the centre of the board is usually very undesirable until the endgame is reached, but the game is so complex that very few rules of this type could be used for phase-tables, and the number of possible chess moves is so vast that the whole approach would be useless. I would be very interested to hear from any reader who successfully applies the phase-table method to a game playing program.

Bibliography

Griffith, A. K.: *A Comparison and Evaluation of Three Machine Learning Procedures as Applied to the Game of Checkers*. Artificial Intelligence, vol. 5 (1974), pp. 137–148.

Samuel, A.: *Some Studies in Machine Learning Using the Game of Checkers*. IBM Journal of Research and Development, vol. 3 (July 1959), pp. 211–229.

Samuel, A.: *Some Studies in Machine Learning Using the Game of Checkers – II – Recent Progress.* IBM Journal of Research and Development, vol. 11 (November 1967), pp. 601–617.

CHAPTER 9
Chess

Of all the games that have attracted the attention of computer programmers, chess must surely rank at the top of the list. This is partly because chess is considered by many to be *the* intellectual game, par excellence, and therefore the creation of a strong chess program can be equated with the creation of an artificial intellect. Another reason is that the writing of a chess program is itself a great challenge.

Because of the enormous interest in computer chess, a lot has been written on the subject. I have decided that this chapter will be a large one. I shall provide a history of the most important milestones in the field, and I shall discuss how the ideas employed in main-frame programs may be applied to micros. I shall also discuss the current state of the art of microcomputer chess programming, with many examples taken from actual games, and will describe some unsolved problems in chess programming.

In the beginning

On March 9th 1949, the American mathematician Claude Shannon delivered a paper at a New York conference. The paper was called *Programming a Computer for Playing Chess*, and it is remarkable that many of Shannon's original ideas have permeated through to the programs of today. He pointed out that there are some 10^{120} possible games of 40 moves (the average length of a master game), and that analysing to this depth at the rate of one game per micro-second would take a computer 10^{90} years to make its first move! A similar, though even more emphatic argument, is that the number of possible chess games so far exceeds the number of atoms in the universe, that even were each atom to be replaced by a Cray 1 computer, it would take the whole system rather a long time to make the first move in a perfect game of chess.

Having dispensed with the notion of perfect play through exhaustive search, Shannon set about defining an evaluation function which would give a reasonably reliable estimate of which side held the advantage in a position, and by how much. His example of a crude evaluation function was:

$$200 \times (K_w - K_b) + 9 \times (Q_w - Q_b) + 5 \times (R_w - R_b) +$$
$$3 \times (B_w - B_b + N_w - N_b) + (P_w - P_b)$$
$$- 0.5 \times (D_w - D_b + S_w - S_b + I_w - I_b) + 0.1 \times (M_w - M_b)$$

where K, Q, R, B, N and P represent the number of pieces of each type (king, queen, rook, bishop, knight and pawn), and the subscripts w and b refer to White and Black. D is the number of doubled pawns (pawns of the same colour on the same file); S is the number of backward pawns (pawns that cannot be defended by a pawn); I is the number of isolated pawns (pawns with no neighbour pawns of the same colour); M is the measure of mobility (the number of legal moves at a player's disposal).

The king is given an arbitrary high value because loss of the king means loss of the game. The values of 9, 5, 3, 3 and 1 for the other pieces are the rule-of-thumb values which chess players learn early in their careers, though bishops are usually regarded as being more valuable than knights so in your chess program you might experiment with values of 3¼, 3⅓ or even 3½ for a bishop.

Shannon's evaluation function is sufficient to provide a reasonable level of performance in a microcomputer chess program. Chess, however, is a complex game, and Shannon recognised the need for the use of many other features if the evaluation function were to result in a strong program, and he suggested the following additional features:

1. Relative control of the centre by pawns (White pawns at c4, d4, e4 and f4; Black pawns at c5, d5, e5 and f5).
2. Weakness of pawns near your own king (e.g. advanced pawns in front of the king after castling).
3. Placing pawns on opposite coloured squares from your own bishops to allow the bishops greater freedom of movement.
4. Passed pawns (i.e. pawns which have no enemy pawns in front of them, either on the same file or on adjacent files). These pawns can often become queens in the endgame.
5. Advanced knights (White knight at c5, d5, e5, f5, c6, d6, e6 and f6; Black knights at c4 etc.), especially if protected by a pawn and free from attack.
6. Rooks on open or semi-open files (an open file is one with no pawns; a semi-open file has one pawn belonging to the opponent).
7. Rooks on the seventh rank. (A White rook on a7, b7, . . ., or a Black rook on a2, b2, . . . , etc., can wreak havoc in the endgame by picking off the opponent's pawns.)
8. Doubled rooks (two rooks of the same colour on the same file).
9. Pieces which are required for guarding functions and, therefore, committed and with limited mobility.
10. Attacks on pieces which give one player the option of exchanging.
11. Attacks on squares adjacent to the enemy king.
12. Pins. (A pin is a setup in which one piece may not move because of the loss of a piece which it is shielding, e.g. White bishop on g5, Black knight on f6, Black queen on e7. Black may not move his knight because of the loss of his queen – the knight is said to be pinned by the bishop.)

The addition of these features would provide a rather sophisticated evaluation function for middle game play, though as Shannon himself pointed out, different factors apply in the opening and (to a lesser extent) in the endgame.

When and how to use the evaluation function

Shannon understood that it is only safe to use this type of evaluation function in positions which are relatively quiescent. If White makes a move capturing Black's queen, it is not sensible to evaluate the resulting position without looking to see if Black might be able to recapture White's queen in reply, or whether he might be able to checkmate. In fact it is meaningless to evaluate a position during a series of exchanges, unless the evaluation mechanism allows for the fact that further meaningful exchanges are possible. Chess players recognise quiescent positions intuitively, but computer programs have more difficulty because they cannot immediately determine which capturing moves and sequences are 'obviously' wrong, in the way that a human chess master can.

Shannon called a fixed depth search strategy a 'type A' strategy. He realised that in chess this type of strategy would lead to weak play, partly because of evaluating many non-quiescent positions once the fixed search depth had been reached, and partly because of the time required for exhaustive search (the alpha-beta algorithm had yet to be invented in 1949). Again he alluded to the thought processes of chess masters, and in particular to the work of the Dutch psychologist De Groot who recorded the spoken thoughts of chess masters as they analysed a number of typical chess positions. Shannon concluded that in order to improve the speed and strength of the program it would be necessary to:

1. Examine forceful variations as far as possible and evaluate only in quiescent or quasi-quiescent situations.
2. Select the variations to be examined by some process so

that the program does not waste a lot of time in totally fruitless variations.

Shannon called this type of strategy a 'type B' strategy, and it is the Shannon B strategy which is used in almost all of the most successful programs of today. The key to the Shannon B strategy is the ability to determine which moves and variations are worth considering, a problem on which much has been written but rather little accomplished during the past three decades. When I examine a chess position I can usually make a reasonably good move after looking at only 50–100 nodes of the game tree. In order to play at the same level, the current world computer champion must examine over one million nodes. If it had the same ability to discern which variations are important, it would be able to defeat Bobby Fischer.

In order to help decide whether a move is worth exploring, Shannon suggested the use of a function which would return a large value for forcing moves (captures, checks and attacking moves), medium values for defensive moves, and low values for all other moves. As the depth of search increased, the requirements of this function would be set higher so that fewer and fewer subvariations would be examined. This approach has proved successful in a number of strong chess programs, and can easily be implemented on a micro. One simple method of doing so would be to examine all moves at the root of the tree, then only the most important 90% of moves at ply-1 ('importance' being determined by Shannon's discrimination function), then only the most important 70% at ply-2, 50% at ply-3, 30% at ply-4 and 10% at ply-5 and beyond, down to the limits imposed by search time restrictions or to quiescent positions. My method would call for an examination of fewer than 10% of the number of nodes normally examined in a 5-ply search, and the 90% saving could be used either to increase the sophistication of the evaluation function (which would also make it slower), or to increase the maximum depth of search in tactical situations.

Another key idea suggested by Shannon was the use of typical chess positions or fragments of positions, for which a particular move or sequence of moves is known to be effective. Chess masters use this type of information all the time. They recognise a situation and immediately start to examine a move which they know has often proved strong in similar positions. Of course it will not always be the case that exactly the same move is best in a slightly different situation, but as we have seen in previous chapters it is extremely important to examine the most likely moves early in the search process. Unfortunately, the only substantial example of this approach was a dismal failure. A strong American chess master, Charles Kalme, implemented a method involving 'snapshots' of chess situations. His work was discussed in a *Scientific American* article in 1973, but shortly thereafter his program fared dismally in the annual ACM computer chess tournament in Atlanta, and little has been heard of the program since then. Perhaps this is one example of a technique used by humans which will be difficult to employ in a computer program. In any event, Kalme's failure should not worry the micro user, since the amount of memory required to use the snapshot approach would be prohibitive at today's prices.

The Bernstein program

Shannon's work was purely theoretical in nature. He did not write a chess program to test his ideas, though if he had done I suspect that his program would have been stronger than some commercially available programs now on the market.

The first example of a program playing full games of chess was seen in the late 1950s. This program was written for the

IBM 704 computer by Alex Bernstein of IBM and three colleagues. Since your own machines will all be considerably more powerful than an IBM 704, any of you who write chess programs ought to be able to do at least as well.

Bernstein *et al* employed four features in their evaluation function: mobility, area control, king defence and material. Area control was defined as the number of squares controlled completely by each side, while king defence counted the number of controlled squares around the king. Their material feature was weighted with the ratio of its own material to that of its opponent, in order to encourage the program to exchange material when ahead and to discourage it from exchanging when behind. This simple heuristic is extremely well known, but not all programmers consider it worthwhile to implement it, possibly because programs play worse in the endgame than they do during the middle game!

Moves were generated in response to a number of questions:

1. Is the king in check?
2. Can material be gained, lost or exchanged (i.e. can the program make an equal or advantageous capture, or is it threatened with material loss)?
3. Is castling possible?
4. Can a minor piece be developed?
5. Can key squares be occupied? (Key squares are those squares controlled by pawns.)
6. Can an open file be occupied?
7. Can any pawns be moved?
8. Can any piece be moved?

If the answer to question 1 is 'yes', the program generates moves that reply to the check, and these moves are put into a 'plausible move table'. If the answer to question 1 is 'no' the program goes to question 2, and so on. If the answer to question 3 is 'yes', no other moves beyond question 3 are examined, as castling was considered so important that no other moves except replies to check and material changing moves are of greater importance to the program.

At the beginning of the game only questions 4 and 7 put moves on to the plausible move list. After the opening stage, the other questions are employed in the move generation process, with questions 2, 5 and 6 being the most often used in the middle game, and questions 5, 6, 7 and 8 during the endgame. Once there are seven moves in the plausible move table, no other moves are generated from that position. This explains why the programmers felt it important to generate the moves in a particular order – they wished to prune off most of the legal moves in every position, and preferred to do so at the move generation stage rather than use the more modern approach of generating all the moves first and then sorting them before finally discarding some.

This simple approach was used to create a tree with a maximum depth of 4-ply, and therefore a maximum of 7^4 or 2401 terminal positions requiring evaluation. In fact a further pruning mechanism was employed: a move is only put on the plausible move list if it results in an increase in score, or at least an equal score, to that which prevailed before the move was made. With a sophisticated, accurate evaluation mechanism this method might work quite well. One problem is that the program may find itself looking at a position in which no move appears to do anything but reduce the score for the side which makes it, and under these circumstances the program will select the best two moves for the inclusion in the plausible move table.

Forward pruning mechanisms go a long way towards solving the problem of having the program examine too many junk variations, but to be effective without being counterproductive a forward pruning program must exhibit sound judgement when deciding which moves to prune, otherwise a superficially bad move which is really quite stunning might easily find itself eliminated from the search.

It is interesting to note that the older Chess Challenger

machines did quite a lot of forward pruning, whereas the current stronger commercially available programs do not. This in itself does not necessarily indicate that forward pruning is difficult to accomplish on a micro, and I would be interested to hear from any reader who thinks he has found a satisfactory way of pruning off a significant part of the game tree. I should remind you that Bernstein's approach of an (essentially) fixed depth search is not to be recommended. Evaluating all positions at 4-ply, irrespective of whether they are quiescent, is certain to result in feeble play unless the evaluation mechanism is sufficiently intelligent to cater for future captures in some way.

The report on Bernstein's work included the moves of a game played by his program against a human opponent. I give the game here, with some comments of my own, to illustrate the standard of play that can be achieved using a primitive search process. Here, and in the next few chess games, I shall familiarise the reader with the notation which is becoming standard for microcomputer chess games, naming the *from* square and *to* square using conventional chess notation – White has the square a1 in his left hand corner and h1 at his right. This is the notation which you will probably use if you write your own chess program.

White: IBM 704
Black: HUMAN

1	e2–e4	e7–e5
2	f1–c4	

The program had not been taught any chess openings and was playing on general principles, hence it developed a piece. It is usually a good rule to develop knights before bishops, so question 4 should have been split into (4a), can a knight be developed?, and (4b) can a bishop be developed?

2	. . .	b7–b6
3	d2–d3	g8–f6
4	c1–g5	c8–b7
5	g5–f6	

Prompted by question 2, but in fact a wasted move. Firstly, the bishop is more useful than Black's knight; secondly, the program ought to give more weight to developing pieces during the opening, and a move such as b1–c3 or g1–f3 is called for.

5	...	d8–f6
6	g1–f3	c7–c6
7	e1–g1	d7–d5
8	e4–d5	c6–d5
9	c4–b5 +	b8–c6
10	c2–c4?	

An excellent example of why the search should not terminate at a fixed depth of 4-ply. White can win a pawn here by playing 10 f3–e5, because if Black recaptures with 10 ... f6 × e5 White will win the queen by 11 f1–e1, when Black must lose his queen for a rook. But the program would only see the variation 10 f3–e5 f6–e5 11 f1–e1 e5–e1 +, and since Black is well ahead in material at this point, the program would evaluate the position as being good for Black, ignoring the fact that White's next move (d1–e1) captures the Black queen. Using Shannon's B strategy, accidents such as this just cannot happen.

10	...	d5–c4
11	b5–c6 +	f6–c6
12	d3–c4	e5–e4
13	f3–g5	c6–g6
14	g5–h3	e4–e3
15	f2–f3?	

Here a strong move would be 15 h3–f4, attacking the Black queen and preventing mate at g2, but again the program would only have examined to the end of the four-ply continuation 15 h3–f4 e3–f2 + 16 f1–f2 g6–g2 (or b7–g2), and seen that it had lost a pawn!

15	...	f8–c5
16	f1–e1	e8–g8

Of course e3–e2+ does not win the White queen because the pawn on e2 is pinned against the Black king. But now 17 . . . e3–e2+ is a real threat.

17 b1–c3??

Which the program overlooks. There is a routine which asks 'am I in check?', but none which asks 'can I give check?', and there is no question of the form 'can I attack a valuable enemy piece?' As a result of these deficiencies, the program would not have put Black's next move in the top seven places on the plausible move list when considering the replies to 17 b1–c3.

17	. . .	e3–e2+
18	h3–f2	b7–f3
19	g2–g3	e2–d1=Q
20	c3–d1	g6–c2
21	b2–b3	a8–d8
22	h2–h4??	

Of course the program is totally lost in any case, but this move is worthy of comment because it illustrates another deficiency of forward pruning. The answers to questions 1–6 were all 'no'. Question 7 generated six legal pawn moves and question 8 generated piece moves, but the plausible move list was full after the first piece move was discovered, and so the program failed to spot the need to defend itself against the threat of d8–d1. Had it done so it would probably have played e1–f1, a move which requires a six-ply search to discover its refutation.

22	. . .	d8–d1
23	Resigns	

So with a crude search strategy and crude forward pruning, the Bernstein program was able to play recognisable chess, but extremely weakly. One important lesson that can be learned about forward pruning from the last mistake, is that your program should look further afield if the first move that it comes up with is seen to be bad. In this case, after examining the 7 chosen moves from the root of the tree, the program could see that it was losing material to 22 . . . d8–d1, but was powerless to stop it. Had it been permitted to continue its search it would have found a 'better' move before too long. There is a parallel here between the drastic forward pruning method employed by Bernstein, and the iterative deepening approach used by many of today's programs. With iterative deepening, a program finds the best move it can after a 1-ply search, then it increases the depth to 2-ply and looks for a better move, then to 3-ply, and so on, until it runs out of time. Similarly, a forward pruning program should be permitted to continue its search by relaxing the pruning requirements, if it cannot find a satisfactory move early on in its search. Instead of searching 7 moves at each level, Bernstein could have examined (say) 5 moves at each level in less than one-third of the time, then when the program discovered that 21 h2–h4 and its four brothers were all dreadful moves, it could have examined all the other moves from the root of the tree, and the best five successors to each of them. This would have resulted in only a slight increase in total computation time for the move, but it would have enabled the program to see the immediate tactical consequence overlooked by the 'best seven' approach.

The modern generation

The first program of the modern generation was written at MIT by Richard Greenblatt, a student, and two colleagues. Work on the program began in November 1966 and by April the following year it had scored two wins, two draws and no losses in a tournament with human players. Based on statistics given in Greenblatt's paper, I would estimate that his program, at that time, was stronger than any commercially available chess machine in 1980 on the market. The name of his program was MacHack VI.

MacHack employed a plausible move generator containing some 50 heuristics. The program was intelligent enough to know that certain heuristics were not always applicable, but depended on the nature of the position. In this way, moves selected by the plausible move generator were not always exactly the same set of moves as those which would have been chosen by a linear evaluation function. From this aspect of MacHack's decision process the microprogrammer can learn an important trick – it is often useful to use one evaluation mechanism (or set of heuristics) to select the plausible moves for the tree, and another one for performing the evaluation of terminal nodes.

The plausible move generator made its decisions by considering the moves themselves, rather than the positions arising after the moves were made. For example, if a move is bad because it blocks the line of attack of another of the player's pieces, the program would recognise the fact rather than look at the resulting position and say to itself 'Hey! This position is bad because my bishop is blocked.' By accepting or rejecting moves for the plausible move list in this way, the program saved a great amount of computation.

During the plausible move computation, each square of the chess board was assigned a measure of importance, corresponding roughly to the estimated value of having an extra piece attacking that square, or the cost of moving away a piece which currently attacked that square. The most important criteria used for assigning these values included how near the square was to the centre of the board or to the enemy king, and whether or not the square was occupied by one of the program's pieces under serious threat.

The value of a piece in strategic terms (as opposed to its actual material value) was related to the number of squares it attacked, i.e. its mobility, and to the number of enemy pieces that it attacked. These strategic values were computed for the piece in its old and new locations and a strategic gain was taken as an indication that the move should be on the plausible move list. In other words, if a move appears to put a piece on a better square, that move is worth further examination.

The program encouraged certain types of attack on squares that were considered possible weak points, for example weak pawns, pinned pieces, and pieces defending other pieces. Moves which fell into these categories were also added to the plausible move list.

MacHack performed an alpha-beta search, with forward pruning. The plausible move generator would select a number of moves at each level of look-ahead, and add to this number any moves which satisfied certain conditions: all safe checks were examined; at the first and second plies all captures were investigated; the moves of a certain number of distinct pieces are examined, so that the program would not ignore most of the board if all of the moves of a single piece were highly plausible. The minimum number of moves selected by the plausible move generator was normally six at each level of look-ahead, but in tournament mode, i.e. when playing at a rate of 2–3 minutes per move, the program would examine a minimum of 15 moves at the first two ply, nine moves at the next two ply, and seven moves at each subsequent level. Only when the minimum number did not exist (for example when one side was in check or had only its king on the board) would the search be narrower, though of course the alpha-beta algorithm would often prune away branches on which there were plausible moves.

One of the few advantages that mainframe programmers have over those writing for a micro, is the availability of an enormous backing store. This enables a program to employ transposition tables, which are advantageous in preventing the program from evaluating the same position more than once. In chess, as in many other games, it is frequently possible to reach the same position by different routes, and we call this phenomenon transposition. As a simple example, if White makes move A, Black makes move B, and White then makes move C, we can reach the same position as if White had made his moves A and C in the reverse order. MacHack produced a hash value for every position evaluated in the tree search, and together with this value the program stored the score for the position and a note of the depth of search at which the evaluation took place. If the position is created again during the search, the program would not recompute the score for the position but would take it from the value stored together with the hash for that position. Even though MacHack stored only 32,000 positions in hashed form, it was able to save considerable computation time and as a side benefit, it was quickly able to detect draws by repetition.

The MacHack program represents the first really significant milestone after Shannon's paper because it was the first program to make good use of the Shannon-B strategy. The strength of the program in 1967 was extremely impressive and created considerable publicity for computer chess among the computing and chess fraternities. This publicity served as the impetus for many of the groups which started programming around 1967 or 68, for example the Slate/Atkin/Gorlen group at Northwestern University and Newborn at Columbia University. In fact Greenblatt and his colleagues probably did as much for computer chess in 1967 as Shannon had done almost 20 years earlier.

I should like to offer you two examples of the playing strength of the Greenblatt program. The first is a position which was shown to several strong American chess players, including Masters, and defeated a number of them.

The position in Figure 31 is a win for Black, who has an extra knight for a pawn. But the task is to find a quick win. If White is allowed to survive he might conjure up counterplay based on the exposed position of the Black king and the weakness of Black's pawns on g6 and a7. How can Black force a quick win?

Black to play

FIGURE 31

MacHack discovered the correct continuation:

1 ... f8–f2+

For the program to play this move it must have been able to see 9-ply ahead, in the crucial variations.

2 f1–g1

The alternative was 2 e2–f2 g4–h2+3 f1–e2 (or 3 f1–g1 b4–e1+4 g1–h2 e1–f2, when Black is a rook ahead) 3 ... b4–b2+4 e2–d1 b2–b1+5 d1–e2 b8–b2 mate.

1 ... f2–e2
3 g7–h8+ d8–c7
4 h8–f6 e2–e1+
5 Resigns

To show that a computer program is a good chess player, it is not enough to give an example of its tactical prowess. The very best programs are extremely adept at tactical combinations but are often let down by their poor strategic understanding. So the proof of the whole pudding must lie in the examination of complete games. The following is the first game ever won by a computer program in a chess tournament. Its opponent was rated 1510 on the USA rating scale, equivalent to a weak club player. The game was played in the Massachusetts State Championship, 1967.

WHITE: MacHack VI
BLACK: Human

1	e2–e4	c7–c5
2	d2–d4	c5–d4
3	d1–d4	

MacHack knew no openings at that time and plays very much as many of today's commercially available machines. This type of opening is bad for White because it allows Black to bring out his pieces 'free of charge', by using developing moves to harass the White queen.

3	. . .	b8–c6
4	d4–d3	g8–f6
5	b1–c3	g7–g6
6	g1–f3	d7–d6
7	c1–f4	e7–e5

A dubious decision. The human was obviously worried about the possible advance of the White pawn from e4 to e5, but Black should have continued 7 . . . f8–g7, and if e4–e5, then f6–h5, attacking White's bishop.

8	f4–g3	a7–a6
9	e1–c1	b7–b5
10	a2–a4	f8–h6+ ?

An ineffective move that weakens an important central pawn. One gets the impression that the human felt he could take risks against MacHack.

11	c1–b1	b5–b4
12	d3–d6	

Black, when making his tenth move, almost certainly overlooked the fact that on the d6 square, White's queen or rook will fork the two Black knights on f6 and c6, thereby rendering harmless Black's threat to the White knight on c3.

12	. . .	c8–d7
13	g3–h4	h6–g7
14	c3–d5	f6–e4
15	d5–c7 +	

Black may have overlooked this response, but in any event his position was hopeless.

15	. . .	d8–c7
16	d6–c7	e4–c5
17	c7–d6	g7–f8
18	d6–d5	a8–c8
19	f3–e5	d7–e6
20	d5–c6 +	

MacHack spots a simple queen sacrifice that forces mate.

20	. . .	c8–c6
21	d1–d8 mate	

A benchmark chess program

It is perhaps worth mentioning in passing the work performed by Jim Gillogly during the early 1970s on a program designed as a benchmark for other chess programs. Gillogly's program, which he named TECH, had a very simple program structure which could easily be emulated by anyone using a micro. Rather than perform strategic evaluation on all terminal nodes in the tree, the TECH program only took a close look at the nodes at the first level of look-ahead. It evaluated all these positions, sorted them into order and only changed this order if a full-width search revealed the forced win or loss of material for a root move. Programs with such a structure can play perfectly recognisable chess and are tactically quite satisfactory but they are hindered in their overall playing performance by a lack of strategic depth.

Those of you wishing to start writing chess programs for your own machines could do a lot worse than employ Gillogly's approach. Because strategic evaluation is only carried out on the (say) 30–40 root moves, the program can perform a quick full-width search, using the alpha-beta algorithm, to detect forcing variations that affect the material status of the board. Such a program is relatively easy to write and should perform at roughly the same level as one of the less strong commercially available machines of 1982, provided that your strategic evaluation function is well thought out.

Gillogly argued that to be of any real merit, a chess program must be able to play better than a TECH type program, given the same amount of time, because the TECH program did not do anything clever. A really good programmer could probably write a TECH type program in little more than 2k of code (assembler) and I would not be surprised to see a program of that size playing better chess than some of the 8k and 16k cassette programs available to personal computer users today.

Deep or shallow search

Not entirely unconnected with the previous section is the question of how essential it is to search the game tree as deeply as possible. There are two distinct schools of thought on the subject: programmers usually prefer to search as deeply as possible, on the grounds that they are more likely to notice neat tactical possibilities; but a minority believe that shallow search, with more attention being devoted to each node, can lead to equally good play. Since human chess players look at a very small tree, this second approach is clearly endowed with some merit, but most chess programmers prefer the exhaustive search technique, possibly because of a lack of confidence in their own ability to create an advanced evaluation function that would be sufficiently sophisticated to perform drastic forward pruning.

Up to now almost all of the world's strongest programs have been the 'brute force' type – searching enormous trees but performing relatively little sophisticated evaluation at the terminal nodes. The TECH program is possibly the supreme example of this genre, performing only a material evaluation at the terminal nodes. We do not yet have sufficient experience with intelligent chess programs to be able to determine which approach is superior but I hope that the following game, despite exhibiting rather passive play by Black, will convince the reader that brute force is not the only possible route to a master strength chess program. For those programming chess on a micro, the intelligent approach offers much scope for original research.

This game was played in a computer tournament in Dortmund in 1975.

WHITE: Schach MV 5.6
BLACK: Fischer/Schneider

1	b1–c3	d7–d5
2	d2–d4	c8–g4
3	f2–f3	g4–f5
4	e2–e4	d5–e4
5	f3–e4	f5–d7
6	g1–f3	b8–c6
7	e4–e5	e7–e6
8	c1–g5	f8–e7
9	d1–d2	g7–g6
10	f1–d3	

So far Black has played rather passively, but White has developed its pieces on sensible squares. White's latest move is, in fact, a mistake, which should lose a pawn to 10 . . . c6–d4 11 g5–e7 d4–f3+ 12 g2–f3 g8–e7, but Black was unable to see this far.

10	. . .	b7–b6
11	g5–e7	g8–e7
12	e1–c1	e8–g8
13	d2–h6!	

Immediately beginning an attack against the Black king. The threat is f3–g5, followed by h6–h7 mate.

13	. . .	e7–f5
14	d3–f5	g6–f5
15	f3–g5	d8–g5 +

Giving up the queen was the only way to prevent mate. If 15 . . . f8–e8 16 h6–h7 + g8–f8 17 h7–f7 mate.

16	h6–g5 +	g8–h8
17	g2–g4	

A fine move, opening up other lines of attack to the Black king.

17	. . .	f5–g4
18	g5–g4	f7–f5
19	g4–h4	f5–f4
20	c3–e4	

Here comes the other knight.

20	. . .	f4–f3
21	e4–g5	f8–f7

Again the only way to prevent mate on h7.

22	g5–f7 +	h8–g8
23	h4–f6	f3–f2
24	f7–h6 mate	

It would be reasonable to deduce, having played over this game, that the program playing the White pieces had a very good idea of what it was doing; that it planned a king-side attack from early on and then executed this attack in a well planned manner. In fact, White did not employ any look-ahead whatsoever. All of its moves were found as a result of a one-ply search. Its king attack feature was obviously well designed but there was no tree search – the planning was all implicit in the evaluation function. This should provide some idea of just how much *can* be achieved without a deep look-ahead and I hope it will encourage some of you to write intelligent programs rather than programs which perform brute force searches of large trees.

The Northwestern program

To conclude this survey I shall give a brief description of the famous program, written at Northwestern University, by David Slate, Larry Atkin and (in the beginning) Keith Gorlen. This program has won most of the important computer chess tournaments of the 1970s, and the interested reader would do well to read a more detailed account of this program, which may be found in Peter Frey's outstanding book *Chess Skill in Man and Machine*.

The Northwestern University program, whose successive generations have been named CHESS 2.0, . . . CHESS 3.0, . . . CHESS 4.0, . . . CHESS 4.9 (the first digit represents a working generation, the second digit is a version within that generation), was born in 1968. When the first computer chess tournament took place in 1970, the program proved itself to be the strongest and it maintained this reputation for most of the decade. Occasionally another program would win an event ahead of the Northwestern program but such occurrences were the exception rather than the rule. This program held the title World Computer Champion, which it took from the Russian KAISSA in 1977. In the World Championship contest in Linz, Austria (25–29 September 1980) we saw a new title holder, BELLE.

Much of the program's power is due to its great speed. The programmers have devoted much effort to the speeding up of essential processes such as legal move generation and to this end the program maintains a data base which includes, among other things, a list of every square attacked by each piece. This list is updated whenever a move is made in the game tree, and by updating it rather than recreating it, the programmers reduce the time taken to provide the attack and defence lists for the newly created position. The program also uses a hash table for transpositions, as described in the section on Greenblatt's work.

For some time, the Northwestern program employed a plausible move generator to restrict the number of nodes in the game tree but various reasons prompted the programmers to a full-width search. One of the prime reasons for doing so was the fact that they noticed certain moves, which appeared good when examined to a depth of (say) 5-ply, but which ranked too low at the root of the tree to be included in the first plausible move list. Chess masters are not faced with this problem because their plausible move generator is much more sophisticated and accurate and I suspect that the chess programs of the future may return to the plausibility approach, unless brute force searching produces an electronic chess master within the next few years.

The program's evaluation function contains a number of terms which quantify the best known chess heuristics. Material is measured in such a way as to encourage the side that is ahead in material to exchange where possible and to discourage the exchange of material if the program is losing. Another feature gives a bonus for attacking enemy pieces and this bonus is enhanced when an enemy piece is doubly threatened.

Pawnstructure is an important feature of the game of chess at higher levels of skill and any program which aspires to master strength must understand the finer points of pawn-structures. If your pawn formation is rotten your whole position is eventually liable to crack under pressure. This program considers doubled pawns (two or more pawns of the same colour on one file); isolated pawns (pawns that cannot be supported by pawns of their own colour); backward pawns (pawns which do have adjacent friendly pawns, but which are less far advanced than their neighbours); passed pawns (those which have no enemy pawn impeding their progress to the eight rank); and advanced pawns.

Knights, bishops, rooks and queens are given bonuses according to the values of the squares they attack, particularly if the squares are near the enemy king or the centre of the board. Rooks are given bonuses for being situated on open files or on the seventh rank (a rook on the seventh rank usually poses a serious threat to enemy pawns which have not yet moved). The kings are discouraged from moving towards the centre of the board, except in the endgame, and there is a safety feature which determines whether or not a king is well sheltered by its own pieces.

The tree searching routines employ all of the techniques that we have encountered in previous chapters: the alpha-beta algorithm, with a 'window', killer moves, etc. In fact the Northwestern program provides us with an excellent illustration of the power of all these neat tree searching tricks – it plays better chess than more than 99.5% of the world's chess playing population and has even won some quick games against International Masters and Grandmasters. These outstanding results have been achieved more through the effects of a cleverly programmed brute force search than as a result of the program's chess knowledge, which is still primitive. The success of the program shows that good programming is even more important than an advanced knowledge of the game, when producing a program of the strength currently being exhibited by microcomputers. Certainly it will be necessary for a human chess expert to be involved in the programming of an electronic Grandmaster but there is absolutely no reason why the readers of this book should not write a program that can play respectable chess.

To illustrate the prowess of the Northwestern program I

shall offer you the following game, which was its first ever win over a human Grandmaster. The game was played at blitz speed, which requires each player to make all of his moves within five minutes. In fact the rules were slightly different for the two participants – Stean was playing in real time but the program was permitted a total of five minutes for CPU time and satellite transmission time, with no penalty for the time taken by its human operator to move the pieces.

WHITE: CHESS 4.6
BLACK: Stean

1	e2–e4	b7–b6
2	d2–d4	c8–b7
3	b1–c3	c7–c5
4	d4–c5	b6–c5
5	c1–e3	d7–d6
6	f1–b5 +	b8–d7
7	g1–f3	e7–e6
8	e1–g1	a7–a6
9	b5–d7 +	d8–d7
10	d1–d3	g8–e7
11	a1–d1	a8–d8
12	d3–c4	e7–g6
13	f1–e1	f8–e7
14	c4–b3	d7–c6
15	g1–h1	

It is peculiar moves such as this one which make it possible to recognise the play of a computer. A strong human player would never move his king on to a diagonal occupied by his opponent's queen and bishop, unless it was forced.

15	. . .	e8–g8
16	e3–g5	b7–a8
17	g5–e7	g6–e7
18	a2–a4	d8–b8
19	b3–a2	b8–b4
20	b2–b3	

If we sum up what has happened so far, it is clear that Black has a dominating position. His pawns control the centre while White's e4 pawn attacks only one central square. Black's pieces are active, White's are passive. But the program has one important advantage – its opponent thinks that to all intents and purposes the game is over and he tries to take the program's position by storm. This is exactly the opposite of the way one should play against a strong program – the tactical search will reveal tricks that the human misses, especially at this breakneck speed.

20 . . . f7–f5?

A mistaken attempt to open up the diagonal to the White king.

21 f3–g5 f5–e4
22 c3–e4 f8–f2

This move appears, at first glance, to be very strong. If now 23 e4–f2, Black's queen immediately gives mate on g2. But the program had seen further in the crucial variation than its opponent.

23 d1–d6!

When he saw this move Stean exclaimed, 'Bloody iron monster'. The point is that Black's queen is needed to prevent d6–d8 mate, and the queen is attacked. If the queen moves to a square that protects d8, White can then capture the rook on f2. So White must win material.

23 . . . c6–d6

The best try.

24 e4–d6 f2–g2

Threatening to move the rook to g5, c2 or e2, with check from the bishop on b7. Any of these moves would win for Black, but . . .

25 g5–e4

Blocking the crucial diagonal.

25	. . .	g2–g4
26	c2–c4	

Blocking off another line of attack.

26	. . .	e7–f5
27	h2–h3	

Stean had hoped for 27 d6–f5 e6–f5, when Black wins the other knight which is pinned against the White king. When the computer played h2–h3 Stean cried out, 'This computer is a genius'.

27	. . .	f5–g3 +
28	h1–h2	g4–e4
29	a2–f2!	

Yet another tactical blow. Black had only expected 29 d6–e4 g3–e4, when he has sufficient material to make the program's task quite difficult. But this latest move, threatening mate by f2–f7 + and then f7–f8 mate, forces an even greater material advantage.

29	. . .	h7–h6
30	d6–e4	g3–e4
31	f2–f3	b4–b8
32	e1–e4	b8–f8
33	f3–g4	a8–e4
34	g4–e6 +	g8–h8
35	e6–e4	f8–f6
36	e4–e5	f6–b6
37	e5–c5	b6–b3
38	c5–c8 +	h8–h7
39	c8–a6	Black Resigns

There was once a time when leading experts in computer science would say that 'Computers can't play chess'.

Up to now I have discussed the most important milestones in computer chess since the time Claude Shannon's famous paper was first published in 1950. Next I shall survey the current state of the art in microcomputer chess programming, as typified by the play in the first World Microprocessor Chess Championship which was held as part of the 3rd Personal Computer World Show in London, in September 1980.

We shall be examining some of the critical moments of the games, and I shall give a deep analysis of a key game between Boris Experimental and Chess Challenger. I hope that from these episodes the reader will learn of a number of important pitfalls that should be avoided in writing chess programs. Remember – it is not necessary to be a strong chess player yourself, but you should get some advice from someone who is at least club strength.

By now the reader should be thoroughly familiar with standard computer chess notation, so from now on I shall employ a more complete form of notation, for ease of understanding.

Checkmate!

We all know that the object of the game of chess is to checkmate your opponent's king, that is to say attack it in such a way that it cannot avoid capture on the next move. One might think that it is a trivial matter to avoid being checkmated (provided that some method of escape exists), but in fact many programs are susceptible to a snap mate. Why can this be?

In the position in Figure 32 it is Black to move. It is threatened with mate at h7, which can be prevented in a number of ways (. . . g7–g6, . . . h5–g6 are the best). But instead Princhess played 22 . . . Ra8–b8, allowing 23 Qf5–h7 mate.

Auto Response Board v Princhess

FIGURE 32

There are two possible explanations for this oversight, apart from a simple programming bug. Those who have read the previous chapter will recall the Technology chess program, which performed only one ply of strategic evaluation. Let us suppose that Black evaluates all the positions at one ply, then performs one more ply of full-width search followed by captures at deeper levels. It considers the move 22 . . . Ra8–b8 and puts it high on the list because it adds an attacker to the White pawn on b2, and puts the rook on a half-open file. The program then considers all second ply moves, and noted the White reply 23 Qf5–h7. From now on the program only examines captures, and since the move 23 . . . Kg8–h7 is an illegal capture it rejects it, but it does not realise that something must be done about the check. Since Kg8–h7 is rejected, the program does not realise that its king must be captured on the next move because the next move (Qh7–g8) is not considered. Thus the program completely ignores the mate and looks only at third ply moves that are legal captures.

Another possible explanation is that the Black program 'saw' the following possibility: 23 . . . Ra8–b8 24 Qf5–h7

Bf6–b2 25 Qh7–g8 (capturing the Black king) 25 . . . Bb2–c1 (capturing the White king). Now Black has won a king and a pawn in return for a king, and is therefore a pawn up. Furthermore, should the program continue its analysis it will discover that its opponent's queen and rook are simultaneously attacked, so if the White queen moves, Black will play 26 . . . Bc1–d2, capturing the rook, while if the rook moves from d2, Black will capture the White queen. Thus the program can come to the conclusion that this variation wins material for Black, overlooking the small technical detail of the illegality of Black's 24th move.

The moral of this story is that your program must always have some means of detecting checkmate. One way is to terminate a search with any move that captures a king, and then look to see if the king capture was inevitable in the previous position. An alternative method is to test every move in the tree to see whether it attacks the enemy king, in which case the program knows that it should only consider moves which are captures of the checking piece, king moves or interposing moves.

The endgame

It has long been recognised that the endgame is the phase which sorts out the Grandmasters from the patzers (the men from the boys). In the science of computer chess programming, too, the endgame has always been the one area where very little progress has been made towards an intelligent player. There have been programs written to play certain basic endings perfectly, including king and queen v king and rook; and queen, king and g-pawn (or b-pawn) v king and queen. But very little has been accomplished in the way of general principles for programming endgames, with the result that programs frequently miss good moves that can be spotted by human players whose overall ability at the game is far from astounding.

Modular Game System 2.5 v Mike III

FIGURE 33

In Figure 33 Mike III had played very well to reach an ending in which a win is very easy for Black to force. Black's advantage may be illustrated by the simple variation 76 . . . Qd6–c7 + 77 Kb7–c7 g4–g3 followed by . . . g3–g2 and . . . g2–g1, promoting to a new queen. Black then has king and queen v king, for a simple win.

The game continued:

76	. . .	Qd6–b4 +
77	Kb7–c6	Qb4–c4 +
78	Kc6–d7	Qc4–d5 +
79	Kd7–e7	Qd5–e5 +
80	Ke7–d7	Qe5–d4 +
81	Kd7–c6	Qd4–c4 +
82	Kc6–d7	Qc4–d5 +
83	Kd7–e7	

The second time that this position has been reached. Black has a quick win with 83 . . . Qd5–f7 + 84 Ke7–d8 (if 84 Ke7–d6 Qf7–e8, then 85 . . . Qe8–c8 and White can never advance the pawn) 84 . . . Kg6–f6 85 Kd8–c8 (or 85 c7–c8 when Black mates by 85 . . . Qf7–e7) 85 . . . g4–g3, etc.

83	. . .	Qd5–e5 +
84	Ke7–d7	Qe5–d4 +
85	Kd7–c6	Qd4–c4 +

This last move produces a position which has now occurred three times. Under the rules of chess the game is drawn under such circumstances.

Drawing by threefold repetition in this way is a frequently overlooked problem in microcomputer chess programs. In order to detect a repetition it is necessary for the program to store the move sequence going back as far as the last pawn move or the last capture, and so a 50 move, or 100-ply sequence must be allowed for. (Another rule is that a game is drawn if 50 moves are played by each side without a pawn being moved or a piece being captured.) The program may then examine the move selected by the tree search (or any move within the tree search) to see if it produces a position that has already occurred. If so, the value of this move is set to a draw, and the move is only made if there is no alternative move which keeps the advantage. Here the program would reject the draw because it would eventually give up its queen for the White pawn, leaving itself with an extra pawn.

Another method for avoiding this problem in the game given above is to have a simple routine which measures whether or not a passed pawn can be caught by the enemy king, before it reaches the promotion square. If it cannot be caught, and if there is nothing else on the board except the kings, the program can set the value of this pawn to the value of a queen. In the final position Black has the advantage of queen and pawn v pawn, or ten pawns to one (for a difference of nine), but if Black gives up its queen for the c-pawn it will be left with an effective advantage of a queen for nothing – still a nine-pawn difference but 9–0 is better than 10–1. Simple ideas like this can often make the difference between a win and a draw.

Mobility

As every chess programmer knows, mobility is the second most important feature in the game, after material. Thus all programs try to maximise the mobility of their pieces. Unfortunately this heuristic can lead to problems if measures are not taken to prevent the queen from being developed too early in the game. The following miniature is a suitable illustration.

WHITE: PRINCHESS
BLACK: K CHESS IV

1	e2–e4	c7–c6
2	d2–d4	e7–e6
3	Nb1–c3	Qd8–h4

Black makes the move that maximises the mobility of his pieces. From h4 his queen attacks most squares in the enemy half of the board. But it is also vulnerable to attack.

4	Ng1–f3	Qh4–h5

Maintaining a mobile stance.

5	Bc1–g5	d7–d5
6	Bf1–d3	e6–e5
7	d4–e5	d5–d4
8	Nc3–e2	c6–c5

Up to now Black has moved nothing but his queen and some pawns, and although his queen at first looked mobile, it is suddenly left without a safe move.

9	Ne2–f4	Qh5–g5

This move might look like an elementary blunder, but in fact the Black queen is lost. If 9 . . . Qh5–g4, White takes away the flight square d7 by 10 e5–e6, and then wins the queen with 11 h2–h3.

10 Nf3–g5 and White soon won.

The moral here is, 'Do not bring out your queen too early in the game, unless there is a very good reason for doing so.' I would advise a penalty of at least half a pawn for exposing the queen to attack before castling.

The state of the art in 1980

How strong or weak were microprocessor chess programs at the start of the 1980s? This question may best be answered by taking a look at a game played between the programs that finished first and second in the 1980 World Microcomputer Championship. The following game was not actually played as part of the tournament, but took place on the final day of the main event as part of a match being played for a stake of £2,500 per side. The reader should be aware that Chess Challenger, which won the tournament, was not commercially available at the time.

WHITE: Chess Challenger
BLACK: Boris Experimental

French Defence

1	e2–e4	e7–e6
2	d2–d4	d7–d5
3	Nb1–c3	Bf8–b4
4	e4–e5	

This move came out of White's opening book but Black's book appeared to end here. How many moves one stores in one's openings library is obviously a matter of availability of memory. In a dedicated unit intended for consumers, memory prices play an important part in such decisions, but when writing a chess program for your own machine you will usually have more memory and consequently you can store more moves. Some people prefer to store openings by keeping a number of variations and branching out at random.

Others store the actual board positions, so that their program can transpose into or back to any variation in the book. Which you do is largely a matter of taste – the trade-off between more moves (when storing moves rather than positions) and the ability to transpose (when storing positions) is not crucial.

4 . . . Nb8–c6

The normal move is 4 . . . c7–c5, to attack White's pawn centre.

5 Qd1–g4 g7–g6
6 Ng1–f3 f7–f5

Although this move looks unnatural, it is quite good in this type of position which often arises in the French Defence.

7 Qg4–g5 Bb4–c3+

I have noticed that micro programs have a greater tendency than humans, or even stronger mainframe computer programs, to exchange pieces. The reasons may vary, but a common one is that the program calculates strategic scores only at the first ply. This leads it to believe that any capture is strategically strong because it deprives the captured piece of its strategic value. At the second ply, when the capturing piece is recaptured (i.e. 8 b2–c3) the program knows that it has lost back an equal amount of material but it does not know that it has also lost some strategic value. It only updates the change in material.

I doubt that this is the reason for the unnecessary exchange of Black's bishop for White's knight in this instance, but it is something to bear in mind when writing a technology type program (see Figure 34).

8 b2–c3
8 . . . Ng8–e7
9 Qg5–h6!

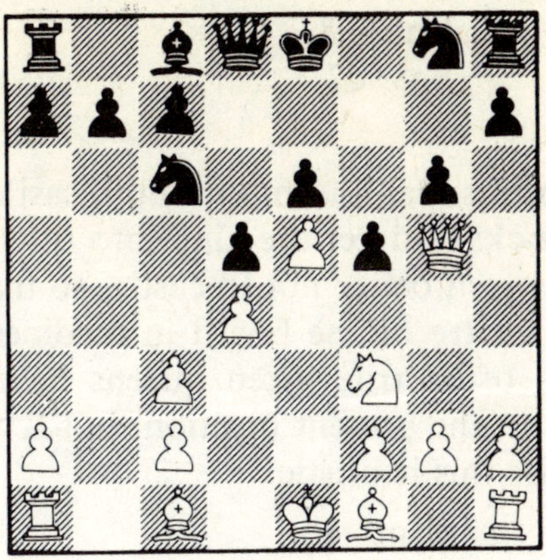

FIGURE 34

A strong move, preventing Black from castling, but I would have been tempted to play a quiet, developing move such as 9 Bf1–d3, and wait for the reply 9 . . . Ke8–g8 which loses at once to 10 Qg5–h6 followed by 11 Nf3–g5. Black must then give up material to avoid being mated.

9 . . . Ke8–f7!

Black realises that it is in a bind and that it must do something about the threat of 10 Qh6–g7 followed by 11 Nf3–g5, attacking the pawn at h7 and simultaneously threatening to fork Black's rook and queen with 12 Ng5–f7.

10 Bc1–g5!

An aggressive move, threatening 11 Bg5–f6, attacking the rook, and if 11 . . . Rh8–g8 12 Qh6–h7, winning at least a pawn.

10 . . . Qd8–f8!

Again Black spots the threat. Now White must retreat or exchange his queen.

11	Qh6–f8 +	Rh8–F8
12	Bf1–d3	Bc8–d7
13	Ke1–g1	

Everyone knows that it is important to castle in chess, so as to unite the rooks and get the king into safety, but in some positions it is much better not to castle, so that the king will be nearer the centre of the board in readiness for the end-game. This is often true when queens have already been exchanged, as in the present position, but few (if any) chess programs utilise this heuristic.

13	. . .	Ra8–d8
14	Ra1–b1	Bd7–c8
15	Bg5–h6	Rf8–e8
16	Rf1–e1	Ne7–g8

A passive and unnecessary move, even though it drives away the bishop (which was no longer doing anything useful on h6). I noticed more than once at the World Championships that when programs get into a passive position they do not understand how to play to improve the freedom of their pieces. Here, for example, Black should try for counter-play on the queen side by means of . . . Nc6–a5, . . . b7–b6 and . . . c7–c5.

17	Nf3–g5 +	Kf7–e7
18	Bh6–g7	

Threatening the pawn on h7.

18	. . .	h7–h6
19	Ng5–h7?!	

A highly dubious plan which deserves to lose material. If Black played carefully it could probably trap one of the White pieces (the knight at h7 or the bishop at g7).

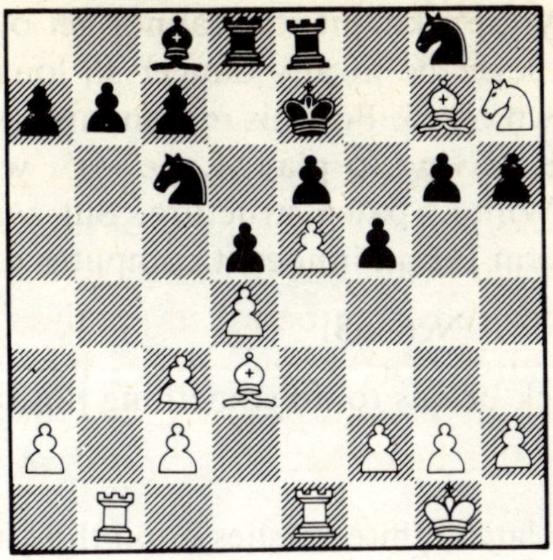

FIGURE 35

19 . . . Ke7–f7!

A good move, but Black misses the main point of the idea.

20 Bg7–f6 Ng8–f6??

A blunder. After 20 . . . Rd8–d7, White would have to go through great contortions even to try to save his knight from permanent incarceration. The immediate threat would be 21 . . . g6–g5, followed by 22 . . . Kf7–g6. If White played 20 h2–h4, to prevent the advance of the Black g-pawn, Black could respond 20 . . . b7–b6, followed by . . . Bc8–b7, . . . Re8–c8 and . . . Kf7–e8, leaving the knight with no place to go. Such plans are not difficult for human players, who realise that entombed pieces are liable to be trapped, but planning is one of the most difficult aspects of computer chess.

21 Nh7–f6 Re8–e7
22 h2–h4 b7–b6
23 h4–h5 g6–g5
24 g2–g3 a7–a6

Although White's knight still cannot get out of the Black camp, it will never be in any danger so long as White can maintain a pawn on e5. For this reason, among others, Black should still be striving to play . . . c7–c5, with the idea of undermining White's pawn structure. But again this plan is far too long term for an innocent computer program.

25 f2–f3 Nc6–a5!

At last, Black begins to do something positive.

26 g3–g4!

But it is too late. White crashes in on the king side. If now 26 . . . f5–f4, 27 Bd3–g6+ Kf7–g7, and White will soon extricate its knight via e8, once Black moves one of his rooks away from its defence of that square.

26 . . . b6–b5
27 Kg1–g2 Na5–c4?

Not understanding the position, Black makes an obvious-looking move which is strategically wrong. In positions of this type . . . c7–c5 is just about the only way to create satisfactory counterplay.

28 Bd3–c4 d5–c4

28 . . . b5–c4 was best, hoping to keep the position closed.

29 g4–f5 e6–f5
30 d4–d5!

Natural and strong. White dominates the centre (see Figure 36).

30 . . . Bc8–b7!

The best way to achieve counterplay. Black attacks the centre.

31 Rb1–d1 Bb7–c8?

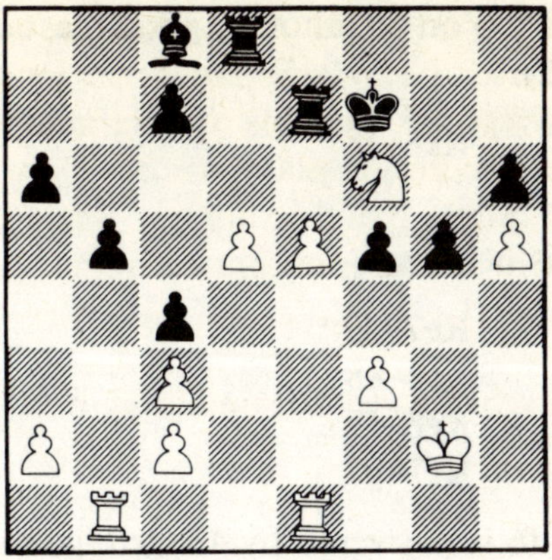

FIGURE 36

After its previous fine move, this is inexplicable. More logical would have been 31 . . . Kf7–g7, defending the h-pawn, so that Black could continue with 32 . . . g5–g4, opening up the king side in the hope of creating counterplay. If White's knight moves off f6 the pawn on d5 can be captured.

32 Kg2–f2 a6–a5
33 Rd1–b1

With the Black bishop on b7 this would not have been possible because 33 . . . b5–b4 34 c3–b4 a5–b4 35 Rb1–b4 Bb7–d5 is probably satisfactory for Black.

33 . . . c7–c6!
34 d5–c6 Rd8–d2+
35 Kf2–g1 Bc8–a6

Black's 33rd move might also be justified by 35 . . . Rd2–c2 36 Rb1–b5 Rc2–c3, when Black has a passed pawn.

36 Nf6–d7 Rd2–c2
37 e5–e6+! Kf7–e8

Not 37 . . . Re7–e6 38 Re1–e6 Kf7–e6 39 Nd7–c5+

winning the bishop on a6 (another good reason for preferring 35 . . . Rd2–c2).

38	Nd7–f6 +	Ke8–f8
39	Nf6–d5	

Now Black is helpless.

39	. . .	Re7–a7
40	e6–e7 +	Kf8–e8
41	Nd5–f6 +	Ke8–f7
42	e7–e8(Q) +	Kf7–g7

42 . . . Kf7–f6 is answered by 43 Qe8–g6 mate.

43	Qe8–g6 +	Kg7–f8
44	Re1–e8 mate	

Some unresolved problems

Amongst the many unsolved problems in chess programming, three stand out in my mind as representing the comparative lack of progress that has been made in reaching Grandmaster level on the computer. I should like to mention

FIGURE 37

these problem areas, so that the reader can gain some grasp of the magnitude of the problem.

The first subject that I wish to discuss in this section is what we call *zugzwang*. It is a German word, whose meaning on the chessboard is that the player whose turn it is to move is at a disadvantage because, and only because, he must make the next move. In such a situation any evaluation function, examining the position as a terminal node on the game tree, would not realise that the very right to move is, in itself, a serious or even fatal disadvantage. The position in Figure 37 will give an idea of what I am talking about.

Imagine that this position is the terminal node on a tree, and the program must evaluate the position. White is a pawn up for nothing, and Black has no pieces on the board other than his king, so the program would indicate a very good, possibly winning score for White. Yet if it is White's turn to move (usually an added advantage!), the game is a draw. Why? Because if White makes the only king move that protects the pawn, Kd6–e6, Black has been stalemated and the game is drawn; while if White makes any other king move, Black can reply by capturing the White pawn and again the game is drawn. So with Black to move, the above position is a win for White, but with White having the extra plus of the right to move, the game is only a draw. How can a computer program know, when evaluating a terminal position, that *zugzwang* is a possibility and that it should search deeper just to see what will happen after another ply or two?

It may seem to the uninitiated, that *zugzwang* is not really very important in chess, but in fact the whole of endgame theory and technique is based on the fact that sooner or later one player is normally forced into a *zugzwang* situation. Even the endgame of king and rook against king involves *zugzwang*: if the defending player were allowed to pass whenever he wished, and miss his move, then the player with the extra rook would never be able to win.

The next problem that I wish to discuss involves the

FIGURE 38

concept of 'never'. Take a look at the position in Figure 38. White has an overwhelming material advantage, a queen up for a knight and three pawns, but the position holds a few surprises. The problem for White is that his queen can *never* extricate itself from the coffin on h6 unless Black obligingly moves his knight, allowing the White queen to capture the pawn on h4, or Black moves his king, allowing the White queen to play safely to h7 or f8. So although White is way ahead on material, and Black has no way to win the White queen, it is Black who has the advantage on material in practical terms, because Black has two active fighting units, the pawns on a7 and e7, while White has only one, the king. If all the pieces on the g-file and h-file remain on the same squares, then Black wins the game by advancing his two pawns in the correct manner. For example, if it is White's move, play might continue:

1	Ka1–b2	e7–e5
2	Kb2–c3	a7–a5
3	Kc3–c4	a5–a4
4	Kc4–b4	e5–e4
5	Kb4 × a4	e4–e3

and White's king cannot get back in time to stop the Black pawn from becoming a queen.

The reason that Black wins this position is that White's queen can *never* get out, and the Black pawns can cope with the White king. To understand that the position is a win for Black, rather than a win for White, a computer program would need to understand two things: that a lone king cannot stop two passed pawns which are separated by 3 or more files, and above all, that the White queen can never extricate itself without Black's help.

The final point which I would like my readers to consider, is how an almost imperceptible difference in position can result in an entirely opposite assessment of the expected result of the game. The previous position is an excellent case in point. Move the Black pawn from e7 to d7, and we now have the position in Figure 39.

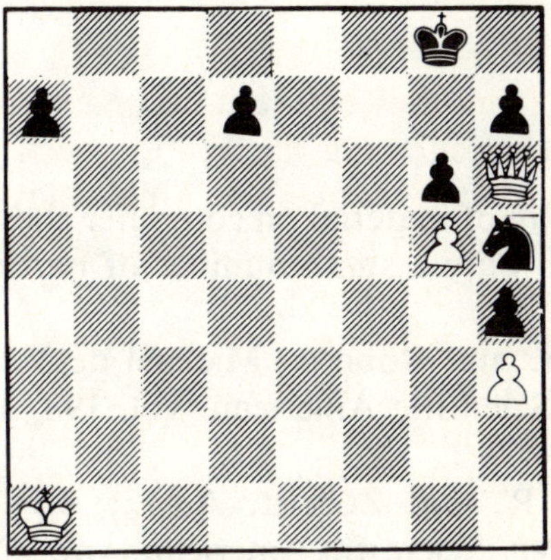

FIGURE 39

If you compare these two positions it appears, at first sight, as though their assessments must lead to identical results, but in fact the opposite is true. Because the Black pawns are only separated by two files, and not three, the White king can stop both of the pawns, capture them both, and then Black is in *zugzwang* and must move his king. So an imperceptible difference in the location of a lowly pawn can make all the difference in the world, even though the opponent has an extra queen. Now just imagine that a computer program is searching a game tree in which both of the two previous positions appear as terminal nodes. It is inevitable that with present-day techniques, the program will assign virtually identical scores to these positions, with the possible result that the search of the game tree might result in quite the wrong move beng made in the root position. In order to avoid such problems, chess programs would need to have the ability to form concepts, and to make logical deductions. Computerised concept formation and deductive reasoning are still in their infancy, and even when they advance dramatically, imagine trying to apply such processes at every terminal node on the tree! The World Chess Champion need not fear for the next 15 years or more.

Bibliography

The bibliography of material on computer chess is enormous. I shall mention only a small number of particularly significant works.

Bernstein, A. and Roberts, Michael de V.: *Computer v. Chess Player*. Scientific American, vol. 198, June 1958, pp. 96–105.

Carlson, F. R. and Zobrist, A. L.: *An Advice-Taking Chess Computer*. Scientific American, vol. 228, June 1973, pp. 92–105.

De Groot, A. D.: *Thought and Choice in Chess*, Mouton and Co., 1965.

Frey, Peter W.: *Chess Skill in Man and Machine,* Springer Verlag, 1977.

Gillogly, J. J.: *The Technology Chess Program*, Artificial Intelligence, vol. 3 (1972), pp. 145–163.

Greenblatt, R. D., Eastlake, D. E. III and Crocker, S. D.: *The Greenblatt Chess Program*, Proc. Fall Joint Computer Conf. 1967, pp. 801–810.

Shannon, C. E.: *Programming a Computer for Playing Chess*. Philosophical Magazine, vol. 41 (7th series), pp. 256–275.

CHAPTER 10
Backgammon

The game of backgammon introduces special problems into the tree search. Some of these problems are caused by the fact that, before s/he decides what move to make, a player must throw a pair of dice and only then will s/he know which 'moves' are legal. The very fact that two dice can be thrown in 21 different ways gives rise to an enormous branching factor, and this is the source of the second major problem. In this chapter we consider how these problems might best be approached. We also examine a strategy for determining when to make or accept a double.

The opening move of a backgammon game is easy for a computer program. Depending on how the dice appear, there are set moves which have been shown by experience to be best. The program merely stores these moves in a table and makes the move corresponding to the particular fall of each die. It is what happens after the first move that is interesting. Let us first consider a program which performs a one-ply search.

The program need not begin to 'think' until after the dice have been thrown, since it is only then that its possible moves are known. For a one-ply search there is little difference between a backgammon program and a chess program – an evaluation function provides a score for the terminal nodes and the program chooses the move which leads to the highest scored terminal node. We shall discuss the evaluation process in more detail later in this chapter. Here it is only necessary to comment on the fact that when one player throws a double (1,1) or (2,2), etc, he makes two sets of moves, as though he had thrown four individual dice. This can be accounted for easily enough by calculating every possible way of playing the double throw, and making each of these ways into one branch of the tree.

Probabilistic trees

Once the search extends beyond one ply, the trees become probabilistic. We have already encountered such trees in another form,. earlier in this book. The tree in Figure 40 will enable the reader to understand the problem.

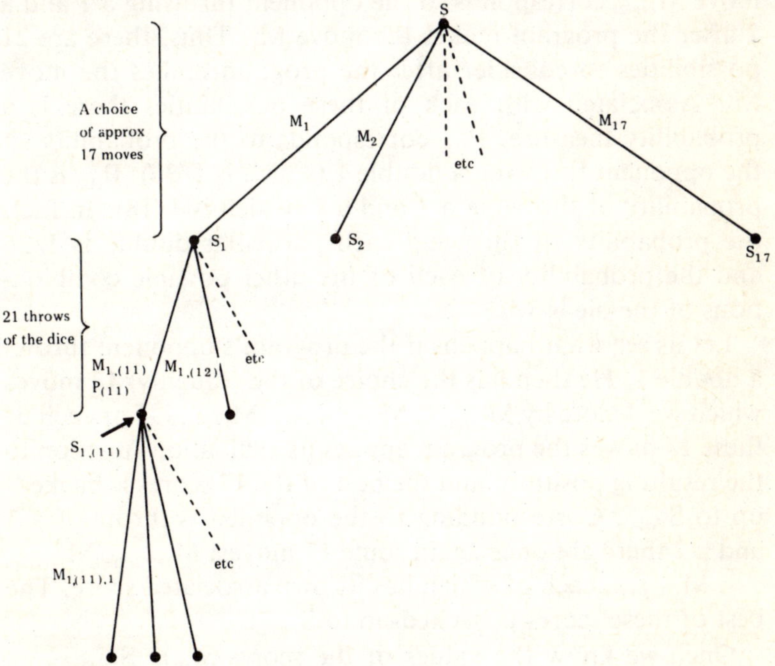

FIGURE 40

Let us assume that it is the program's turn to move from the root of the tree after the dice have been thrown. Berliner has calculated that in an average board position there are roughly 40 possible ways of making each move but that in typical game positions (assuming sensible play) the number drops to around 17. So from the root of the tree the program can choose from the moves M_1, M_2, . . ., M_{17}. Let us assume that we first examine move M_1. In a one-ply search we would apply the evaluation function to the resulting position and back-up the score S_1 to the root of the tree, assigning to S the value of the best score found so far.

After the program makes move M_1, its opponent throws the dice. The move $M_{1,(11)}$ corresponds to the opponent throwing double 1 after the program has played M_1. The move $M_{1,(12)}$ corresponds to the opponent throwing a 1 and a 2 after the program makes the move M_1. Thus, there are 21 possibilities to consider after the program makes the move M_1. Associated with each of these possibilities there is a probability measure. $P_{(11)}$ corresponds to the probability of the opponent throwing a double 1 (which is 1/36). $P_{(12)}$ is the probability of throwing a 1 and a 2 (which is 1/18). In fact, the probability of throwing each particular double is 1/36 and the probability of each of the other possible combinations of the die is 1/18.

Let us see what happens if the program's opponent throws a double 1. He then has the choice of the (roughly) 17 moves which we denote by $M_{1,(11),1}$, $M_{1,(11),2}$ . . . $M_{1,(11),17}$. For each of these 17 moves the program applies its evaluation function to the resulting position, and the best of the 17 scores is backed-up to $S_{1,(11)}$. Corresponding to the opponent's throw of a 1 and a 2 there are once again some 17 moves: $M_{1,(12),1}$, $M_{1,(12),2}$ . . . $M_{1,(12),17}$, each of which has its own associated score. The best of these scores is backed-up to $S_{1,(12)}$.

Once we know the values of the scores $S_{1,(11)}$, $S_{1,(12)}$, . . . $S_{1,(66)}$, we would like to back-up these scores to S_1 so that S_1 represents the best of these scores. But the program's opponent cannot choose how the die will fall and so he is unable to choose whether S_1 has the value of $S_{1,(11)}$ or some other backed-up value. The actual merit of the node at a depth of one ply is, therefore, not the merit of the best node at two ply, but a weighted sum of the two-ply scores – the weightings corresponding to the probabilities of the various throws of the die. Thus, there is a probability of 1/36 that the program's opponent will be able to choose for his value of S_1 and backed-up score $S_{1,(11)}$. There is a probability of 1/18 that the program's opponent will be able to choose for S_1 the value of $S_{1,(12)}$. And so on. The actual score which should be assigned to S_1 is therefore:

$$S_1 = (1/36 \times S_{1,(11)}) + (1/18 \times S_{1,(12)}) + (1/18 \times S_{1,(13)}) + \ldots$$

The size of tree and how to cope with it

It will already be clear that, in order to perform the equivalent of a two-ply search, the program must do a lot of three-ply work. Some of this work is very fast: the moves at the second ply are nothing more than the throw of the dice and these remain fixed for the whole game, as do their probabilities; they can be stored in a simple table. But the choice that arises after the throw requires a legal move generator, which may also be table driven but which increases the branching factor to approximately 17 × 12, or 357, though this number *can* rise to over 800. Since it is impossible to choose how the dice will fall, the alpha-beta algorithm has no place in the tree search. The program must examine every possibility from a node before backing-up. There is, however, another method of pruning the tree, which in some ways is analogous to alpha-beta pruning.

Let us assume that M_1 is, in fact, the best move that the program can make. After calculating the scores and backing-up to S_1, the program knows the value of making the move M_1. It then begins to look at the move M_2, and it calculates the score S_2 by adding:

$$(1/36 \times S_{2,(11)}) + (1/18 \times S_{2,(12)}) + (1/18 \times S_{2,(13)}) + \ldots$$

and since M_1 is better than M_2, the scores S_1 will be higher than S_2 (I have assumed that we are following the normal convention under which high scores are good for the program and low, or negative, scores are good for its opponent).

To determine that S_1 will be higher than S_2, if we examine M_1 before M_2, it will be necessary to sum all 21 terms in the expression for S_2. But what happens if we examine the moves in the reverse order, with the worst move being examined first? To show that M_{16} is better than M_{17} it will not necessarily be essential to add all 21 terms in the expression for S_{16}. It might be the case that after adding only 18 of the terms, the score would already be better than that of S_{17}. From that point on it is no longer important in the relationship between M_{16} and M_{17} whether the three remaining terms in the expression for S_{16} add up to a relatively small or large number. We know for certain that S_{16} is larger than S_{17}. Unfortunately, the whole of the pruning process is not this simple. In order to know that S_{15} is greater than S_{16} we *do* need to know the exact total of the 21 terms in S_{16}. So how can we afford to prune certain parts of the tree?

The answer lies in an analogy argument, which involves some approximation and hence some risk. But I doubt that it will give rise to serious errors.

It seems reasonable to argue that if, in position A, the results of n of the 21 possible throws add up to something better than the results of the same n throws in position B, then position A is better than position B. This is certainly true when $n=21$, and it is least likely to be true when $n=1$. Readers can experiment to see how large n can become without producing large errors in comparing two nodes. The important thing to remember is that we choose a 'cross section' of possible throws – at least one throw with a 1, one throw with a 2, and so on. The absolute minimum number of throws to be compared is three, for example 1 and 2, 3 and 4, 5 and 6. I would expect it to be true that if:

$$S_{1,(12)} + S_{1,(34)} + S_{1,(56)} > S_{2,(12)} + S_{2,(34)} + S_{2,(56)}, \text{ then } S_1 > S_2.$$

Of course there would be exceptions to this generalisation, but the number of exceptions ought to be a small price to pay for cutting down the possible throws of the dice from 21 to only 3.

When we consider a deeper tree, which takes into account the first two moves by the program and the first reply by its opponent, instead of examining a three-ply sequence we are, in fact, looking at a five-ply probabilistic tree. The number of nodes on this tree will already be so large that, without alpha-beta pruning, it is very doubtful whether a microprogram can search it within an acceptable time span, and alpha-beta pruning is not possible because of the nature of the tree – a player does not have complete freedom of choice because of the dice. The tree in Figure 41 will illustrate the magnitude of

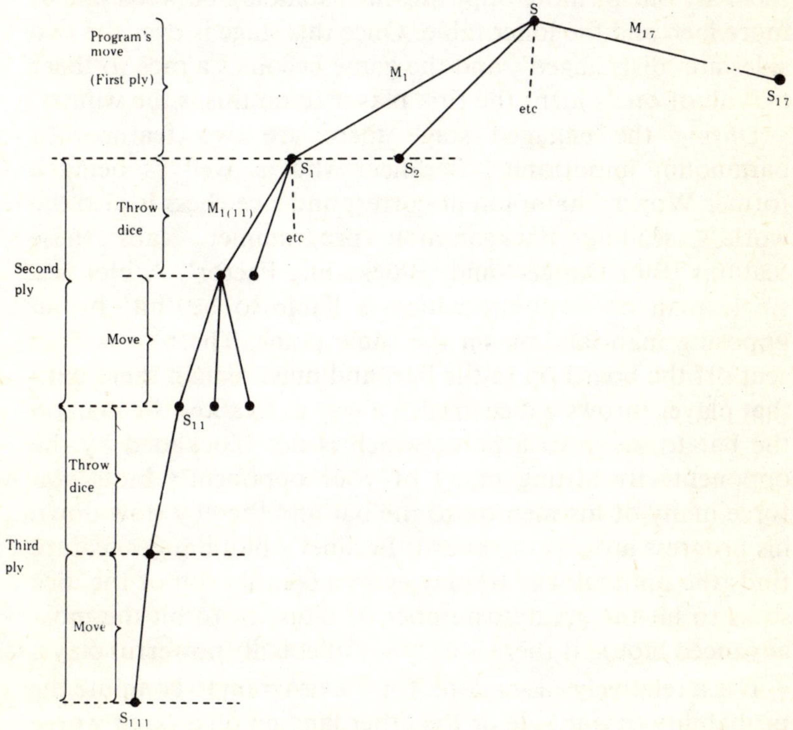

FIGURE 41

the problem. Since none of the scores at any ply can be known until *all* successor moves from that node have been examined, there is no way that alpha-beta can be employed. Of course forward pruning is always possible, using either the apparent merit of a node measured by the evaluation function or the backed-up merit as determined from an extra ply of look-ahead (which would be slow) but this is all that one can do.

The evaluation function

Backgammon can be divided into two distinct stages. For most of a game the two sides are 'engaged'. That is to say, there are one or more opposing men standing between one or more men and the inner table. Once this stage is over the two sides are 'disengaged', and the game becomes a race to 'bear off' all of one's men; the first player to do this is the winner.

During the engaged stage there are two features of paramount importance. Berliner, who as well as being a former World Champion at correspondence chess is also the world's leading backgammon programmer, calls these features 'Blot Danger' and 'Blockading Factor'. A blot is a single man on a point, which is liable to be 'hit' by an opposing man landing on the same point. The blot is then sent off the board on to the bar, and must remain there until that player throws a dice in such a way as to allow the man on the bar to move to a point which is not blockaded by the opponent. By hitting many of your opponent's blots you force many of his men on to the bar and thereby slow down his progress around the board. Berliner's blot danger feature finds the optimal way to play every potential roll of the dice so as to hit the greatest number of blots, or to hit the most advanced blot(s) if there is a choice of equally powerful plays.

It is a relatively easy matter for the program to compute the probability of one side or the other landing on a point where his opponent has a blot. Clearly the blot danger feature must use such a calculation in order to arrive at an accurate estimate of danger, which in turn will discourage the program from making moves which leave vulnerable blots. In any game where chance plays a part it is impossible to be sure that a particular strategy will be foolproof, but it makes good sense to play with the odds.

The notion of a blockade is very important in impeding the progress of your opponent's men, since an enemy man cannot land on a blocked point (ie a point with two or more of your own men on it). Setting up a succession of adjacent blockades is a particularly powerful strategy if it can be successfully adopted because it prevents the opponent from moving unless he is lucky enough to roll high numbers from a point just on one side of the blockade. Berliner's program considers every combination of from zero to seven blockading points (seven is the maximum number possible, since each side has only 15 men), at a distance of from one to 12 points in front of each man. It employs a table of these blockading patterns to store the number of rolls of the dice that could legally be played by the side which is trying to pass the blockade. This number indicates the extent to which each man is blockaded.

When the two sides' men become disengaged, the 'running game' begins, so called because each player's men run as fast as possible towards the inner (or home) table. At this stage of the game it is possible to estimate fairly accurately the probability that a particular player will win the game by bearing off all his men before his opponent is able to do so. One method of doing this is to 'count' the position – simply add up the number of steps each man must take before he can bear off, assuming no wasted motion. This count can be employed in a simple table to determine the odds of winning, and such tables are found in most backgammon books. For example, the books will tell you that if your count is 60 and your lead over your opponent is four when it is your turn to roll, the odds are eight to five in your favour. Until the last few moves of the game, when special heuristics apply, it is relatively simple for the program to decide which men to move and in many situations it will make no difference. But it is just in this stage of the game that the complication of the doubling cube becomes of paramount importance.

Backgammon is traditionally played for stakes. One of the essential elements of a backgammon set is a cube with the numbers 2, 4, 8, 16, 32 and 64 on the faces. If a player feels that he has a good chance of winning he may put the cube with the 2 face uppermost, at which point his opponent must either resign or agree to play the game for double the usual stake. Having accepted a double a player may, later in the game, double again, by turning the face 4 uppermost. This process may continue until the players are wagering 64 times the original stake – people have won and lost fortunes through the doubling cube.

Not surprisingly, statisticians have calculated formulae which indicate when a player should double and when a double should be accepted and these formulae are obviously easier for a program to apply than for a human. There is, however, an important psychological aspect to doubling. If most players double when their probability of winning is around 0.6, it will be better to double at 0.7 and keep your opponent in the game (if he assumes that he still has some chance he will be less likely to resign, and you will win twice as much).

Backgammon books give quite a lot of useful information on when a player should double and when a double should be accepted. This makes the programmer's task easier, and helps to reduce the element of skill in the game below its normally tiny amount. My own view of the game is that it is rather shallow, with virtually no scope for brilliant or imaginative play but with features that allow a fast mind to score a steady though slight advantage against a player with a lesser facility for calculation. It can be a fun game to program, with plenty of scope for neat graphics work and the problem of coping with the enormous trees certainly makes it a challenge to the serious games programmer.

Bibliography

Berliner, H.: *Experiences in Evaluation with BKG – A Program that Plays Backgammon*. Proceedings of the fifth International Joint Conference on Artificial Intelligence 1977, pp. 428–433.

Keeler, E. B. and Spencer, J.: *Optimal Doubling in Backgammon*. Operations Research, vol. 23, No. 6, Nov.–Dec. 1975, pp. 1063–1071.

CHAPTER 11
Stud Poker

For some reason which I fail to understand, poker is one of the most widely misrepresented games ever invented. Most people who do not know how to play poker consider it a game of luck, in which the person who gets dealt the best cards wins. I have even heard highly intelligent people refer to poker as a 'base, gambling game'. And there are those who associate poker with the card sharps of the 19th-century Mississippi steamboats and assume that every poker player is some sort of low life. These opinions could not be further from the truth and, in my opinion, there is no less skill in poker than in chess or bridge.

The game of poker that became famous during the days of the Wild West is now known as five-card draw and is still popular. But there is another family of poker games which require even greater skill and which are much more interesting to play: these go under the generic name of stud poker. I shall describe in some detail how a stud poker program might be written and next I shall write about the older form of the game – draw poker.

Five-card stud

Briefly, each player is dealt one card face down and one card face up, and may look at his own down card. A round of betting takes place, and all those who put in the necessary amount of money on this round will stay in the game and receive a second face-up card (the others drop out of the hand). After receiving the second up card, the players indulge in another round of betting and, once again, those who put in the necessary remain for a further round, while the others drop out. The third up card is followed by another round of betting, and then comes the fourth and final card up and the fourth and final round of betting. When the last round of betting is over, those remaining in the hand turn over their one down card, and the player with the best five cards wins the money. In order to determine whose cards are the best, the following ranking applies to the hands:

Straight flush: This is the best type of hand to have, and most regular poker players will only have such a hand a few times in their life. A straight flush is five cards of the same suit which are in an unbroken sequence, for example the 6 7 8 9 and 10 of Hearts.

Four of a kind: As its name suggests, this type of hand has four cards of the same denomination.

Full house: Three cards of one denomination and two of another, for example three 6s and two Aces.

Flush: All five cards of the same suit but not in an unbroken sequence.

Straight: All five cards in an unbroken sequence, though not all of the same suit.

Three of a kind: Three of the cards are of one denomination, the other two are not of the same denomination as each other.

Two pairs: For example two Aces and two 7s – the fifth card is of no importance unless two players have the same two pairs, in which case the fifth card breaks the tie.

One pair: Aces is the highest pair, then Kings, Queens, and so on down to 2s.

High card: If a player has none of the above hands, then his holding is valued in accordance with the highest denomination card in his hand (Ace is high) and then if two players have the same high card their second highest cards are compared and so on.

So much for the procedure and the ranking of the hands. Various betting options exist in most forms of poker, the most common ones being:

Bet: At the start of a round of betting, one player is first to speak. There are various methods for deciding who is first to speak and in stud poker it is usually the player with the highest face-up cards. He has two options, he may bet or he may 'check'. If he wishes to add to the money in the pot, the player bets, by putting into the pot any amount of money that is in accordance with the house rules. We shall assume that we are playing 'pot limit', which means that the size of the bet may be anything from one unit up to the total amount of money already in the pot. So if the pot stands at £10 and we are playing in £1 units the first person to speak may, if he wishes to bet, put in any amount from £1 to £10.

Check: If the person whose turn it is to speak does not wish to bet and no one else has put money in on that round of betting, he may say 'check', which means that he does not wish to put money in at this stage but he may decide to do so when it is next his turn. If, at any time in a round of betting, all the players check in succession, then the round of betting is over.

Call: Once someone has put some money into the pot during a round of betting, the next player must put in at least the same amount if he wishes to remain in the game. Putting in the same amount as the others is known as calling. When all the players have put money into a particular betting round, that round may only end when all of the players bar one have called – at that point everyone has put in the same amount.

Raise: It is possible to put in more than the previous bettor and this is known as raising. If the first player puts in £1 and the second player wants to put in an extra £1, he will say something like 'your £1 raise £1', and put £2 into the pot. Once there has been a raise it is necessary for all the players after the last raiser to call the bet before the round is at an end, so that everyone will have contributed the same amount to the pot. The maximum that can be raised is the amount in the pot before the raise takes place. So if the pot stands at £1, and the player bets £1, making the pot £2, the second player can put in the £1 to meet the bet and then raise £3 (the current size of the pot).

Pass: Sometimes known as 'fold'. This is what happens when a player decides that he no longer wishes to take part in this particular hand – he turns his cards face down and relinquishes all claim to the money. Beginners often think that passing is cowardly but in fact more hands are passed by good players than by bad ones.

Some basic principles

Two essential principles should be followed in a game of stud poker. On card two and card three (ie when you have a total of two or three cards, including the down card), you should *never* put money into the pot unless your cards so far, including the down card, can beat every hand that you can see on the table. The reason for this is obvious enough – if your up cards are a 6 and an 8 of different suits, and your down card is a 2, and if your opponent is showing a 5 and a 9 of different suits, you should not be putting money into the pot because you are beaten 'on the table' and your opponent has a hidden card which may well go nicely with the others. Many beginners make the mistake of assuming, in a situation such as this one, that they have just as much chance of 'hitting a pair' (ie getting another 2, 6 or 8 on the fourth or fifth card) as their opponent and so it is almost an even money shot if they stay in the pot. But this is false accounting. Firstly, your opponent may already have a pair – his down card might be another 5 or a 9. In this case he will certainly beat you if you do not draw a pair; he may beat you even if you do draw a pair because his pair of 9s or 5s may be higher than your eventual pair; and if he does not yet have a pair and you both draw a pair, he has better chances than you because his cards at the moment are higher than yours, so it will be odds on that his pair will be higher than yours. The only way that you can win is if he does not make a pair and you do, but then your pair may be 'open' (ie both cards face up) in which case he will not put any money into the pot on card five. If you don't believe me, try it for yourself.

The second golden rule is that when betting on card four, don't put money into the pot unless you have 'equity', that is to say, unless the ratio of the money already in the pot to the money you are now putting in is no less than the odds against you having a winning hand when the last card is dealt.

A simple example will explain this principle. Suppose that you hold the 2, 3, 4 and 8 of Hearts (the 2 is the down card) and that your opponent is showing the 5 of Clubs, the 5 of Diamonds and the 10 of Spades. The pot stands at £10 and your opponent bets £10. What should you do? In order to win the hand, and to be sure that you are winning the hand, you need to hit a fifth Heart to make a flush. Then, unless your opponent already has three of a kind or two pairs, and makes a full house on the last card, you must hold the winning hand. And if he does have a chance of making a full house you will see it from his fifth card, so there will be no danger of your betting too heavily on the fifth round.

Since you need to hit a Heart to win and you have already seen four Hearts (the ones in your hand), you know that of the 45 unseen cards remaining (the 44 in the deck and the one down card in your opponent's hand) there are nine Hearts. The odds against your hitting a Heart are therefore (44-9):9, or 35:9 (almost 4 to 1). But your equity, or investment odds, are only 2:1, because there is £20 currently in the pot and you must put in £10 to stay in. In making this calculation it is important to remember that the money in the pot does not belong to you in any way, even though you put some of it there – the money belongs to the pot until someone wins it. It is also important to remember that you cannot usually count on winning any more money on the fifth round of betting, because your opponent will not be obliged to put in any more money, but there will be some occasions when it *is* reasonable to assume that your opponent will put money in the pot after the fifth card.

It is precisely because of this concept of equity that it is vital to make a good-sized bet when you are in the lead, because otherwise you are making it cheap or free for your opponent to stay in the pot, and then he may hit better cards than you do later on in which case he will 'steal' the pot. In the above situation, for example, if your opponent bets only £1 instead of £10, he is playing like a sucker. You call his £1 bet and now you have 11:1 money odds while the odds against hitting a winning card are only about 4:1. If your opponent plays like that often enough, in the hope of 'sucking you in' to the pot when you really should be out of it, he will be sorry to see his financial empire crumbling as you get better cards than him on one hand out of five.

These two golden rules provide the basis for solid play in a game of five-card stud. Of course like most rules of thumb, there will be occasions when they should be broken, but it takes a good player to recognise these situations and, until you or your program is a regular winner, you should play it safe. There is one exception, and that is concerned with bluffing, about which I have written a little earlier on. To play good poker it is essential to bluff occasionally, but the good player will judge when to bluff by taking careful note of his opponents' styles of play and their mannerisms. I shall write more on the subject of bluffing in the next chapter, when we will be looking at draw poker, so for our stud poker program let us assume, for the time being, that there will be no bluffing. I shall give an algorithm for programming stud poker but its parameters are subject to variation at the reader's discretion. In order to illustrate the algorithm, I shall describe one hand of stud poker in some detail and for the sake of simplicity I shall assume that the program is playing against only one opponent – you may extend the principles of the algorithm to a higher number of players and I would recommend five or six as being the right number for a personal computer program.

The algorithm in action

Our stud poker algorithm is based on a system for estimating the probability that our opponent's down card is of a certain denomination. These probabilities are adjusted in the light of information obtained from his play, or more precisely, from the way that he bets during the hand. Other factors, such as bluffing and poor play by the opponent, could also be included in such an algorithm but for the purpose of this example I shall keep things as simple as possible. The reader ought to have little difficulty in generalising from this example, to produce a routine that implements the algorithm successfully.

Let us suppose that when the cards are dealt the program receives the Ace of Clubs as the down card, and the 9 of Hearts as the up card. The opponent has the 8 of Diamonds as his up card.

PROGRAM: (A C) 9 H
OPPONENT: (??) 8 D

Before the betting begins, we can already make certain probability estimates about our opponent's down card. We have seen one Ace, one 8 and one 9, and there are 49 unseen cards at this stage in the proceedings. Of these 49 cards three are Aces, three are 8s and three are 9s and there are four of every other denomination. So without any more information to go on, we can estimate the probability of the opponent's down card being an Ace as 3/49, of its being a King as 4/49, a Queen 4/49, and so on, giving us the table in Figure 42.

DENOMINATION	PROBABILITY
Ace	0.061
King	0.082
Queen	0.082
Jack	0.082
10	0.082
9	0.061
8	0.061
7	0.082
6	0.082
5	0.082
4	0.082
3	0.082
2	0.082

FIGURE 42: *Probabilities for opponent's down card before first round of betting (correct to three decimal places).*

The program has the highest face-up holding (9 is higher than 8), so it opens the betting. There is an 'ante' of £1 in the pot, so the program bets £1 and the opponent decides to call, putting in £1 to make the total amount of money in the pot £3. From the fact that our opponent called, it is reasonable to make two deductions: (a) he almost certainly has a down card which can beat a 9, otherwise he was very foolish to call the bet; (b) he may have another 8, giving him a pair of 8s but if he did have a pair of 8s he might well have raised the bet, so he is probably less likely to have another 8 than to have a 10, J, Q, K or A. (This deduction can be made into a learning mechanism, so that after playing a long session against the same opponent, the program could estimate the number of hands in which the opponent had not raised with a pair on card two.)

We must now apply some formula to adjust the old probabilities in the light of the new information received. This must be done in some way that weights the importance of the old information relative to the new. Since the information that we had prior to the first round of betting was all *a priori* information, whereas we now have some *a postori* information, I would give the new information something like four times as much weight as the older information. Furthermore, I would suggest that we assume it to be twice as likely that the opponent's hole card was an A, K, Q, J or 10 than another 8. So from the assumptions made on the basis of the one called bet we can estimate the probabilities of the various denominations being the opponent's down card as in Figure 43.

Ace	King	Queen	Jack	10	9	8	7	6	5	4	3	2
2/11	2/11	2/11	2/11	2/11	0	1/11	0	0	0	0	0	0

(2/11 = 0.182; 1/11 = 0.091)

FIGURE 43

These fractions came from the fact that we wish to estimate the probability that he holds an Ace, King, Queen, Jack or 10 as being twice as much as the probability of his holding an 8, and we must have all the probabilities adding up to 1. We estimate the probabilities of his holding a 9, 7, 6, 5, 4, 3 or 2 as being zero, on the assumption that he is not playing badly, though as I mentioned before, this presumption can be varied by the program itself.

We must now combine the old and new probabilities in accordance with their weightings (new:old = 4:1), and so the new measure for the opponent holding an Ace as his down card is given by:

$$(0.061 \times 1) + (0.182 \times 4) = 0.789.$$

The measure for the King is given by:

$$(0.082 \times 1) + (0.182 \times 4) = 0.810$$

The Queen, Jack and 10 have the same old estimates and the

same new estimates as the King, so their revised measures are all given by:

$$(0.082 \times 1) + (0.182 \times 4) = 0.810$$

The measure for the 9 is given by:

$$(0.061 \times 1) + (0 \times 4) = 0.061$$

The measure for the 8 is given by:

$$(0.061 \times 1) + (0.091 \times 4) = 0.425$$

And the measure for the 7, 6, 5, 4, 3 and 2 are all given by:

$$(0.082 \times 1) + (0 \times 4) = 0.082$$

Finally, to arrive at the new probability estimates for all the denominations, we need to normalise these figures so that the total probability adds up to 1. So we sum the above measures:

$$0.789 + (4 \times 0.810) + 0.061 + 0.425 + (6 \times 0.082) = 5.007$$

and divide each of them by 5.007 to arrive at the new probability estimates (Figure 44).

DENOMINATION	PROBABILITY
Ace	0.789/5.007 = 0.158
King	0.810/5.007 = 0.162
Queen	0.162
Jack	0.162
10	0.162
9	0.061/5.007 = 0.012
8	0.425/5.007 = 0.085
7	0.082/5.007 = 0.016
6	0.016
5	0.016
4	0.016
3	0.016
2	0.016

FIGURE 44: *Probabilities for opponent's down card after the first round of betting.*

The first round of betting is now over, and the dealer gives each of the players one more card. The program receives the 7 of Spades while its opponent gets the 10 of Clubs, so the situation on the table now looks like this:

PROGRAM: (A C) 9 H, 7 S
OPPONENT: (??) 8 D, 10 C

and there is £3 in the pot. The opponent is now 'high', ie he has the highest cards shown on the table, since 10, 8 is better than 9, 7, and so it is the opponent to open the betting on this round. He may check, or he may bet anything from £1 to £3. Let us assume that he bets the maximum of £3.

The first thing that the program must do is to determine whether or not, on the basis of the probability estimates that it had before his £3 bet, the opponent is likely to have the winning hand and if so, by what margin of probability. In order to be winning at this stage, the opponent must hold, as his down card, an Ace, an 8 or a 10. An Ace would give him A, 10, 8 against A, 9, 7, while a 10 or an 8 as the down card would give him a pair. From Figure 44 the program can determine that the probability of its opponent's down card being an A, 8 or 10 is:

$$0.158 + 0.085 + 0.162 = 0.405$$

So the probability that he does not hold the winning hand is $1 - 0.405 = 0.595$, and the odds against the program having the winning hand are 0.405:0.595, or 1:1.47. If the program calls the £3 bet, since the pot now stands at £6 the program will be getting 2:1 money odds, so the program definitely has enough equity to call the bet because 2:1 is better than 1.47:1. From this calculation the program may determine that it is safe to call the bet. The algorithm ought to have some randomly-based adjustment in its calculations to determine when to raise rather than call – possibly this might be a probability function whose input parameters are the actual odds against the opponent having the better hand, and some measure of how the opponent sees the situation. It is clearly better for the program, when raising the pot, to have its strength hidden in the down card if it wants the opponent to stay in the hand, while it is better to have all its strength on the table (with the 'threat' of more strength in the down card) if it is trying to bluff its opponent out of the pot.

Having made the above calculations, the program has determined that it is safe to call the £3 bet, but since the odds against the opponent having the best hand at this stage are only 1.47:1, it would be a little imprudent to raise at this stage. What the odds should be is not an easy question to answer but I would recommend not raising unless the odds are at least 2:1. (In fact I would recommend an over-riding heuristic, under which the program would never raise when the opponent could have a cast iron cinch, as here, if he has another 10, the opponent knows for sure that he is winning.)

The program therefore calls the £3, making the total in the pot £9 and the dealer gives out another card to each player; this time the program gets the 6 of Diamonds and its opponent the Jack of Spades, so the situation on the table is now this:

PROGRAM: (A C) 9 H, 7 S, 6 D
OPPONENT: (??) 8 D, 10 C, J S

and there is £9 in the pot. The opponent is still high, since J, 10, 8 is a better holding than 9, 7, 6, but the program's hidden Ace is still an important card, because unless the opponent already has a pair or an Ace, the program is still winning. The situation has now been made even more complicated because the latest cards to be dealt give each player, in theory at least, the chance for a straight if the fifth card is exactly right. For example, if the opponent's hole card is a 9, 7 or Q, he can make a straight on card five by hitting a 7 or Q (if he holds a 9), or a 9 (if he already holds a 7 or Q).

The opponent's betting situation has improved somewhat since his highest face-up card is better than the program's highest face-up card, the opponent's second highest up card is better than the program's, and so is his third highest up card. So the opponent happily tosses in £9 with a smile on his face that the poor microcomputer cannot see. What should the program do now? Answer: stay calm and calculate the odds. In order to be winning at this stage, the program's opponent must hold an Ace, 8, 10 or J as his hole card. The probability of this, from Figure 44, is:

$$0.158 + 0.085 + 0.162 + 0.162 = 0.567$$

This means that the program probably doesn't hold the winning hand at the moment, but the odds against it holding the winning hand are only 0.567:0.433, or 1.31:1, whereas if it calls the £9 bet it is getting 2:1 money odds, since the £9 bet has made the pot up to a total of £18. Therefore, the program should still call this bet, even though the odds indicate that at this stage it is probably not holding the best cards. So the program calls the bet, the pot stands at £27, and the fifth and final card is dealt. The program gets an Ace while its opponent gets another Jack, so the players have the following cards showing:

PROGRAM: (A C) 9 H, 7 S, 6 D, A D
OPPONENT: (??) 8 D, 10 C, J S, J H

and there is £27 in the pot. The human opponent now feels very smug, with a pair of Jacks showing, and says, 'I suppose I ought to bet something – here is £20.'

The principles apply here, just as they did on the previous rounds of betting, except for the fact that this is the final round, after which whoever has the best cards will take the money. The program calculates that to beat it the opponent must have a Jack (for three Jacks) or a 10 or 8 in the hole (for two pairs). The probability estimates indicate that the total probability of the opponent having the winning hand is:

$$0.162 + 0.162 + 0.085 = 0.409$$

therefore the odds against the program are 0.409: (1–0.409) =0.6921:1, well below the money odds, so there is every reason to call the final bet.

Refinements to the algorithm

There are various ways in which the reader might care to modify this algorithm. To begin with, there is the fact that when, for example, the opponent hit a 10 at card three, the program knew that its original, *a priori* estimate of the probabilities wasn't accurate because the 10 of Clubs was actually still in the deck. At that point it could have recalculated the original *a priori* probabilities in the light of the news that the 10 of Clubs and the 7 of Spades were still in the deck after card two and this would have the effect of making the calculations of the probability estimates more accurate from card three onwards.

Another useful idea is to modify the probabilities all the way through the hand on the basis of the opponent's betting. If the opponent shows strength (ie raises when he could call, or bets when he could check) the program could assume that it was more likely that he held a good card, and adjust the probabilities for the good cards upwards by (say) 10 per cent, normalising the others as necessary. If the opponent showed weakness by checking when he might have been expected to bet, then the probabilities for the good cards could be adjusted downwards by 10 per cent.

Bluffing plays an extremely important part in poker, so it would be as well to assume that on a certain percentage of occasions the opponent will bluff and then adjust his percentage over a number of hands in the playing session. The program can then allow for the possibility of the opponent bluffing when making its calculations, possibly by calculating a suitable proportion of slightly adverse equity situations.

More players

If you want to get the most fun out of a poker program, I would suggest that you write one for six players, five hands being played by the program and one by the user. You can use similar probability estimates, although the actual calculations will be more complex, and you will find the game with more players is more stimulating than the two-handed game.

CHAPTER 12
Draw Poker

We have discussed the game of stud poker in a simplified, two-handed, form, and have seen how it is possible to predict an opponent's hidden card from information gained during the betting and, from these predictions, we developed an algorithm for deciding whether or not to bet. Now we shall turn our attention to draw poker.

One major difference here is that we shall consider a game for more than two players. Draw poker for two would be extremely dull, and the ideal number is six or seven players. When writing your program I would suggest that you vary the number of players at your discretion. The principles that I am about to outline are applicable for any number of players.

The rules of the game

At the start of a hand, each player is dealt five cards face down, which he may look at. No one else sees any of these cards. The player on the dealer's left usually opens the betting – there are various ways in which this is done; in some cases it is mandatory to bet, in other schools it is illegal to bet unless holding at least a pair of Jacks. We shall assume that the first player may bet or check at will.

The betting proceeds with each player having the option, when it is his turn to bet, of either dropping out of the pot ('passing' or 'folding') or putting in at least as much money as has been put in since the last bet ('calling' or 'raising'). When all of the active players have put the same amount of money into the pot, the first round of betting is over. The remaining players may then discard some of the cards in their hand and receive, in their place, an equal number of new cards from the unseen deck. This process, known as the draw, is concluded in a clockwise order starting on the dealer's left, so the dealer is the last player to draw new cards.

Once all the players have taken their turn to draw, a second round of betting takes place. When all remaining players have put the same amount of money into the pot, this second round is complete. The players all turn their cards over, and the one with the highest hand takes the pot. The order of importance of the hands is exactly the same as for five-card Stud.

The basis of the algorithm

At the start of a hand of draw poker, no one *knows* anything about anyone else's cards, unlike stud poker in which at least one of the opponent's cards is visible from the outset. But by employing simple probabilities, it is possible to make certain estimates about the type of hand which a player is holding.

The probability of being dealt a straight flush is one in 64,974, or 0.0000153. The probability of being dealt the various other types of hand is shown in Figure 45.

Four of a kind:	one in 4165 or 0.00024
Full House:	one in 694, or 0.00144
Flush:	one in 509, or 0.00196
Straight:	one in 255, or 0.00392
Three of a kind:	one in 47, or 0.02128
Two Pairs:	one in 21, or 0.04762
One Pair:	one in 2.37, or 0.42194
No pair (high card only):	one in 1.99, or 0.50251

FIGURE 45

From this table we can determine the probability that an opponent has a certain type of holding after the cards are dealt, and it is an easy matter to work out the probability that the program holds better cards. For example, if the program holds a pair of Aces, the probability of a particular opponent having been dealt better cards is simply the sum of the probabilities of being dealt two pairs, three of a kind, straight, flush, full house, four of a kind and straight flush. If the program was dealt a full house – Aces and (say) twos – the probability that it was already beaten is the sum of the probabilities of the opponent being dealt four of a kind and a straight flush.

Thus, without any information gleaned from the betting or the other aspects of play, the program already knows something about the probability that it is winning at this stage of the game.

To employ such probabilities with any real degree of accuracy throughout the game, we must introduce a greater degree of discrimination than that achieved by dividing all possible hands into the nine categories listed above. I am indebted to my friend Stewart Reuben, one of Britain's leading poker players, for the division into 109 categories. This list (Figure 46) should be coded into your poker program in such a way as to assign a two-byte probability estimate to each holding for each player in the game (apart from the program itself, which of course knows what it is holding).

A few comments are required on this division into 109 types of holding:

(1) Hand number five – four cards to an inside straight or a straight open at only one end: in a situation with 4, 5, 6, 8, J, by discarding the Jack it is possible to draw one card which will make a straight, provided that card is a 7. Similarly, when holding 8, J, Q, K, A, by discarding the 8 and drawing a 10 it is possible to make the straight. In each of these situations there is only one card denomination which will suffice to make the straight, whereas with a holding such as 2, 6, 7, 8, 9, it would be possible to discard the 2 and make a straight by drawing *either* a 5 or a 10. We must therefore distinguish between a situation in which either of two cards

will bring joy to our hearts. The reason for this distinction is obvious – it is twice as easy to make a straight when any one of 8 cards will work, as it is when any one of four cards will do.

(2) There are more Ace high flushes than there are flushes with any other card high (think about it if you don't believe me). So to have an Ace high flush in the making is much better than to have a chance of making just any old flush. Hence the distinction between hands 7 and 8.

(3) When holding three Kings it is useful to have an Ace as one of the two remaining cards, as this substantially reduces the chance of an opponent having or drawing three Aces. This explains the distinction between holdings 49 and 40, and for a similar reason you must distinguish between holdings 83 and 84, since it is very useful when holding a full house of Kings to know that one of the Aces is already denied your opponent, who therefore has much less chance of holding or drawing a full house of Aces. Similarly, the distinction between hands 98 and 99.

Numerical designation of the various possible holdings in five cards:

No hand	1
Three cards to a flush	2
Three cards to a straight flush	3
Ace high	4
Four cards to a straight missing inside card or open only at one end (ie only cards of one denomination will make the straight)	5
Four cards to an open ended straight	6
Four cards to a flush without an Ace	7
Four cards to a flush with an Ace	8
Four cards to a straight flush missing inside card	9

Four cards to a straight flush including Ace low	10
Four cards to a straight flush including Ace high	11
Four cards to an open ended straight flush	12
Pair of 2s	13
Pair of 3s	14
Pair of 4s	15
. . . etc.	
Pair of Aces	25
Two Pairs 3s and 2s	26
Two Pairs, 4s high	27
Two Pairs, 5s high	28
. . . etc.	
Two Pairs, Aces high	37
Three 2s	38
Three 3s	39
Three 4s	40
. . . etc.	
Three Kings with an Ace	50
Three Aces	51
Straight (A, 2, 3, 4, 5)	52
Straight (2, 3, 4, 5, 6)	53
Straight (3, 4, 5, 6, 7)	54
. . . etc.	
Straight (10, J, Q, K, A)	61
Flush (7 high)	62
Flush (8 high)	63
Flush (9 high)	64
. . . etc.	
Flush (Ace high)	69
Flush (Ace, Q high)	70
Flush (Ace, K high)	71
Full House (2s)	72
Full House (3s)	73

Full House (4s)	74
. . . etc.	
Full House (Ks)	83
Full House (Ks over Aces)	84
Full House (Aces)	85
Four 2s	86
Four 3s	87
Four 4s	88
. . . etc.	
Four Ks with an Ace	98
Four Aces	99
Straight Flush 5 high	100
Straight Flush 6 high	101
Straight Flush 7 high	102
. . . etc.	
Straight Flush A high	109

FIGURE 46: *The 109 types of hand*

Since we know the probability of a particular opponent being dealt a particular type of hand, we can calculate the probability of his holding any of the above 109 hands after the cards are first dealt. To do this accurately we would need to calculate exactly how many hands exist of each of the 109 types, and then divide this number by 2598960, which is the total number of possible hands in a 52 card deck with no wild cards.

The approximation that we shall use in this chapter is based on taking the probability of being dealt a particular category of hand (see Figure 46) and then dividing this by the number of types of hand within this category. Special calculations may be made for designations 1–12, but I doubt that this would improve the performance of the program, as any player holding a hand worse than 13 after the draw would (or should) certainly fold.

The probability of being dealt one pair is 0.42194. Since there are 13 possible pairs that one can have, the probability of being dealt a pair of 2s is $0.42194 \times 1/13$, or 0.0325.

The probability of being dealt a pair of 3s or a pair of anything else is also 0.0325, so we can assign to holdings 13 through 24 initial probability values of 0.0325. Up to now we have not used any approximation.

The probability of being dealt two pairs is 0.04762, but this total probability is not evenly split between two pairs (3 high), two pairs (4 high), . . . , two pairs (Ace high), because while there is only one way that a player can have two pairs 3s high (ie two 3s and two 2s), there are two ways that he can have two pairs 4s high (ie two 4s and two 3s, or two 4s and two 2s). It is easy to see that if you do not wish to follow my approximation, you can assign accurate probability estimates to holdings 26 through 37 by dividing the total probability of 0.04762 in the ratio 1:2:3:4:5: . . . :12. Alternatively, you can start with equal probability estimates for each type of hand, making all of them $0.04762 \times 1/12$, or 0.00397.

When this process has been completed, your program will have probability estimates for each of the 109 designations, these probabilities representing the likelihood that a player will be dealt a hand of this type in his first five cards.

These probabilities form the basis of our draw poker algorithm.

How the algorithm operates

Let us assume at the outset that there is no bluffing in our game. We can therefore deduce that when a player bets or raises he is indicating a strong hand, relative to some arbitrary point, and that if he checks or calls he is indicating a weak hand relative to that arbitrary point. As the betting proceeds, during the first round, players are repeatedly faced with a situation in which they must either fold, or put in more money *knowing that the other players have bet or raised*. This point is very useful – a player who puts in money knowing that other players have indicated strength, must himself be indicating more strength than he would be indicating if no one else had yet bet. In other words, the arbitrary point has moved upwards. A player who raises during the betting when there have already been ten raises before him, must have a fairly strong hand: after all, the other players are raising each other, and with each raise there is an implicit 'I think that my cards are better than yours.' So, to be in the pot after a number of raises requires a strong hand.

When the cards are dealt, each player will have, on average, a hand whose designation lies somewhere just below 13. This is known from Figure 46, which indicates that there is a slightly less than 50 per cent chance of being dealt a pair or better. So at the start of each hand the program should assign to each of his opponent's designation lists, a pointer which is set on 12 or 13 (12 if you want the program to be slightly optimistic, 13 if you wish it to be slightly conservative). As each player puts in money, the program should adjust the position of that player's pointer, to indicate what it thinks is the player's *minimum* holding. This process can be accomplished in the following way, though the reader may find it preferable to vary the size of jump made by the pointer, in accordance with how his program reacts.

When a player checks his pointer is not moved. If he calls or raises however, his pointer is moved up by: 5 per cent × (number of designations between present and 109) × number of raises, where number of raises indicates how many players have raised the pot since this particular player last put in money. If he himself is raising, this raise is included in the number of raises.

The following example should explain how the method works. We assume that there are five players, called A, B, C, D and E. Each of them has his pointer set initially at 12. A is the first to speak, since the player on his right (E) dealt.

A checks, pointer remains at 12;
B bets, pointer moves up by 5% × (109–12) × 1 = 4.85, to 17 (rounded);
C raises, pointer moves up by 5% × (109–12) × 2 = 9.7, to 22 (rounded);
D calls, pointer moves up by 5% × (109–12) × 2 = 9.7, to 22 (rounded);
E raises, pointer moves up by 5% × (109–12) × 3 = 14.55, to 27 (rounded);
A calls, pointer moves up by 5% × (109–12) × 3 = 14.55, to 27 (rounded);
B raises, pointer moves up by 5% × (109–17) × 3 = 13.8, to 31 (rounded);
C calls, pointer moves up by 5% × (109–22) × 2 = 8.7, to 31 (rounded);
D calls, pointer moves up by 5% × (109–22) × 2 = 8.7, to 31 (rounded);
E calls, pointer moves up by 5% × (109–27) × 1 = 4.1, to 31 (rounded);
A calls, pointer moves up by 5% × (109–27) × 1 = 4.1, to 31 (rounded).

Since the last four players have all called, the first round of betting is now at an end. The program has set the pointer for each of the players at 31, indicating that it expects each of them to have not less than two pairs, 8s high. The next stage is to adjust the probabilities for all the hands of designation 31 through 109, so that they add up to one. The ratio of these probabilities is already known, it is simply the ratio of the initial probabilities as calculated from Figure 46 by dividing categories of hands into the 109 types of hand. The program merely adds up all the probabilities for hand designations 31 through 109, and then divides each of them by the total, to arrive at a new measure for each. This new measure will keep the probabilities in the same ratio as before, while ensuring that their sum is 1.

In fact this adjustment can be made during the betting

process. As a player bets, calls or raises, his pointer is adjusted and the probability measures can also be adjusted in the manner described in the preceding paragraph. The program may then make its betting decisions based on up-to-date information about the estimated strength of each of its opponents' hands.

What happens during the draw

The program, if it is still in the pot after the first round of betting, must then make a decision as to how many cards to throw away in the hope of drawing a better hand. This decision is often obvious and unambiguous, for example holding four cards to a straight or a flush and a completely disconnected card, it will always throw the disconnected card and hope to make a straight or flush. On the other hand, when holding three of a kind, many players prefer to discard one card rather than two, since the reduced chance of making four of a kind is partly compensated for by the fact that a single discard disguises your hand (you might have four cards to a straight, four to a flush, four to a straight flush, or two pairs). Your program should have a set of rules telling it what to discard according to what designation holding it has. Where there is a choice of discard, it should choose at random between two possible discards to disguise its play and confuse the opposition.

A certain amount can be learned from the number of cards discarded by the opponent, and I would suggest adjusting the probabilities for players who discard certain numbers of cards. For example, a player discarding three cards must be assumed to be holding a pair. Make the probabilities for all other holdings zero, and adjust the pair probabilities so that they add up to one.

A player discarding one card can be assumed not to have a

pair, so set all of his pair probabilities to zero and adjust the other probabilities accordingly. (If his pointer is already at 26 or higher you need take no action, since it is already assumed that he does not hold less than two pairs.)

A player who discards four or five cards (five is prohibited in some schools) should be assumed to have designation 4 (if he discards four cards – assume that he has kept an Ace), or designation 1 (if he discards five cards).

A player who stands pat, ie takes no cards at all, should be assumed to have at least designation 52, though when bluffing is added to your program you should allow for the 'no card bluff' in a certain proportion of hands, and assume a lower minimum designation.

Estimating how hands improve during the draw

All good books on poker give tables to show the odds against making various types of improvement to your hand during the draw. For example, Irwin Steig's *Poker for Fun and Profit* teaches that when holding a pair and discarding three cards, the probability of making a full house is 0.0102, of making four of a kind 0.00278, of making three of a kind 0.1149, and of making two pairs 0.1587. We can use this information to adjust the probabilities still further.

Let us assume that, after the first round of betting, the pointers are all on 24 (a pair of Kings). A player discards three cards, so we assume that he does indeed have a pair, and the designation probabilities are adjusted accordingly. We must then assume, after the draw, that the probabilities of his holding four of a kind, a full house, three of a kind and two pairs, are given by the above figures, and that the balance (0.7143) is the probability of his holding a pair after the draw. Having determined the probabilities for each of the feasible categories of hand, we can divide them up to indicate the probability of his holding each of the feasible types of hand (remember that some types, such as straights and flushes, are no longer feasible after the three card draw).

After the draw is over

The program now has at its disposal an updated list of probabilities and a pointer – all this for each player. The second round of betting now ensues and the pointers are adjusted as before, according to whether the player checks, bets, raises or calls. As the pointers move up and the probabilities are adjusted, so the program forms a changing picture of how its own hand compares to those of its opponents. If the program holds two pairs and there are four other players in the pot, all raising each other, the program will soon conclude that it is very probably beaten, and will fold. On the other hand, with a good full house, and only one other player raising, the program has more reason to be optimistic about its chances. How can this optimism be made into a betting strategy?

The program decides whether or not to remain in the pot in a similar manner to the method employed in stud poker. It calculates the probability that it holds the best cards, and compares this with the 'pot odds', the ratio of the amount of money that it must put in the pot: the amount of money already in the pot. If the odds against winning are less than the money odds, the program should play. If the odds against winning are greater than the money odds, it should fold. To determine the odds against it winning, the program first identifies the designation of its own hand. It then adds up, for each player, the probabilities corresponding to all the hands of higher designation. This gives the probability that this particular player has a better hand than the program. If the probability that player A has better cards than the program is PA, then the probability that the program has better cards than player A is (1–PA). The probability that the program holds the best hand of all is therefore:

$$(1-PA)\times(1-PB)\times(1-PC)\times\ \ldots\ \text{etc.}$$

Bluffing

If nobody bluffed in poker, the game would immediately lose its appeal. A program could play super-accurate poker because it could calculate the odds much quicker and more accurately than its human adversaries. But bluff is an essential element of the game.

Your program may determine when to bluff by making a decision that it will do so in a certain proportion of situations in which its opponents all appear to have weakish hands, and the program has already shown strength by its first round betting and by drawing a small number of cards (two or less). What this proportion should be is very much up to the reader, and depends on what style of game he wishes his program to play. I would suggest that your program only bluffs when all of its opponents have a less than 0.1 chance of holding three of a kind or greater. Even 0.1 may be a little on the high side for a game with seven players (six plus the program), but it can be made a variable to be set at the user's discretion at the start of play.

An important part of the program will be a routine to estimate the proportion of occasions when the opponent is bluffing. This can only be done by examining the opponents' cards when the showdown takes place, ie all the money is in the pot and everyone turns over their cards. At this point the program can make certain deductions about whether the opponent may have over-represented his hand during the betting. For example, if a player turns out to have only a pair of 6s at the end of a hand, but has been betting in such a way as to make the program think that he had at least three of a kind, then either the player is very bad, or he has been bluffing. In either case we should allow the program to reduce the value that it places on information gained from that player's betting habits.

The program should keep track of the betting, and remember how each player bet until the hand is over. If the player turns out to have a worse hand than the program believed possible, the program should analyse how the player's pointer was adjusted, and count how many times the player bet, called or raised after this stage was reached. This number of 'illicit' bets will be called BADBETS, and the total number of bets made by a player during a hand will be called ALLBETS. For every hand that is played out to a stage where the program sees the player's cards, BADBETS and ALLBETS are counted and then added to variables called BADBETSTOTAL and ALLBETSTOTAL. The quotient BADBETSTOTAL/ALLBETSTOTAL is an indication of the extent to which that player bluffs, and is called the 'bluff factor' (BF).

When the program next comes to adjust the pointer for that player, it multiplies the calculated adjustment by (1–BF). This means that if the player is known to bluff all the time (ie BF = 1), no inference about the strength of his hand will be made from his betting. But if he is known to bluff very rarely, BF will be low and the pointer adjustment will be very little changed from the calculated one.

To make the program more sophisticated it would be relatively easy to weight recent experience more than past experience when calculating the bluff factor. For example, BF could be calculated from the relation:

$$\text{NEW BF} = (0.9 \times \text{OLD BF}) + (0.1 \times \text{latest hand BF})$$

This technique would have the effect of detecting recent changes in playing style by the opponent. A player who had bluffed little or never, but who suddenly changed his betting style and began to bluff at every opportunity, would get away with it for two or three hands at the most, but then the program would 'suspect' and BF would soar to nearly 1.

Making draw poker a many player game

You will almost certainly be playing against your program using a VDU of some sort, or even a primitive LED for output. It is not really practical under these circumstances for more than one human being to take part in the game at any one time, but you can make the program into an interesting recreation by having it play all the hands apart from your own. The program must not cheat, otherwise it will always win, and it can make its probability calculations from each player's 'seat' each time there is any action, either betting or drawing cards. Start each of the players off with the same amount of money, say £1 million, and play pot limit poker with £10 ante by the dealer. If you discover that the program is consistently too conservative for your liking, lower the 5 per cent multiplicative factor. If the program plays too loosely, raise the 5 per cent. If you wish to play in a poker game with players of varying styles, some loose some 'tight', have different factors for different players.

Bibliography

The following articles on draw poker should be considered more advanced reading for those interested in a more sophisticated approach.

Findler, N. V., Klein, H., Gould, W., Kowal, A. and Menig, J.: *Studies on Decision Making Using the Game of Poker*. Proceedings of IFIP Congress 1971, Vol. 2.

Findler, N. V.: *Studies in Machine Cognition Using the Game of Poker*. Comm. ACM, Vol. 20, pp. 230–245 (1977).

Findler, N. V.: *Computer Poker*. Scientific American, Vol. 239, No. 1, July 1978, pp. 112–119.

It will also be essential for a poker programmer to find a book on the game which gives tables showing the odds against making certain improvements when drawing cards. The Steig book mentioned in the text is one such volume, but there are very many others.

CHAPTER 13
Othello

In this chapter we are going to take a look at the game of Reversi (which has recently become known as 'Othello'). This is a superb game simply because the rules can be learned in less than one minute, yet it can take years to master. It is more complex than draughts (checkers) but far less so than chess. And it is great fun to play.

Reversi was invented in England during the early 1880s, and so it should now be celebrating its centenary. The game is played on an 8 × 8 board with discs which are coloured black on one side and white on the other. The players move alternately until the board is full or until neither side may make a move, at which point the player with the most discs on the board is the winner. If a player reaches a position in which he has no moves at his disposal, he must pass and the right to move is returned to his opponent.

In order to make a legal move, a player must put down a disc with his own colour uppermost, so that the disc being put down and another of his discs which is already on the board contain between them an unbroken line (horizontal, vertical or diagonal) of his opponent's pieces. These pieces showing the opponent's colour are then flipped over and now belong to the player who has just moved, but they may be flipped back later by a move made by the opponent. If the disc being put down forms more than one 'sandwich', all the sandwiched discs are flipped.

The first four moves must all be made in the four central

squares of the board, d4, e4, d5 and e5, and herein lies the one and only difference between Reversi and 'Othello'. In Reversi, the two players may choose where they play within these four central squares. Thus, the player who moves second may either force his opponent to make the first two moves in a horizontal or vertical line or offer his opponent the choice between that and a diagonal line. Black moves first and if he decides to put a disc on (say) d4, White could force him to play in a horizontal or vertical line by himself playing on the only diagonal spot, e5. Or White could leave the choice open by playing on e4 or d5.

In Othello, which was 'invented' in Japan during the early 1970s, Black starts the game with discs on d4 and e5, White with discs on e4 and d5. If this really is a new game then I have just invented a wonderful game called David Chess, in which the rules are exactly the same as in normal chess except that White must make his first move on the King's side. (Incidentally, Kevin O'Connell has invented another game, almost as interesting as my own, called Kevin Chess, in which White must make his first move on the Queen's side, and we are both going to patent our games and try to make as much

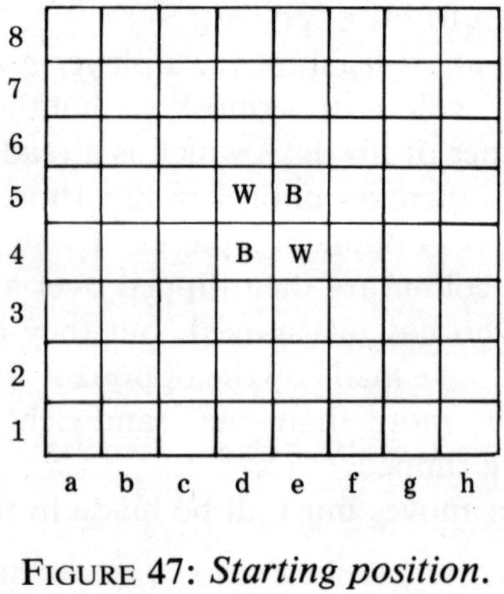

FIGURE 47: *Starting position.*

money out of the licensing fee as did the man who 'invented' Othello.)

Since the principles of playing Reversi and Othello are identical, we shall now refer to the games under the combined name of Reversi/Othello.

How to play a good game of Reversi/Othello

Having explained the rules of the game, we should now examine some of the more important principles or heuristics of good play. Figure 47 shows the initial position of Othello, in which Black may play on d6, c5, d3 or f4. All of these moves are nothing more than reflections of each other, so the decision as to where Black should place his next disc is completely immaterial. I would suggest that your program choose between the four squares at random, so that the human player will be faced with a visually different board position more often.

The first principle of the game is that it is the end result that counts, not who has most discs on the board during the earlier parts of the game. In fact, it is very often the case, particularly in games between beginners and experts, that the beginner has the vast majority of discs until near the end of the game, and he finally loses by an absolutely enormous score. One reason for this is that until the very final stages of the game, material (ie, the relative number of White and Black discs on the board) is much less important than structure (where your discs are situated) and mobility (how many moves you have at your disposal). If you have a lot more discs than your opponent, he will tend to have the greater mobility, so it is usually the case that a strong player will try to minimise the number of discs that he turns during the first part of the game. Of course, this strategy can be taken too far. One Othello program which is commercially available recently lost two games in a Paris tournament when it turned so few discs that its opponent scored a clean sweep during the first 20 moves. Such accidents are rare, but your program should prevent them.

Material and mobility are easy to measure, but structure is much more complex. Certain aspects of structure are obvious, and these help us to formulate a sensible strategy. For example, a disc on a corner square can never be captured, so it can form an ever growing base from which its owner can expand outwards unmolested. For this reason, the player who first captures a corner very often wins the game. Since a corner square is so desirable, it is very disadvantageous to place a disc on any of the squares b2, b7, g2 or g7, since this almost always leads to the loss of the adjacent corner, when the opponent gets one of his own men on the long diagonal for just long enough to make a sandwich that includes the b2/g2/b7/g7 square. Similarly, the squares b1, a2, g1, h2, b8, a7, g8 and h7 are undesirable, as they allow an opponent to creep along the edge and finally capture the adjacent corner. On the other hand, since a1 is such a good square, and b1, b2 and a2 are so bad, it is obviously desirable to have discs on c1, c3 and a3, so that one day the opponent will be forced to capture these discs, putting his own disc on b1, b2 or a2, and you will be able to recapture, putting your disc on a1.

This analysis of structure can be continued by placing greater value on the squares d3 and e3 than on c2, d2, e2 and f2, on the grounds that if a player occupies the third rank, when his opponent occupies the second rank, he will be able to make a capture on the edge of the board, and edge squares are worth having. In fact, the value of edge squares is an extremely complex subject, well beyond the scope of this book, but suffice it to say that a lot of erroneous ideas have been expressed about edge squares. Certainly b1 and a2 are bad squares to occupy from the structural point of view, but in fact it is edge formations that are really important, and not individual edge squares.

How the game changes

The nature of the game changes as more and more discs are added to the board. In the early stages (the opening) and the middle game, structure and mobility are all important, but in the final analysis it is the player with the most discs on the board who wins the game. It is therefore clear that up until a certain point in the game, structure and mobility should be the most heavily-weighted features in the evaluation function, while during the last few moves the evaluation should become more and more oriented towards the number of Black and White discs actually on the board. One way in which this might be accomplished is to have an evaluation function of the form:

$$W_1 \times (\text{MOBILITY} + k \times \text{STRUCTURE}) + W_2 \times \text{MATERIAL}$$

where $W_1 = e^{-nz}$ and $W_2 = (1 - e^{-nz})$
n = number of discs on the board
k and z are constants

When the number of discs on the board is low, ie during the early stages of the game, W_1 might be just below 1, while near the end of the game, when n approaches 64, W_1 approaches 0.

Quantifying the features

Mobility is easy to measure, being merely the number of moves available, but in a tree-searching program the matter is not so simple. The reason for this is that after a White move, it is possible that White has a very low mobility because he has just made a number of captures (ie flipped a number of Black discs), whereas after Black's reply move, White might have a much higher mobility because Black has flipped a number of discs back. It is therefore rather meaningless to compare mobility evaluations at odd and even ply, so the tree should be searched to a uniform depth, or at least all terminal nodes should be either at odd or even ply. In this way the program can happily compare its mobility in different positions, whereas were it to compare the mobility after a White move with the mobility after a Black move, the answer would be meaningless.

Material is also easy to measure, being merely the count of how many White and Black discs are on the board. The most difficult problem is how to measure the structural aspects of the position. One obvious method, which has gained wide support, is to weight the squares of the board in some way that reflects which ones are desirable and which ones should be avoided. A simple weighting map is shown in Figure 48.

	a	b	c	d	e	f	g	h
8	16	−4	4	2	2	4	−4	16
7	−4	−12	−2	−2	−2	−2	−12	−4
6	4	−2	4	2	2	4	−2	4
5	2	−2	2	0	0	2	−2	2
4	2	−2	1	0	0	2	−2	2
3	4	−2	4	2	2	4	−2	4
2	−4	−12	−2	−2	−2	−2	−12	−4
1	16	−4	4	2	2	4	−4	16

FIGURE 48: *Possible square weightings to reflect good and bad squares.*

All things being equal, which they never are, the above map represents an acceptable valuation of individual squares, but the problem is made more complex by the fact that occupation of one square may well change the desirability of occupying some other square, and this change might have an effect of fatal proportions. A simple example is the question of the b2 square. It is very bad to occupy it, because occupation of b2 might lead to the loss of a1, but if you already occupy a1 then b2 can do you no harm. A map of square values must therefore change dynamically as the game progresses, and your program shoud be able to cater for these changes.

The openings

Reversi/Othello is not yet sufficiently well analysed for us to be able to tabulate the best and worst openings, but that is not to say that we cannot make some definite remarks about opening play. Indeed, it is quite possible for your program to build up its own openings library, given one or two elementary principles.

We have already discussed the subject of mobility. Another important aspect of opening play is the apparent undesirability of being the first player to place a disc outside the central 16 squares. The reason for this is rather obvious – if you are the first to place a disc one rank or file away from the edge, your opponent will probably be the first player to place a disc on the edge of the board, and the edge squares are important. Therefore, if your program could analyse exhaustively the first 12 moves of the game (remember that there are 4 discs on the board at the start), it could determine which side was ahead in mobility in every variation, and it could also select the move or moves which gave itself the best chance of being the first player to place a disc on the edge of the board. This exhaustive 12-ply search might take a great deal of time, but it would only need to be done once, and the results could be printed so that you would be able to construct an openings book comprising optimal play (at least, optimal in the context of this strategy). Then, even though your program might only be able to perform a 3-ply or 4-ply search during the game, it could play the first few moves on the basis of the exhaustive 12-ply search.

I should perhaps add that it is not yet known the extent to which the 'Sweet 16' strategy is likely to be successful, but that, combined with a mobility feature, should enable your program to write a strong openings book.

The middle game

We have examined the form that a Reversi/Othello evaluation function might take, and it only remains for the reader to select his weightings, which he can perhaps do on a learning basis. The small number of independent parameters (W_1, k and z) makes it relatively easy and quick to play a large number of test games in which one version of the program employs one set of parameters while its opponent uses another set. At the end of a series of such games, the programmer can select optimal weightings. (Once again, let me remind you to ensure that, in its quest for high mobility, your program does not give away all of its discs.)

The endgame

Since the total number of discs on the board is the final and absolute criterion for determining the winner, it is clear that your program should, during the last few moves, search the game tree to its very end, and apply only material as its evaluation feature. How far from the end of the game an exhaustive search is possible will depend upon the speed of your processor and the efficiency of your program. For this reason it is doubly important to have an efficient move generation routine. The advantage of being able to search the whole of the game tree from six to eight moves prior to the end of the game, are rather obvious.

Writing the program

This chapter contains all that you need to know to be able to devise a suitable evaluation system for the game. Your program will be a traditional tree-searching program, employing the alpha-beta algorithm and all the tricks associated with it (alpha-beta window; killer heuristic; iterative deepening; move sorting; etc).

Examples of computer play

Just how strong are the best Othello programs compared to the strongest human players? Since the game is quite complex, and humans have more difficulty envisaging board positions after a number of discs have changed colour (and changed back again), the relative difference between the best humans and the best programs should be much smaller than is the case in, for example, the game of chess. And that is exactly how things are. The world's strongest human players are not demonstrably better than the best Othello programs and I would guess that within a year or two there are programs which will never, ever lose a game to a human.

In order to test the world's best human players against good Othello programs, Professor Peter Frey, of Northwestern University, Evanston, Illinois (home of the famed CHESS 4.n programs), organised a man v machine tournament on June 19 1980 at the Northwestern campus. Six Othello programs were pitted against the two top-ranking human players in the world, Hiroshi Inouie of Japan (the current World Champion), and Jonathan Cerf of the USA (runner up in the previous World Championship but winner of the title in October 1980). The result of the tournament was a win for Inouie, but he did lose one game, to a program written in London named The Moor*. Cerf also lost a game, to a program written by Dan and Kathe Spracklen of Sargon fame. Since then the programs have been debugged to some extent, and I imagine that if the tournament were to be replayed the humans would have more difficulty finishing at the top.

To produce programs that can play this well, normally requires a substantial commitment in man hours. But there is no reason why the readers of this book cannot write a program to play at or near expert level. Mike Reeve, who programmed The Moor, didn't even know how the pieces moved when he began working on the game, so some advice from a strong player is very useful; with it you can achieve quite a lot.

The following games show The Moor in action and illustrate some of the finer points of Othello/Reversi.

******The Moor was written by Mike Reeve, a postgraduate student at Imperial College, University of London. Expert advice was provided by Michael Stean, a chess Grandmaster who is also a very strong Othello player. The program was written for Philidor Software, a company owned by myself and Kevin O'Connell.*

Game one

First a position, taken from a game in the third Othello/Reversi tournament for computers organised by the French magazine *L'Ordinateur Individuel*, in May 1980. In this game, The Moor, searching to a depth of only 2-ply, had fallen foul of a program looking to 6-ply (The Moor was a development version, written in Pascal). Black, our opponent, had just made a mistake, and I give the position shown in Figure 49 only to illustrate the point that having a large number of discs on the board is not always a good idea, even near the end of the game. Look what happens now,

8	B	B	B	B	B	B	B	
7	B	B	W	W	W	B	B	B
6	B	B	W	W	B	B	B	B
5	B	B	W	B	B	B	W	B
4	B	W	B	W	B	B	B	B
3	B	B	B	B	W	B	B	B
2			B	B	B	B	B	
1			B	B	B	B	W	
	a	b	c	d	e	f	g	h

FIGURE 49

from a position in which Black is 'winning' by 46 discs to 11, with only seven squares left to play on. We begin with White's play at move 58 (White moves are W, Black moves are B):

54 W b1 55 B PASS 56 W h8
57 B PASS 58 W h2 59 B PASS
60 W h1 61 B PASS 62 W b2
63 B a2

and now neither side may move again, so the game ends, with White having 39 discs to Black's 24.

The previous episode shows just how easy it is to be deceived into thinking that having a big material advantage is decisive. In the next game, for which you will need an Othello set if you wish to follow it properly, Black gets into serious trouble from early on, and then makes a serious mistake which costs him the first corner. This game was played at the finals of the 1980 British Othello Championships in London, immediately after Neil Cogle won the Championship title. It illustrates my argument that a computer program can already play at the same level as top human players.

Game two

Black: Neil Cogle (1980 British Othello Champion – for humans!)
White: The Moor (4-ply look-ahead)

1 B c5	2 W e6	3 B f5
4 W c4	5 B c3	6 W d3
7 B f4	8 W b3	9 B b4
10 W c6	11 B d6	12 W a4

So The Moor has gained the first disc on the edge of the board, and to redress the balance Black takes the dangerous square a2.

13 B a2	14 W f6	15 B e7
16 W f8	17 B b5	18 W e3
19 B f7	20 W a5	21 B a6

Black was already in a bad way, with a disc on a2 and a deficit in mobility, but this move is a fatal mistake which puts his position beyond repair. See if you can spot The Moor's killing reply (Figure 50).

22 W a3

Now you can see the danger of playing on a2. Black must lose the a1 corner.

23 B d8	24 W b6	25 B c7
26 W a1		

Now that The Moor has a corner, it uses it as an impregnable base from which to expand its control of the board.

	a	b	c	d	e	f	g	h
8						W		
7					W	B		
6	B		W	W	B	B		
5	W	B	W	W	W	B		
4	W	W	B	W	W	B		
3		B	W	W	W			
2	B							
1								

FIGURE 50

27 B f3 28 W g3 29 B f2
30 W g4 31 B h5 32 W e2
33 B e1 34 W d2 35 B h4
36 W d7 37 B c8

White can afford to concede virtually every edge square at this stage of the game, in the knowledge that his corner anchor on a1 will eventually allow a clean sweep of the edges.

38 W g1 39 B d1 40 W g6
41 B h6 42 W g5 43 B c2
44 W b1 45 B b2

Now that a1 is already occupied, putting a disc on b2 is unimportant.

46 W a7 47 B g2

There is no way that White can be kept out of h1. If Black plays on f1, White replies on c1 and then Black is forced to play on b7 and g2 within the next few moves.

48 W h1 49 B h2 50 W f1
51 B b7 52 W c1 53 B PASS

Black has no moves, and White continues its march around the edge of the board.

54 W h3	55 B PASS	56 W h7
57 B PASS	58 W g8	59 B g7

Black's problems are aggravated by the fact that by now The Moor is examining the whole of the game tree exhaustively, and is always making the very best move.

61 B PASS	62 W e8	63 B PASS
64 W b8		

Neither side may move to a8, so the game comes to an end with The Moor winning by 61 discs to 2, which is rather like being several queens up at the end of a game of chess.

Finally, I shall give without comment the game won by The Moor against World Champion Hiroshi Inouie of Japan, on June 19 1980. The final score in this game was 36-28 in favour of the program, and not 34-30 as reported in the tournament bulletin.

Black: The Moor
White: Hiroshi Inouie

1 B d6	2 W c6	3 B c5
4 W c4	5 B b3	6 W e6
7 B c7	8 W b5	9 B a6
10 W c3	11 B c2	12 W b4
13 B f4	14 W f5	15 B f3
16 W e3	17 B a3	18 W d7
19 B d3	20 W g4	21 B f6
22 W a4	23 B d8	24 W b6
25 B a5	26 W e7	27 B h3
28 W e8	29 B f8	30 W f7
31 B c8	32 W g5	33 B h6
34 W h5	35 B h4	36 W g6
37 B h7	38 W c1	39 B d2
40 W b2	41 B d1	42 W e1
43 B e2	44 W f1	45 B f2
46 W b1	47 B g8	48 W g1

49 B b7	50 W a7	51 B g2
52 W g3	53 B h1	54 W h2
55 B a1	56 W h8	57 B g7
58 W b8	59 B a8	60 W a2

Black wins by 36-28.

To the best of my knowledge, this is the first time that a computer program has ever defeated a human World Champion in a game of pure skill.

CHAPTER 14
Go-Moku (and Renju)

We shall now look at a game with an enormous number of possible moves at every juncture. The game is known as Go-Moku (or 5-in-a-row) in most Western countries, and in Japan there is a popular variant called Renju, which involves considerably more skill. Go-Moku is a two-person game played on a Go board using Go stones; it is the size of the Go board (19 × 19) that gives rise to the enormous branching factor of the game tree.

Black always starts and makes a move by placing a black stone on any of the intersections. Thereafter, the players move alternately and the player who first completes a horizontal, vertical or diagonal line of five of his own stones is the winner.

Since five men in a row is enough to win, if you get four men in a row with the two adjacent intersections (at each end of this row) vacant, then on the next move you can complete a row of five (unless your opponent can do so immediately). So an unblocked row of four men is a winning formation. It is now easy to understand that if you have a completely open row of three you are threatening to force a win by making it into an open row of four on the next move and then a row of five on the following turn. The threat to convert a completely open row of three into an open row of four can normally be blocked, simply by closing the row of three at one end and then, when the opponent places a stone at the other end of the row to make a row of four, it is possible to block the only open end of the row of four to prevent it becoming a row of five.

Although it *is* possible to counter the threat of making one completely open row of three into an open row of four, it is obviously impossible to counter two such threats if they exist simultaneously. Thus, the most fundamental winning tactic in Go-Moku is to try to force a position in which you have, simultaneously, two completely open rows of three stones. The simple examples of Figure 51 will help to illustrate these principles.

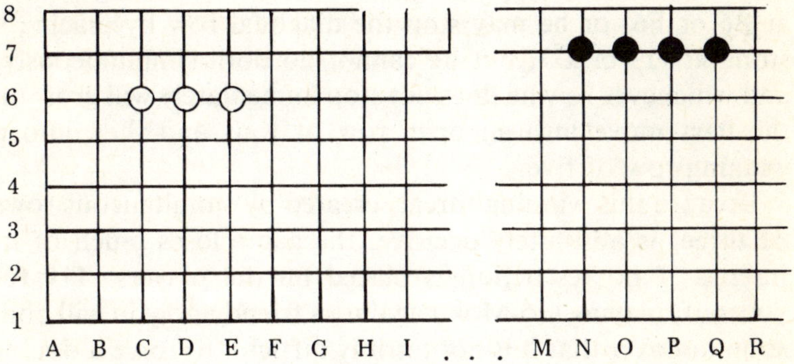

FIGURE 51

The following rather obvious statements should be sufficient to teach the absolute beginner enough so that he can understand the principles of the game:

(a) The four black stones at N7, O7, P7 and Q7 in Figure 51 form an open row of four. Unless, on his next move, White can complete a row of five stones elsewhere on the board and thereby win the game, White has no way to avoid defeat. If he plays on M7 then Black will play on R7 and win, and vice versa.

(b) The white stones at C6, D6 and E6 form a completely open row of three. Unless Black takes remedial action against this row, or unless Black can himself force a win on some other part of the board, this row of three threatens to win by becoming an open row of four. For example, if it is now

Black's turn and he plays a stone on some useless point, White may place a stone at B6 or F6, in either case creating an open row of four which next move will become a winning row of five.

(c) If we now add to the board two more white stones, on F5 and G4, we can see that unless Black has a win on some other part of the board, White will win by making one or other of these rows of three into an open row of four on his next move. Black may stop the horizontal row by placing a stone at B6 or F6, or he may stop the diagonal row by placing a stone at H3 or D7, but he cannot do both simultaneously; and whichever row he does not stop immediately will grow on the next move into an open row of four and then into a winning row of five.

Because this winning threat, created by simultaneous rows of three, is absolutely decisive, the game loses much of its interest if no restriction is placed on the players. Try for yourself, playing Go-Moku against a friend and you will both soon discover that it is not terribly difficult to force a double threat situation early in the game.

For this reason, the Japanese have made the game more difficult and more interesting, by creating a version called Renju, in which the player of the black pieces has certain restrictions placed on his moves. These restrictions are:

(a) A move which simultaneously creates a double or triple line of 3 is illegal for Black, but legal for White.

(b) A move which creates a double or triple line of 4 is illegal for Black, but legal for White.

(c) A move which creates an overline (more than 5 in a row) is illegal for Black, but legal for White (though it does not win for White). Note that in Go-Moku, overlines are legal but do not win.

Renju is only played on a 15×15 board, whereas Go-Moku can be enjoyed on a board that is 19×19 (the traditional Go board), or any size down to 9×9.

Program design

Since Go-Moku is a zero sum, two-person game, we can employ most of the tricks of the trade that have been discussed in earlier chapters. The program will grow and search a game tree, using some sort of evaluation function to evaluate terminal nodes on the tree. The obvious problem is the size of the tree itself – with 361 intersections on the board, even the alpha-beta algorithm will need to evaluate at least a quarter of a million terminal nodes when performing only a 4-ply search, and that assumes almost perfect ordering. The true number is likely to exceed five million terminal nodes in a 4-ply search, which puts the whole concept of full-width search under a big cloud where Go-Moku is concerned. We will therefore need to find some way to prune the game tree, but more about that later.

Evaluation

As I mentioned in an earlier chapter, there is always a trade-off between selecting a sophisticated but slow evaluation function, which provides a relatively accurate score for a game position, and the other extreme which is a fast but simple evaluation function which permits the search of a larger tree but which does not 'understand' so much when it is looking at a terminal node. William Blake once wrote: 'A fool sees not the same tree that a wise man sees' and his words of wisdom were clearly intended for programmers working on computer games.

In the case of Go-Moku, since the size of the game tree is so enormous, the use of a simple evaluation function with a deep tree search is clearly out of the question. In this sense, an important decision has been made for us by the very structure of the game itself. We must look at a relatively shallow tree, so we ought to ensure that our evaluation mechanism is wise rather than foolish.

Let us start by considering what features might usefully be incorporated in our evaluation function – we shall expand their scope a little further on in this chapter.

The key to a successful strategy is obtaining some of your own stones, in an unbroken row, in such a way that they could *conceivably* be extended into a row of five. Let us first define some variables.

W1 = the number of single white stones which are in a row, column or diagonal in such a way as to allow the stone to be extended into a row, column or diagonal of five stones.

Using the notation of Figure 51, imagine a white stone on D1 and black stones on A1, F1 and D5. There is no way that the stone on D1 can ever form part of a row or column of five stones, because the horizontal and vertical directions are sufficiently well blocked off by Black, but it is conceivable that the stone on D1 could form part of a diagonal of five stones, if White were to be able to place stones on E2, F3, G4 and H5. So in this case W1 would be 1, because this is the number of possible 5-rows that can be made using D1. If there were no black stone on A1 then the value of W1 would be 2 because D1 could be part of a horizontal or diagonal 5-row, and if there were no stone on D5 either the value of W1 would be 3, since 5-rows could be constructed horizontally, vertically and in one diagonal direction.

Similarly, B1 = the number of single black stones which are in a row, column or diagonal in such a way as to allow the stone to be extended into a row, column or diagonal of five stones (which we call a 5-row).

And W2, B2, W3, B3, W4, B4, W5 and B5 are the corresponding variables for situations in which White or Black has a row, column or diagonal with 2, 3, 4 or 5 of his own stones in an unbroken row.

Let us assume for the sake of simplicity that all terminal nodes are at even depth, that is to say we only evaluate a position in which it is the program's turn to move. We shall further assume that the program is White. It is now necessary to assign weights to the features of the evaluation function in such a way as to reflect the worth of a 1-row, a 2-row, a 3-row, a 4-row and a 5-row. Of course a 5-row has infinite value, in the sense that if you make 5-row you have won the game, so the weighting assigned to W5 and B5 should reflect this fact, in the same way that a chess-playing program would have an infinite value assigned to the kings.

Let the weightings which we assign to these variables be as follows:

AW1 is the weighting assigned to W1;
AB1 is the weighting assigned to B1.

Then the whole of the evaluation function takes the form:

$$(AW1 \times W1) + (AW2 \times W2) + (AW3 \times W3) + (AW4 \times W4) + (AW5 \times W5) - (AB1 \times B1) - (AB2 \times B2) - (AB3 \times B3) - (AB4 \times B4) - (AB5 \times B5)$$

By ensuring that the weightings increase as the indices increase (ie AW5>AW4>AW3, etc.) we are using our evaluation function to represent the statement:

5-rows are more valuable than 4-rows which are more valuable than 3-rows which are more valuable than 2-rows which are more valuable than 1-rows.

And if we ensure that AB5 lies between AW4 and AW5, and that AW4 lies between AB4 and AB5, and that AB4 lies between AW3 and AW4 . . . etc., we are using the function to represent the statement: Make a 5-row if you can, otherwise prevent your opponent from making a 5-row of his own if you can, otherwise make a 4-row of your own if you can, otherwise prevent your opponent from making a 4-row of his own if you can, otherwise . . . etc. The actual values of the AWi and the ABi should be chosen by intelligent guess-work to begin with, and then modified in the light of experience. I have discussed how this might be done, manually and automatically, in earlier chapters.

Refinements to the evaluation function

The function described above is simple to understand and to program, yet it encompasses the most important aspects of the game of Go-Moku. Nevertheless, it is rather unsophisticated and I should like to point out ways in which it might be improved.

Consider an empty board on which we place one solitary white stone on the intersection E1. This stone can conceivably form part of four different future 5-rows, or to be more accurate it can form part of 5-rows in four different directions: horizontal, vertical, diagonal towards J5 and diagonal towards A5. So the value of W1 produced by that stone is 4, one for each direction. Now let us remove this stone from E1 and place it on J1. Is the stone of the same value on J1 as it was on E1? Since the value of W1 for the stone on J1 is also 4, just as it was for the stone on E1, it might seem at first as though the two stones *are* of equal value but they are not. Until the game nears its conclusion, much of the value of a particular 1-row, 2-row or 3-row lies in its potential as a threat – the opponent must react in some way to counter the threat. Therefore, part of the strategy of the game lies in placing a stone in such a way as to compel the opponent to reply to one threat and then taking advantage of a different threat which the opponent was unable to meet because he had to attend to something more immediate.

Let us consider the situation of two white stones on E1 and D1, with the rest of the board being irrelevant. If we add a third white stone to C1, a serious threat since a white stone on B1 or F1 would now force a win, the opponent would have to react to this threat by placing a black stone on B1 or F1.

White has then not accomplished anything in the horizontal direction because his play has now been blocked and if he puts a stone on F1 Black can counter on G1, and if he plays on B1 Black can counter on A1. But the placing of the third white stone on C1 might well have much deeper implications – it might be part of a plan to create a strong formation over on the left hand side of the board, with a view to extending this formation into a winning threat later in the game.

Now we come to the important difference between having a single stone on E1 and having it on J1. If the planned future activity is in the area of the A-column, B-column and C-column, it is less likely to be successful than if it is in the E-column, F-column and G-column, simply because in the former case this activity is bounded by the left hand edge of the board. If your area of activity is bounded in some way, either by an edge of the board or by a strong (or even impregnable) formation of your opponent's stones, you will be less likely to win than if your area of activity is not bounded. In the latter case you have more opportunity to use the area of activity to create further threats.

What does all this mean in relation to our evaluation function? The obvious implication is that the weighting should vary in some way that reflects the number of vacant intersections to each side of a 1-row, 2-row or 3-row. (The number of vacant intersections to each side of a 4-row is not important, since the 4-row itself will determine the outcome of the game at once.) In the above example it might appear as though the small number of intersections to the left of E1 might be compensated for by the larger number of vacant intersections to the right of E1, and that therefore, E1 and J1 *are* of equal value. But if we think about the nature of the game it is clear that having a formation near the centre of a row, column or diagonal, gives greater flexibility than having that same formation near one or more edges of the board. We should therefore adjust our weightings in some suitable manner, to reflect the desire to have useful formations nearer the centre than the edges. One possible way of doing this is to subtract from a weighting AWi (or BWi), an amount Ci, where Ci is inversely proportional to (1 + number of vacant intersections between the end of a formation and its nearest edge of the board (or enemy stone) in the same direction). Thus, for a single black stone on the D1 intersection of an otherwise empty board, the weighting AB1 would actually be AB1 – (1/3), for the component of the score that is related to the horizontal 1-row. This is because in a horizontal direction the nearest edge intersection to the 1-row on D1 is the intersection on A1, which is two vacant intersections away from D1. The weighting of AB1 in the diagonal direction towards the left hand edge would be AB1 – 1/1; the weighting in the diagonal direction towards the right hand edge would be AB1 – 1/1; and finally the weighting towards the top edge would be AB1 – 1/1 (these last three values are due to D1 being on the edge of the board).

The suggestion to subtract a value that is inversely proportional to the 'freedom of movement' of a formation is given here as an indication of the shape that this part of the evaluation function should take. You might find it more satisfactory to subtract the square of that number, or some other function.

Another important refinement of the evaluation function is needed to take care of those situations in which a stone of one colour may have a nearby neighbour of its own colour. For example, white stones on E1 and G1 with no other stones on the first horizontal row. The value of these two stones is clearly more than the value of two individual 1-rows, because the two stones can easily combine into a 3-row if White is permitted to play on F1. On the other hand, two white stones with one vacant intersection between them are worth slightly less than a 2-row because with a 2-row there are four distinct ways of creating a 5-row, whereas with two separated 1-rows there are only three distinct ways (since the vacant intersection between them *must* be occupied). This leads me to suggest that in a situation of this type we employ a weighting mid-way between that of a 2-row and the sum of two 1-rows. If there are two vacant intersections between the two 1-rows, use a weighting one quarter of the way between that of two 1-rows and that of one 2-row, and if there are three vacant intersections take a weighting one-eighth of the way between them. Similar logic can be used to suggest weightings for (say) a 1-row separated from a 2-row (in the same horizontal, vertical or diagonal) by one or two vacant intersections, though here as usual, your first guesstimate as to the size of the weighting will almost certainly need to be changed in the light of experience.

The two refinements discussed here are probably necessary for a very strong program, but those of you who wish to keep things simple will, I'm sure, get an entertaining game from a program which employs only the most primitive form of the evaluation function.

Combating enormous tree growth

The potential size of the Go-Moku tree forces us to introduce some sort of forward pruning from the very first ply of search. The simplest way to do this is to employ the evaluation function also as a plausibility indicator. First your program generates a list of all the legal moves in the root position. (In fact it has this list readily available and updates it whenever a move is made in the tree – the updating consists simply of removing a now occupied intersection from the list of legal moves.) The program then evaluates all the resulting positions at ply-1, using the evaluation function, and sorts the moves into descending order of merit based upon these evaluations. The worst n per cent of the moves on the list may then be discarded (n can be chosen to suit the execution speed of your program – I would suggest that you start with n = 90). You will now have a list of some 36 moves (at the start of the game) and from each of the 36 positions you again generate and evaluate, discarding the worst (say) 92 per cent of the moves at the next ply. The percentage of moves discarded goes up as the tree gets deeper and deeper, and this parameter can be adjusted, dynamically if necessary, so that the program is made to respond in any desired time frame.

Your tree will now be no larger than the tree for a chess program, and move generation will be faster than for chess, so provided you code the evaluation routine in an efficient manner, you ought to be able to perform a search of 4–6 ply within a minute or two, if your program is written in assembler.

We have already encountered the concept of the alpha-beta window and the killer heuristic, both of which should be employed in your Go-Moku program. In a large tree the killer heuristic is particularly useful and the fact that you sorted the moves prior to generation of the replies at each level will help considerably in the optimisation of the alpha-beta routine itself. One other method of speeding the search is to avoid the need to re-evaluate those parts of the board that are not affected by a move in the game tree. You might, for example, keep several different components of the evaluation, and update only those affected by a move. For example, let us assume that the evaluation function has separate components for each horizontal, each vertical and each diagonal. If the program considers a move on the intersection A1, this move will in no way affect the evaluation of a formation in the J column, so part of the evaluation process need not be repeated – it is known to be unchanged. The more you speed up the evaluation process, the deeper the tree can grow, so any technique which updates the evaluation function in an incremental way is certain to be useful.

Tactical search

In most board games it is possible to distinguish strategic play from tactical play. We have discussed this point before, with particular reference to chess, and it is well known that the tree search should look deeper in those parts of the tree that are of greater tactical interest. In Go-Moku, tactical play is represented by threats, counter threats and moves that defend against threats. We have seen how the very existence of a 3-row constitutes a threat and it would be possible to argue that the creation of a 2-row is a veiled threat since the 2-row can easily grow into a 3-row. But I would recommend that we assume the evaluation function will be sufficiently smart to provide scores that represent fairly accurately the value of having a 2-row. It is the tactical value of a 3-row that is not so easy to measure and your program should therefore consider any move which creates a 3-row as being worthy of further consideration, even if it would otherwise be a terminal node.

My suggestion for a tactical search is to examine any move which creates or blocks a 3-row or a 4-row or which creates a 5-row. This means that having grown the tree to what would normally be its full depth, the program examines the board to see if any 3-rows exist and if so, whether the opponent can block them. The program also examines moves which themselves create 3-rows. It does the same for 4-rows and it looks for moves which create winning 5-rows. This process can, particularly during the later stages of the game, lead to a substantial increase in the size of the tree, but tactics are extremely important in Go-Moku and it is essential for a strong program to have a good command of tactics. In order to be able to extend the tactical search to (say) 4 or 6 ply beyond the usual depth of search, it may be necessary to reduce the depth of the first part of the search. To ensure that your program responds within an acceptable amount of time, you should make your tree search iterative, with a mandatory cutoff after a certain maximum number of seconds. Your program might then perform a full 1-ply search, plus (say) 6-ply of tactical search; then if it has not consumed all of its thinking time it can sort the 1-ply moves as suggested above, prune off 90 per cent of them, generate the replies to the remaining 10 per cent and then perform a 6-ply tactical search from the resulting positions at depth 2-ply. Once again, if the search time is not exhausted, prune 92 per cent of the second-ply moves and perform your 6-ply tactical search. In order to optimise the performance of your program, try playing around with the various parameters (not only the weightings in the evaluation function, but also the percentage of moves pruned at each level and the depth of tactical search).

Bibliography

Elcock, E. W. and Murray, A. M.: 'Experiments with a Learning Component in a Go-Moku Playing Program', *Machine Intelligence 1*. Collins, N. L. and Michie, D. (Eds), Edinburgh University Press 1971, pp. 87–103.

Murray, A. M. and Elcock, E. W.: 'Automatic Description and Recognition of Board Patterns in Go-Moku', *Machine Intelligence 2*. Dale, E. and Michie, D. (Eds), Edinburgh University Press 1971, pp. 75–88.

CHAPTER 15
Bridge Bidding

Contract bridge is one of the most interesting and skilful of card games, ranking alongside poker in its complexity. Many computer programmers are also bridge enthusiasts, so I expect that many of my readers will, at some time or another, have considered the possibility of writing their own bridge program. Let me warn you from the outset – this is a most daunting task. I would expect a competent programmer to take three times as long to write a bridge program as to write a fairly respectable chess program, and the size of the bridge program would be much larger – with less than 32 kbytes you might as well forget it. But since most of you who own or have access to computers *will* have at least 32k at your disposal, writing a bridge program is a task that can be undertaken by anyone who is prepared to devote a lot of time and effort.

In writing about computer bridge I shall attempt only to outline some simple principles which will enable the reader to write a working program. The game is sufficiently rich in ideas that stronger bridge players will be able to extrapolate from my suggestions and include a number of more advanced concepts in their programs. Anyone who writes a 'simple' bridge program based on Chapters 15 and 16 will be able to enjoy an undemanding game without the need to find three other (human) players.

How to play bridge

I do not wish to go into a detailed description of the rules of the game, but some of my readers may not know how to play, so some explanation is essential. This will also enable those of you who play other bidding games to learn the principles of programming the bidding phase, which can be carried over to other games. The principles of playing the cards might also be useful in programming other games which are based on taking tricks. So don't give up if you are not attracted to the idea of programming bridge – what you learn here may help you in other games.

Contract bridge is played by four players, who form two partnerships. A normal deck of 52 cards is used, and at the start of a hand each player is dealt 13 cards. The players start by bidding for the right to play the hand, and whichever side makes the highest bid then tries to make the number of tricks indicated by that bid. If the partnership is successful in making the desired contract it scores points according to the size of the bid, and the number of extra tricks (overtricks) made by the partnership. If the contract is not made, the partnership which was playing to make the contract loses penalty points, the number of penalty points depending upon the number of tricks by which the contract failed, and whether or not the defending partnership decided to 'double' the contract (doubling, as one might expect, doubles the number of points gained or lost on a hand, and also affects bonus points which can be scored in certain situations).

The player who deals the cards opens the bidding. He may say 'pass' or 'no-bid' if he doesn't wish to make a positive bid at this stage, or he may make a bid of the form 1 Club, or 2 No-Trumps – the number part of the bid indicates the number of tricks that must be made if this bid is the final contract (number of tricks = number bid + 6); the suit part of the bid indicates what will be the trump suit if this bid is the final contract.

After the first player has made his bid or passed, it becomes the turn of the player sitting to his left. This player may also pass; or he may make a higher bid; or he may double the opponent's previous bid. In order to make a higher bid he must indicate a greater number of tricks, or he must bid a higher ranking suit (or No-Trumps) than the previous bid. The ranking of the suits goes (from lowest to highest) Clubs, Diamonds, Hearts, Spades and then comes No-Trumps. So one Heart is higher than one Diamond; one No-Trump is higher than one of any suit; and two Clubs is higher than any bid at the one level.

The bidding proceeds in this way, moving round the table in a clockwise direction and coming to an end only when three successive players pass. Even if a player doubles or redoubles an opponent's bid, there must then be three successive passes before the bidding is at an end. Once the bidding is over, the players who won the bidding (ie made the final bid) are obliged to play the contract, or to be more precise, whichever of them first bid the suit (or No-Trumps) of the final contract – he is the one who must play the cards for his partnership. He is referred to as 'Declarer' and his partner as 'Dummy'.

The player on the declarer's left leads any card that he chooses and, at this point, dummy places all of his cards on the table, face up so that everyone can see them. From now on dummy has nothing to do until the hand is over. His partner, declarer, must play the cards for both of them.

The rules of play are very similar to those of Whist and many other trick-taking games. The player who wins one trick leads the first card to the next trick, and the players must follow suit if possible, or if this is not possible they may trump a card if they possess any trumps. (In a No-Trump contract this is not applicable.) Cards rank in the usual order, from Ace, King, Queen, and Jack down to 4, 3 and 2.

The bidding phase

The point of the bidding phase is to try to reach the optimal contract, partly by conveying information to your partner about the strength and 'shape' of your hand. In order to be able to determine what contract you and your partner should be playing, it is important for you to know something about each other's hand. This is accomplished by bidding, but because every bid must be higher than the previous bid, a partnership does not have a completely free licence to pass information back and forth during the bidding, as this would lead them into an impossibly high contract. So the most important thing to do during the bidding is to try to reach the ideal contract by conveying the maximum information about your hand in the most economical manner. Let us examine the bidding of a hand of bridge to see how information is conveyed (Figure 52).

Spades: K 8 7 4 2
Hearts: 2
Diamonds: A J 9 5 3
Clubs: K 10

Spades: 10
Hearts: Q J 10 7 6
Diamonds: Q 8 2
Clubs: Q J 4 3

N
W E
S

Spades: 9 5
Hearts: K 9 4
Diamonds: K 10 7
Clubs: A 9 8 6 5

Spades: A Q J 6 3
Hearts: A 8 5 3
Diamonds: 6 4
Clubs: 7 2

FIGURE 52

For the sake of convenience we usually refer to the four hands by the four points of the compass: North, South, East and West. We shall assume that West was the dealer, and that the bidding goes like this (players' thought processes in brackets):

West: Pass (I have a weak hand);
North: One Diamond (I have a stronger-than-average hand with two good suits. I shall bid the lower-ranking suit first to give my partner a chance of bidding Hearts at the one level);
East: Pass (I also have a hand that is no better than average, and since my partner is weak we will not have enough combined strength to make any contract);

South: One Spade (I have two biddable suits, but I have more Spades than Hearts so I shall bid Spades first);
West: Pass;
North: Two Spades (My partner has at least four Spades in his hand so we have at least nine Spades out of 13 between us. Obviously Spades will be a good suit for us to play a contract in);
East: Pass;
South: Three Hearts (I must show my partner that I have another biddable suit);
West: Pass;
North: Three Spades (My first Spade bid indicated only that I had reasonable Spade support for my partner. Now I should tell him that I have more than minimal Spade support and that I do not have enough strong cards in the unbid suits to make a No-Trump contract possible);
East: Pass;
South: Four Spades (My partner has at least four Spades and probably holds the King of Spades. He also has four or five Diamonds so he does not have many Clubs and Hearts. I have the Ace of Hearts so we are unlikely to lose more than one Heart trick, and I only have two Clubs, so we cannot lose more than two Club tricks before I can trump any further Clubs that are led. So we ought to be able to avoid losing any more than three tricks, and four Spades seems quite possible);
West: Pass;
North: Pass (Enough is enough);
East: Pass.

The above bidding and thought processes represents an over-simplification of what was going on in the minds of the players. But it does serve to explain the type of thought processes that one goes through when bidding in a simple fashion. I ought perhaps to mention at this stage that by reaching certain contracts a partnership may qualify for a 'game bonus' if the contract is made. These game contracts are: three No-Trumps; four Hearts or four Spades; five Clubs or five Diamonds. Making a lesser contract allows you to score the game bonus later on if you can make another contract that counts, together with the earlier contract, for enough points to make a game. I will not go into the scoring system in this chapter, but you should study an elementary book on bridge before writing your program, so that the scoring will be correct.

In order to make the bidding phase easier and to ensure that information is conveyed economically, various bidding systems have been invented. In a bidding system, each bid has a fairly precise defined meaning, and by correctly interpreting a bid, a player will understand more about his partner's hand. One useful tool employed in many bidding systems is what are known as 'high card points'. This points method usually counts 4 points for holding an Ace, 3 for a King, 2 for a Queen, 1 for a Jack or singleton (a suit with only one card, other than the Ace), 4 for a void (a suit with no cards), 1 for each card after the first five in a suit. Using this point count method, various rules of thumb have been developed, including:

(a) Do not open the bidding with fewer than 12 points;

(b) If you hold 12–15 points you should open one of your best suit;

(c) If you hold 16–18 points you should open one No-Trump;

(d) In order to make a three No-Trump contract the combined hands should have no less than 24 points, preferably 25 or more.

The above rules can all be broken, under the correct circumstances and, in fact, the same bid can mean many different things in the same situation, depending on which system of bidding the partnership is employing. The most important thing to remember about bidding is that bridge is a partnership game, and you should be trying to help your partner during the bidding by making meaningful bids that he will understand. There is no point in making a brilliant bid on one bidding system if your partner is using a different system – he will not understand what you mean and before you know what is happening you and your partner will have overbid, and found yourselves in an impossible contract.

How to program a bidding system

Before writing your program, decide what bidding system will be used in the program and make a long list of what the various bids can mean in different circumstances. Whenever the program must make a bid it determines the circumstances and makes the appropriate bid. Whenever the program must interpret a bid made by its partner, it determines the circumstances under which the partner's bid was made, and then looks at the list of bids to see what the particular bid should mean in those circumstances. These two processes, the making of the correct bid and the interpreting of the partner's bid can each be aided by keeping a number of important variables and updating them in the light of new information transmitted and received. The following variables might usefully be employed when deciding what bid to make or when interpreting a bid made by one's partner:
Max Clubs (what is the maximum number of Clubs that have been shown so far by the player who is bidding this hand);
Min Clubs (the minimum number of Clubs shown by the bidding);
Max Diamonds;
Min Diamonds;
Max Hearts;
Min Hearts;
Max Spades;
Min Spades.

By storing values for all the above variables, the program can build up an idea of the way in which the suits are distributed in his partner's hand, or he can keep track of the extent to which he has described the distribution of the suits in his own hand. In addition to knowing how long a suit might be, it is also very useful to have some indication as to how strong a particular hand might be.

This can be accomplished using two variables called Max Points and Min Points, which indicate the known limits of strength of a hand as indicated by the number of high card points in the hand. For example, if a partnership is using a bidding system in which 13 points is the minimum number for making an opening bid, a player who makes an opening bid is known to have at least 13 points so his Min Points is initially adjusted from 0 (the default value when the hand is dealt) to 13.

Adjusting the distribution variables is not a particularly difficult matter. At the start of a hand the four Max variables are set at numbers which may be deduced from the holding of the hand under scrutiny. For example, if the computer is making the first bid for West in the above hand, it sets Max Spades for North, East and South at 12, since it has one Spade and knows that no other player may therefore have more than 12. Similarly, Max Hearts is set at 8, Max Diamonds is 10 and Max Clubs is 9. The minimum values of the suit variables are all set at 0 since no bids have been made and therefore nothing is known about the distribution in each of the hands other than the program's 'own' hand.

If we follow through the bidding of the above hand again, assuming that the computer is playing South, we can see how easy it is to adjust the distribution variables for the other hands. (Here I shall make certain assumptions concerning the bidding systems employed by the N-S pair and the E-W pair.)
West: Pass (West's Max Points is set to 11, as he would open the bidding on 12 or more.) West's Min Points remains at 0;
North: One Diamond (North's Min Points is set at 12, Max Points is set at 15, since with 16–18 points North would have opened one No-Trump, and with 19 or more he would have opened two of a suit. Also, Min Diamonds is set at 4, the minimum number needed to bid, and Max Diamonds is set at 7, since with 8 he would have opened higher);
East: Pass (East's Max Points = 11, Min Points = 0);

South: One Spade (South, the program, has indicated that he holds at least 7 points, otherwise he would have passed. So Min Points = 7, Max Points = 11, otherwise he would have made a stronger bid to indicate that he, too, held an opening hand. Min Spades = 4 and Max Spades = 6, since with seven or more Spades, South would have made a stronger bid than one Spade);
West: Pass;
North: Two Spades (Min Spades = 3, Max Spades = 5, since with six or more Spades North would be able to bid higher in Spades, and would have opened in Spades rather than Diamonds. Also Max Hearts = 4 and Max Clubs = 4, by subtraction from 13);
East: Pass;
South: Three Hearts (Min Hearts = 4, Max Hearts = 6 and, by subtracting from 13, we find that Max Diamonds = Max Clubs = 4. Note that neither Clubs nor Diamonds can be longer than a four-card suit, as this would have required South to bid the suit before now);
West: Pass;
North: Three Spades (Min Spades = 4);
East: Pass;
South: Four Spades (Min Spades = 5);

This example is not intended to indicate exactly how the variables should be adjusted, nor is it intended to be complete in the summary of information conveyed by each bid. The sole *raison d'être* for the example is to show the reader the type of information that can be gleaned from a bid, and how this information may be used to update some of the more useful variables. When you have decided on the bidding system that will be employed in your program, the method for updating each of the variables will suggest itself.

Special conventions in bidding

There are a number of special bidding conventions, each of which may be used in a particular situation. Often these

conventions take the form of a question and an answer. For example, the Blackwood convention is a method of asking your partner how many Aces he holds, and how many Kings. This information is particularly useful if your partnership is hoping to make a small slam (12 tricks) or a grand slam (13 tricks). The asking bid in Blackwood is four No-Trumps, and the replies are:
Five Clubs, when holding no Aces (sometimes this reply is given when holding all four Aces);
Five Diamonds, when holding one Ace;
Five Hearts, means two Aces;
Five Spades, means three Aces.

In order to ask how many Kings your partner has you simply bid five No-Trumps, and he bids the number of Kings at the six level (six Clubs is 0 or maybe 4), six Diamonds is 1, etc.

When the Blackwood convention is employed, the program can update variables such as: Number of Aces, Number of Kings, and the tri-state variables Ace of Clubs, Ace of Diamonds, etc, which can indicate yes, no or don't know, depending on what may be deduced from the bidding. For example, if you hold two Aces and find that your partner holds the other two, you know which Aces he holds and so you can set the values of the tri-state variables (Ace of Clubs, etc) accordingly. This detailed use of variables can be most helpful when making a slam decision.

Another popular convention is known as Stayman, and consists of a two Club asking bid after your partner has bid one No-Trump. The asking bid enquires whether the partner has at least four cards in either Hearts or Spades (or both), in which case he should respond by bidding the appropriate suit (or the better suit if he holds at least four cards in each of the two suits). If the program asks this question of its partner, it can use the reply to update the variables Min Spades, Max Spades, Min Hearts and Max Hearts, according to the reply bid.

Deciding what to bid: a simple algorithm

When faced with the decision of what bid to make, a number of complex factors enter the thought processes of a good bridge player. Here we are discussing the problems of writing a relatively simple bridge program, and so we must try to employ a relatively simple bidding algorithm. I have devised such an algorithm, which lacks the subtlety of an advanced bridge player, but which ought to provide the computer with the ability to make bids that are reasonably intelligible and reasonably sensible. The algorithm applies to any bidding system, so you may choose any system that you like, preferably from a good book on bidding. One word of advice – try to use a 'natural' bidding system (one in which the bids tend to reflect the obvious features of the hand) rather than an 'artificial' system (in which most of the bids form an apparently obscure code).

Most books on bidding will offer advice on how many high card points are needed to make contracts at various levels. In *Bridge for Beginners* (by Victor Mollo and Nico Gardener), for example, we find that a useful guideline is:

22–25 points are needed in the combined hands to make any contract;

26 points are needed to make three No-Trumps, four Hearts or four Spades, or five Clubs or five Diamonds;

34 points are needed to make a slam (12 or 13 tricks).

These guidelines are extremely useful, inasmuch as they can set an upper limit on the program's bidding. In our earlier example, once the program knows that it and its partner (playing North-South) hold less than 34 points, which is when his second bid is made (South's one Spade), it is immediately obvious that a slam is not a real possibility, so the maximum contract is a game contract and the highest possible bid is five Diamonds.

The manner in which the algorithm operates is simplicity itself. The program first asks the question 'Can I bid again without exceeding the safe limit?', where the safe limit is defined by the above guidelines. If the answer to this question is 'yes', the program simply examines every one of its legal bids, determines what would be meant by each of these bids, and then performs some sort of matching exercise to produce a numerical score that represents the accuracy with which each bid describes the hand (bearing in mind what has already been bid). In a situation where the program is responding to an asking bid (eg, Blackwood or Stayman) there is no problem – the program simply gives the correct answer to the asking bid. But in the general case the program must evaluate each bid and then choose the bid with the highest score, or, if two or more bids have a similarly high score, the program selects the lower bid so that it can convey information in an economic manner.

How exactly this matching procedure is programmed will depend entirely on the type of bidding system you employ in your program, but a few hints may be useful for setting you on the right track. Firstly, we should consider a situation in which the program ought to make an asking bid. This might happen when it has discovered that it and its partner have 34 points or more between the two hands. The program may wish to know how many Aces and Kings are in its partner's hand (unless it has all the Aces and Kings itself), in which case it bids four No-Trumps. If the answer indicates that its partner has all the missing Aces, the program can then ask how many Kings are in its partner's hand. It will then find out whether the partnership is missing any of the important top cards and make its decision as to whether it can afford to bid seven (for a Grand Slam) or only six (a Small Slam). Asking bids and their responses are as easy for a computer program as for a human player.

In a more general situation, the program must decide the extent to which a bid conveys information that has not already been conveyed. One way to do this is to count the number of variables which can be updated after making a particular bid. If a bid provides information which gives useful information about three of the variables, then the bid is, in some sense, more useful to the program's partner than a bid which gives useful information about only two variables.

One final point, which is important to implement because of the necessity of playing a contract in the best suit (or in No-Trumps if that is better than a suit contract): throughout the bidding the program should keep some kind of measure for each suit and for No-Trumps. This measure should indicate the desirability of playing a contract in that suit. At the start of the hand, when the cards are dealt, the measures might simply be the number of high card points in each of the suits (excluding the points for singletons and voids). For No-Trumps the measure should be zero. When the program's partner makes a bid, the number of high card points for the suit bid should be increased by (say) 8 for the first time that partner bids the suit, 4 for the second time and 2 for the third time. If the program's partner bids all of the suits in which the program does not have adequate control (either an Ace, or a King and one other card, a Queen and two other cards or a Jack and three other cards), then the number of points assigned to No-Trumps can be adjusted to some high value (say 15). Each time that the partner bids another suit, which he has not yet bid, this score is increased by 2. The program then has a relatively easy measure of whether each suit is worthwhile, and whether No-Trumps is a possibility. Then, as the level of the bidding gets nearer and nearer to the guideline limits, the program can easily make a decision about the final contract. It is then only important to avoid making a bid which is so high that partner can no longer make a safe bid (ie, a bid within the guideline limits) in a suit which is deemed to be acceptable.

Now find a good book on bidding and select an easily programmable system.

CHAPTER 16
Bridge Play

In the previous chapter we looked at one of the most popular card games, contract bridge, and we examined some of the problems involved in writing a bidding program. Here we shall consider the even more difficult task of writing a program that can play a bridge hand, both from the declarer's seat and from the seat of one of the defending players. Let us begin by looking at the nature of the problem.

Contract bridge differs from most of the games that we have discussed in one respect that is not immediately obvious. (The fact that it is not a perfect information game is quite another matter.) In a game such as chess, it is not important to win in any specific number of moves – the important thing is to achieve the desired result and it is more pleasant to win in 25 moves than to win in 100. A program can win a good game of chess if it can avoid tactical oversights and play reasonably sensible strategic moves. Its overall performance will not be optimal, but that does not matter – it is the result that counts.

In bridge, and similar card games that have a trick-taking stage, there are only a limited number of 'moves' (ie tricks) in the game. A hand of bridge lasts for 13 tricks, never more and never less, and so it is essential to achieve the desired result within those 13 tricks. For this reason, a bridge playing program must aim to determine a hopefully optimal strategy in order to maximise its chance of success. Even if bridge were a full-information game, the number of 'moves' would make an exhaustive tree search prohibitive. There are 13 cards that can be led to trick one, 12 cards which can be led to trick two, and so there are 13(!) ways of selecting the card to be led to each trick. This number must be multiplied by the number of cards that may legally be played by the second, third and fourth players who play to a trick, and the result is a number so enormous as to make exhaustive search unfeasible.

A subset of this problem was solved by Berelekamp many years ago. He wrote a program to play 'double-dummy' bridge hands in No-Trumps. Double-dummy means that everyone can see all of the cards in all of the hands, so declarer is playing a full-information game, and need make no estimate or guess of where particular cards lie in the defending hands. By reducing the problem still further, so that only No-Trump contracts were attempted, it was possible to write a program that performed satisfactorily. The approach adopted by Berelekamp was to create a hypothesis for playing the contract from declarer's hand, then to try to refute this hypothesis and to create an improved hypothesis.

This approach is really an intelligently directed exhaustive search. The intelligence, or bridge knowledge, is used to guide the search, and hopefully any contract which can be made *will* be made before the program runs out of time. The serious reader will find it useful to read the original paper on this particular program.

In the real world of bridge, where the situation of the defenders' cards is not known exactly, programming becomes far more difficult. An expert bridge player will often be able to make an intelligent guess, after the bidding, as to how the suits are distributed between the defending hands, and he may also know or be able to guess the exact location of certain key cards, particularly the missing Aces. He does this by gleaning information from the bidding, and those of you who studied the previous chapter will have realised that some of the information passed during the bidding can actually be used during the play of cards.

Very little has been done in the way of programming the play of the cards at bridge. There are two commercially available bridge computers, neither of which plays at the same level as the best chess programs, and there are a few other programs around which readers may have come across in the micro literature. One of America's leading computer bridge experts, Thomas Throop, has done much to popularise the subject in North America. He has a regular column in *Personal Computing* in which he describes how various hands were played by his own program, which runs on a mainframe, and on George Duisman's program, which is available for Apples and other personal computers. So far Throop has not discussed how his program works, so there is no available literature on the detailed programming of bridge play. But hopefully this situation will improve as more people become interested in computer bridge. In Britain, Dr Alan Stanier wrote his PhD thesis on the subject of bidding a bridge hand and then planning the play from declarer's seat, and much of my own understanding of the problem stems from my reading of his thesis. The ideas expressed in the present chapter represent a simplified distillation of Stanier's ideas and one or two of my own.

Stanier correctly emphasised the importance of having the playing program learn from the bidding. Perhaps the most obvious application is in trying to decide which way to play a *finesse*. Consider, for example, the following situation:

Spades: A J 5

Spades: ? Spades: ?

Spades: K 10 3

South is declarer and wishes to try to make three Spade tricks. No Spades have yet been played, so the defenders have seven Spades between them, including the Queen. There are two ways of trying for three Spade tricks, both involving a finesse. South can guess that the missing Queen is in West's hand, in which case South plays the King of Spades, discarding the 5 from dummy, then the 3 – and if West does not play the Queen then dummy's card is the Jack. If South guesses that East has the Queen, the play is different: the 3 is played from South, dummy plays the Ace and leads back the 5 – if East does not play the Queen on dummy's 5 then South plays the 10, otherwise he plays the King, taking the Queen and winning the third trick with the 10.

If the defenders have bid, declarer might be able to make some deduction from the bidding which helps him decide which way to take the finesse. If West has bid Spades, then it is a reasonable assumption that he holds the Queen. If East is the only defender who bids, and late in the hand he has already played cards with sufficient point values to justify his bid, it is not unreasonable to guess that West holds the missing Queen. Deductions similar to these are not difficult to program, and the reader can use his own knowledge of bridge (and what he can find in books) to suggest various deductive routines which might help the play of a hand.

How to decide on a strategy

The most difficult problem for a human bridge player will often come at the very start of a hand, before he decides which of dummy's cards to play on trick one. At that stage he must plan his strategy, and an incorrect strategy can result in the wrong card being played as early as trick one. We shall now examine a simple strategy which could be programmed on a micro.

When the bidding is over and the defender leads a card to trick one, declarer should count the number of sure tricks that can be seen. It is possible that the contract can be made simply by playing 'winners' until the required number of tricks has been taken. Such hands are not really interesting, as they require no particular skill or thought, apart from ensuring that the cards are played in the correct order so that the program does not get itself blocked (when it is forced to play from, say, dummy's hand when it really wants to play from its own).

If it is not possible for the program to make a contract merely by playing off top winners, it must try to create extra tricks in some way. Various techniques exist in bridge, whist and similar games for creating these extra tricks; some of them are simple, such as the finesse that we examined earlier, others are more complicated, such as squeeze plays – playing out so many winning cards that the defenders are unable to keep all their important cards. Our simple strategy will be to explore three different methods of creating extra tricks: the finesse, establishing extra tricks in long suits, and cross-ruffing. If one or more of these techniques appears likely to be successful, and the program 'thinks' that it has found a method of creating a winning plan, then it should follow this plan unless and until it is forced to re-think, ie until the plan goes wrong. If the defending players deviate from the plan at any point, the program must reassess how declarer should play the hand, and this reassessment will usually result in a new plan. The flow chart for this strategy is given in Figure 53.

As I mentioned earlier, this strategy is rather simple, and will not provide a challenging game for strong bridge players. It should, however, allow the reader to write a program that plays an entertaining game for players below club strength. You will note that if the program is unable to generate a plan that either guarantees the required number of tricks, or at least gives some chance of making the desired number of tricks, then it will cut its losses and employ whichever plan results in the smallest number of penalty points.

Executing the strategy

Once the most promising plan has been found, the program must decide in which order it is going to play the cards. Here

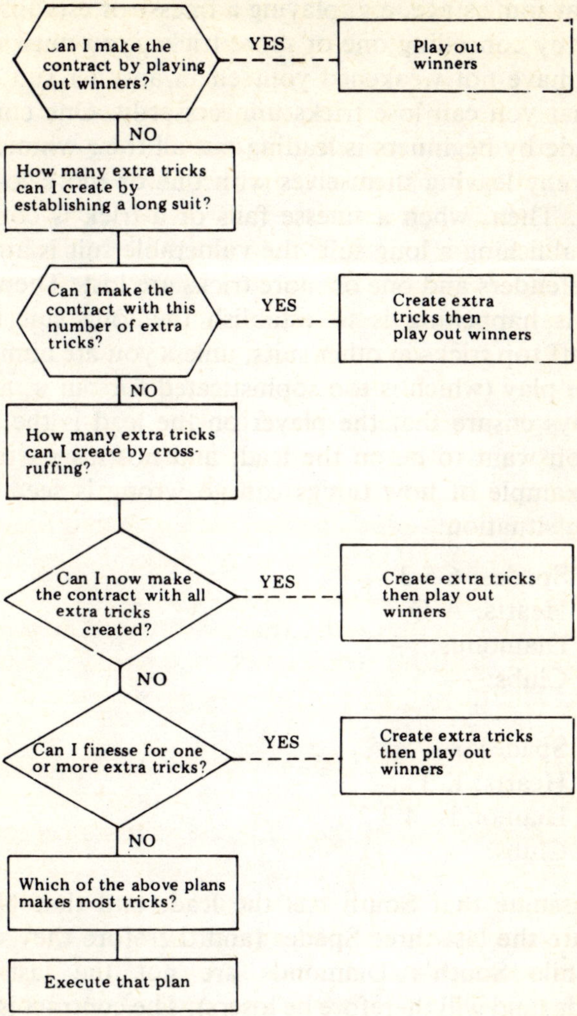

FIGURE 53: *Simple declarer strategy – flow chart.*

the normal heuristics of bridge (and other trick-taking games) apply. The two most important principles to follow are:
(a) When you are following a plan that involves giving away

the lead at some stage, e.g. playing a finesse or establishing a long suit by conceding one or more tricks, you must ensure that you have not weakened yourself in another suit to the extent that you can lose tricks unnecessarily. One common error made by beginners is leading out all their winners in a suit, thereby leaving themselves with one or more losers in that suit. Then, when a finesse fails or a trick is conceded while establishing a long suit, the vulnerable suit is attacked by the defenders and one or more tricks are lost. The way to avoid this happening is to establish the long suit before playing off top tricks in other suits, unless you are aiming for a squeeze play (which is too sophisticated for our strategy).

(b) Always ensure that the player on the lead is the player whom you want to be on the lead, and not his partner. A simple example of how things can go wrong is seen in the following situation:

Spades: 6 5 3
Hearts: A Q
Diamonds: —
Clubs: —

Spades: —
Hearts: K J
Diamonds: 4 3 2
Clubs: —

Let us assume that South has the lead, and that North's Spades are the last three Spades (and therefore they will all win), while South's Diamonds are not the last three Diamonds (and will therefore be losers). The contract is being played in No-Trumps. South leads the J of Hearts, North plays the A, then North plays the Q of Hearts and suddenly notices what he has done wrong. South must now take his trick with the K and then he is forced to lead a Diamond, losing the last three tricks instead of winning with the remaining Spades. Of course, there are various ways that the cards could be played in a different order, so that North-South would make all five tricks, but this example shows you how a careless mistake can cost several tricks and turn a good contract into a bad one.

Endplay situations

When a number of tricks have been played, the number of cards remaining in each of the player's hands becomes small enough to allow for some sort of exhaustive search of the game tree. How many tricks must be played before this type of situation arises will depend largely on two factors: the certainty with which the program is able to place all the remaining cards in the correct player's hands, and the speed of execution of the exhaustive search routine.

In the previous chapter, when we discussed the way that a hand might be bid, we saw how it is possible to put upper and lower bounds on the number of cards in each suit that is held by each of the players. These bounds can often be made more constrained during the bidding and once play begins they are constrained still further, as the exposure of dummy's cards provides more information. Finally, as one player shows out (ie shows that he has no more of) a particular suit, the exact number of cards in that suit remaining in a player's hand can be determined.

Sooner or later, the program will be able to estimate the exact number of cards of each suit in each of the two unseen hands. Furthermore, from information gained during the bidding and the play, it may be able to arrive at an intelligent guess as to the location of some specific, high-value cards. It is then in a position to play what will have become a full-information game or, to be more precise, an almost full-information game (since it is likely that the exact location of one or two cards will remain unknown). When this stage is reached, the program can construct a two-person game tree of how the remaining cards might be played, and by searching this tree it can find the optimal way to play the last few tricks. This technique applies when the program is playing from either the declarer's seat, or from one of the defenders' seats.

During the play of the cards, the program should ask itself, as it is about to decide on its play to each trick, whether or not it has sufficient information to enable it to perform such a tree search. For this purpose, we should divide cards into 'important' and 'unimportant' cards. Loosely speaking, an important card may be defined as one which, if its location is guessed incorrectly, will affect the result of the succeeding tree search. All other cards are 'unimportant'. Simple examples of both types of card are easy to find. If the defenders each have two remaining Clubs and declarer has two Clubs, both of which are higher than all of the defenders' Clubs, then it is quite immaterial which way round the defenders' Clubs are distributed, since declarer is bound to take both of the last two Club tricks. But in the case of a missing Queen, which must be caught by a finesse carried out

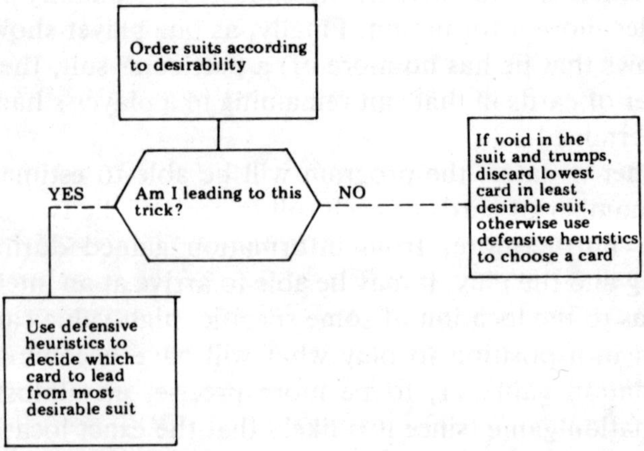

FIGURE 54

in the correct direction, a wrong guess as to the location of the card will result in the finesse going wrong, and at least one trick being lost which should not have been lost. So the missing Queen will be an 'important' one.

As a general rule, I would suggest that the program should not try an exhaustive tree search until the number of 'important' cards remaining is no more than one.

Having written your tree search routine, you will have an opportunity to try it out after different numbers of tricks have been played. This will enable you to time the execution of the routine where there are 3, 4, 5 . . . tricks remaining to be played. You can then decide what sort of time delay is acceptable to you, and set the 'endplay parameter' so that the exhaustive search does not begin until such time as the computer's delay in calculating its optimal play is acceptable. Remember – the computer can determine the optimal endplay strategy for defending players as well as for declarer, and since you will be playing one of the hands and the computer will be playing the two unseen hands, you must allow for a delay by both of the other players. Unfortunately, there can be a substantial difference between the times needed to search trees with the same numbers of cards (or tricks). This is because one tree search might be performed in a near optimal ordering (ie the search heuristics provide a good ordering of the 'moves') while another tree search might be highly non-optimal in its ordering. Another reason for a large disparity in the search times is that even with the same number of *tricks* to be played, there can be vastly differing numbers of nodes on the search tree because of the way that the suits are distributed. If all the suits are evenly distributed among the players, the branching factor at each node will be small. If the suits are unevenly distributed, the branching factor at some nodes will be small and at others it will be large. The combinatorial effects of these differences might result in two trees having the same number of tricks but widely differing numbers of terminal nodes.

How to play the defence

Bridge books are full of useful defensive heuristics which can be used by your program, particularly at the very start of a hand when it is necessary to decide what to lead to trick one. Perhaps the best known such 'rule' is: when defending against a No-Trump contract, lead the fourth highest card of your longest suit. This type of lead tells your partner something about your longest suit and he can then decide how to play that suit. Another simple heuristic is that if you only have two cards in a particular suit, and declarer is playing a trump contract in another suit, you normally play the higher of your two cards first, then the lower of the two, so that if your partner gets the lead he can play another card in that suit and you will be able to trump (if you have any trumps) because by then you will be void in that suit.

Defensive heuristics can be employed to update the information that the program is keeping about the number of cards of each suit in each hand, and in certain cases it might also be possible to update information about specific cards. For example, if your partner leads the 8 of Spades against a No-Trump contract and you can see the Ace, Jack and 9 of Spades (in your own hand and dummy's hand), then if partner's lead was the fourth highest Spade in his hand he must hold the King, Queen and 10.

The simplest strategy to program for defensive play is one which orders the suits in their 'desirability' from the defenders' point of view. A defending player should be able to decide which suit or suits will not be profitable for him to lead, and he can then rank the other suits so that when faced with a choice of what to lead at the start of a trick he can lead a card from the suit at the top of the desirability list. Reasons for putting a suit high on the desirability list are varied: a player may wish to lead a card merely to transfer the lead to his partner's hand; or he may wish to lead a card in his weakest suit so as not to give away any tricks by a bad lead;

or he may have one or more winners in a suit and may wish to take them. The order of desirability will usually change quite often during the course of a hand, as more information is revealed about the distribution of the suits and the locations of certain cards. But the concept is not a difficult one to program.

Having ordered the suits in this manner, the program decides which card in the suit should be played on the basis of the various defensive heuristics that you have programmed. For this you will need to read some good books on defensive play. When the program must lead to a trick, it chooses the appropriate card from the suit at the top of the desirability list. If it must play second to a trick it will normally play the lowest card of the led suit, while playing third it will play the highest card unless that card has already been beaten. When forced to discard from a different suit (ie the card that was led is from a suit in which the defending player is void), the program should discard a card from the suit that is currently bottom of the desirability list.

Bibliography

Berelekamp, E. R.: 'A Program for Playing Double-Dummy Bridge Hands', *Journal of the Association for Computing Machinery*, 1963, No. 3.

CHAPTER 17
Shogi

I would now like to introduce you to a game which you will almost certainly never have come across. It is related to chess, but has an added dimension of complexity which can result in exciting sequences being sustained for very many more moves than in chess. This game is so popular in its country of origin (there are some 19 million players) that those who excel at the game often become millionaires, and are held in greater esteem than Bjorn Borg in Sweden or Kevin Keegan in England. I am referring to shogi, or Japanese chess, and I can recommend the game very highly to anyone who enjoys 'western' chess. My shogi-playing friends have been trying to persuade me for some time that 'western' chess is an inferior form of the game and, although I have yet to be firmly convinced by their arguments, I must confess that shogi does have enormous appeal. Since it is well known that computer programmers usually show great aptitude for chess, it is likely that among the readers of this book there are many potential shogi masters (or dans as they are known in Japan), and many thousands who would enjoy the game if they took an hour or so to learn to play it.

Japan is the Mecca of shogi, but during the past few years an organisation has grown up in the western world whose aim is to popularise the game outside its native country. The Shogi Association, PO Box 77, Bromley, Kent, England, welcomes new members and will supply shogi sets and elementary literature to those who cannot find them elsewhere. It also publishes a regular magazine and holds meetings in London. Through the efforts of the Shogi

Association there have been shogi tournaments held in London, for which leading Japanese players have flown half way round the globe, and in the 1980 tournament I was able to see my colleague Larry Kaufman, an International Chess Master from the USA, who seems to have abandoned the 'inferior' form of the game for its Japanese counterpart. I understand that he has now become completely addicted, to the extent of travelling to Japan in the hope of becoming a professional shogi player.

How to play shogi

The best way to learn the game of shogi is to buy a copy of *How to Play Shogi* by John Fairbairn, and to study this slim volume with a shogi set in front of you. Although shogi sets normally have the pieces inscribed in Japanese characters, the Shogi Association imports sets in which the pieces also have westernised lettering as well as arrows to show you how each of them moves. It should take no longer to learn the moves at shogi than to learn how to play western chess, and I am reliably informed that one can even get used to the Japanese symbols rather more quickly than one might suspect. Since the main point of this chapter is to enable the reader to write his own shogi-playing program, I must begin with a precis of the rules and moves of the game.

Each player starts the game with 20 pieces made of wood or plastic. These pieces are uniform in colour, but for the sake of convenience we call them Black and White, as in chess. The game is played on a 9×9 board (does anyone know of a 9-bit processor?) with the two armies set up in the starting position seen in Figure 55.

The pieces and their moves

KING: Each player has one king and, as in chess, the object of the game is to checkmate the opposing king. As in chess

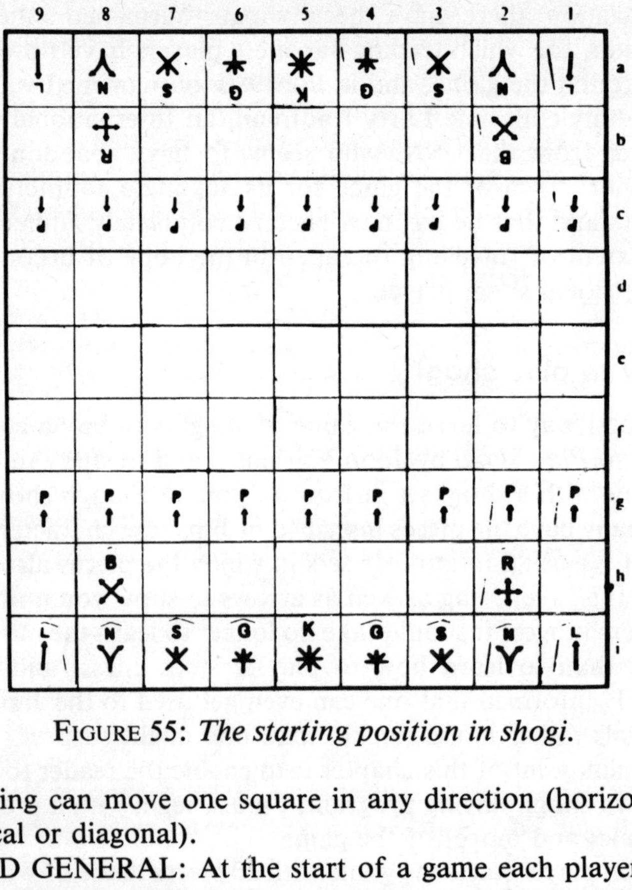

FIGURE 55: *The starting position in shogi.*

the king can move one square in any direction (horizontal, vertical or diagonal).

GOLD GENERAL: At the start of a game each player has two golds. The gold moves one square at a time, vertically, horizontally, or diagonally forwards. It may not move diagonally backwards.

SILVER GENERAL: Each player has two silvers. The silver moves one square at a time, diagonally or forwards. It may not move sideways and it may not move straight backwards.

KNIGHT: Each player has two knights, whose move has the same form as the knight in chess but with the restriction that it may only move two squares forwards and then one square to the left or right. So whereas a chess knight has eight moves at its disposal from a central square on an empty board, a shogi knight will have only two possible moves, but as in chess it may jump.

LANCE: Each of the two lances moves straight forwards as far as it likes, but it may not jump.

ROOK: The shogi rook moves exactly like its counterpart in western chess, in a straight line as many squares as it wishes. There is no queen in shogi, so the rook is usually regarded as the most powerful piece.

BISHOP: Again this piece moves just like a chess bishop – any number of squares in a diagonal direction.

PAWN: As in chess, the initial shogi position has a row of pawns across the board. Since shogi is played on a 9×9 board, each player begins the game with nine pawns, which can move one square forwards. There is no double pawn move when a pawn makes its first move; there is no diagonal capturing move; and there is no such thing as an *en passant* capture.

Promoted pieces

One of the most interesting aspects of shogi, as compared to chess, is the fact that whereas in chess only the pawns can promote to a piece of higher value, in shogi some of the other pieces can also promote. A promotion move is made by moving a piece partly or wholly within your promotion zone (the last three ranks or rows furthest from you). Promotion takes place at the conclusion of the promoting move, and it is important to remember that in shogi it is not always compulsory to promote, as we shall see. The following pieces have the ability to promote:

SILVER: The promoted silver moves exactly like a gold. On your shogi set the silver can be turned over and on the reverse side you will see the symbol for a promoted silver.

KNIGHT: The promoted knight also moves exactly like a gold.

LANCE: The promoted lance moves exactly like a gold.
PAWN: The promoted pawn moves exactly like a gold.
ROOK: When the rook is promoted it retains its original ability to move any number of squares horizontally or vertically, and acquires the extra ability to move one square in a diagonal direction.
BISHOP: Similarly, when the bishop is promoted, its original move is retained and it has the new ability to move one square vertically or horizontally.

If a pawn or lance moves to the last rank, or if a knight moves to either of the last two ranks, promotion is compulsory. At all other times, promotion is optional.

Capturing

If a player moves one of his pieces on to a square that is occupied by one of his opponent's men, the opponent's piece is captured as in chess. But here lies one essential difference between the two games, and it is this difference that adds an extra dimension to the game of shogi.

In chess, when you capture one of your opponent's pieces it is removed from the board forever. In shogi you keep this piece 'in hand', and later in the game you may drop it on to any vacant square (subject to a few restrictions). The drop is made instead of moving a piece from one square to another, and it is important to remember that a piece may only be dropped in its unpromoted state, even if it had been promoted before it was captured. When you drop a captured piece on to the board it becomes your own piece, and for this reason the capture of an enemy piece has a double significance. One interesting aspect of the drop is the fact that you might well decide to sacrifice a valuable piece on one part of the board in return for an inferior one, simply because you want to be able to drop that inferior piece on another part of the board within the next few moves.

Check and checkmate

When a king is attacked it is said to be in check, just as in chess, and the player who is in check must take evasive action – moving his own king, capturing the checking piece, or interposing a piece between the two. If the king is attacked and there is no way to save it, the player has been checkmated. Since all of the pieces are, in practical terms, in play throughout the game, it is extremely rare for a game of shogi to end in a draw. In chess the number of the pieces on the board is gradually reduced as the game progresses, and when sufficient reduction has taken place the game will inevitably end in a draw. Those who find master chess games boring because too many of them (some 55 per cent or more) are drawn, need have no such fear regarding shogi.

How to program shogi

There is no reason why most of the principles that apply to chess programming cannot also be applied to shogi programming. Growing and searching a game tree is the obvious approach, the most serious problem being the large branching factor caused by the increased number of pieces (40 instead of a maximum of 32) and the possibility of the drop. If you hold just one type of captured piece 'in hand' you will have 42 or more squares on which it may be dropped. It is easy to see how the number of legal moves at one's disposal can easily increase to 150 or 200, once two or three enemy pieces have been captured. Clearly it is necessary to find some way of reducing the list of legal moves to produce a list of manageable size. The answer to this problem lies in the use of intelligent shogi heuristics, or 'proverbs' as they are known in the trade.

Anyone who is interested in writing a chess program need only refer to the enormous wealth of chess literature in order to find a number of heuristics which can be employed in a plausible move generator or an evaluation mechanism. A lot has also been written about shogi, but unfortunately for most readers of this chapter it is almost entirely published in Japanese and if your Japanese is anywhere near as bad as mine is you will not relish the thought of ploughing through tomes of mysterious symbols. Here I have space for only a very small number of heuristics, and I must recommend the reader to take a look at the extensive list which can be found in the back of Fairbairn's booklet. In addition, those of you who would like to make your shogi programs as strong as possible ought to join the Shogi Association and try to obtain all the back numbers of *Shogi* magazine in which the most important proverbs are explained. Once you understand a proverb, it is an easy matter to convert it to numerical form so that it can form part of the evaluation/plausibility mechanism.

Shogi openings

The exact order in which the opening moves are played does not appear to be so critical in shogi as in chess. The most important aspect of opening play in shogi seems to be the squares on which one places one's pieces, and not the exact order in which they are moved there. The only source of shogi openings that I can find in any language other than Japanese is, once again, that published by the Shogi Association.

Since it is not necessary for your shogi program to have access to large tables of opening variations, you need only devise some method of encouraging the program to make moves that will lead to its pieces being on the right squares. A simple method of accomplishing this is to examine each of the pieces in a desired formation and determine how many moves away from its target square it is at the moment. The 'opening' feature in the evaluation function can then be penalised by (say) 1 point for each piece that is one move away from its target square, 2 points for each piece that is two moves away, and so on. This method, or any similar pattern-matching process, will provide a useful measure as to the degree to which a desired opening formation has been achieved.

The middle game: a few heuristics

As in chess, the middle game in shogi sees most of the manoeuvring and struggling for a strategic advantage. This is the part of the game for which an evaluation function will be of the greatest use. The players must fight for control of important squares, and in particular for control of the area near their opponent's king. In shogi the initiative is just as important as it is in chess, and by building up a strong attack in the area near the enemy king, a player may develop an initiative which can later be converted into a win. Many of the heuristics that you will find in *Shogi* magazine will relate to the initiative and to the concepts of king attack and king safety.

Perhaps the most difficult problem that you will encounter when writing a shogi program is that nobody has written one before you, so there is absolutely no published literature on the subject. In order to convert a shogi heuristic into a feature for your evaluation function you will therefore be compelled to make various guesses and estimates, and then improve the weightings of your function in the light of experience.

Possibly the most surprising aspect of shogi heuristics is the fact that there is no recognised scale of values for the pieces themselves. Almost every schoolboy knows that in chess a bishop or knight is worth roughly three pawns, a rook five pawns, and a queen nine pawns, but to the best of my knowledge there is nothing reliable in the shogi literature to compare. (Readers should be warned that in one book, published in English, the rook is said to be more valuable than the king – ignore this book and, probably, anything else not published by the Shogi Association.)

Those of you who have read the chapters on chess will know that the second most important feature, after material, is mobility. In fact the chess pieces have material values which are not entirely disproportionate to their average mobilities, so it would be possible to write a chess program that was governed by present and potential mobility, rather than by material and present mobility. In shogi, since material values cannot be defined in the same way as they can in chess, mobility is possibly the most important feature. We define mobility in shogi in the same way as we do in chess – the number of squares attacked by a piece.

The attack on the enemy king is of greater importance in shogi than it is in chess. For this reason, two features which are employed in many chess programs are absolutely vital in a shogi program: King Attack and King Safety. A primitive measure for King Attack is found by adding 2 points for every attack on a square which is not more than three squares distant from the enemy king, and 1 point for every possible move to a square from which such an attack can be made. The sum of these attacks and potential attacks provides a measure of the extent to which a player's pieces can operate within the vicinity of the enemy king, and the extent to which they control possible flight squares that might be used by the enemy king to escape from a strong attack.

King Safety can best be measured by taking into account the number, nature and proximity of friendly pieces that are situated near the king. If your king is surrounded by many of its own pieces it will be much safer from attack than if it is on an exposed part of the board, with few of its own pieces nearby. As in chess, it often pays in shogi to keep the pawns in front of your own king as defensive pieces, obstructing the attack of the advancing enemy. In addition, it is useful to have two or three generals (golds and silvers) near your king for added protection. The different shogi openings usually define a particular defensive formation for the king, so by reading about the openings you will learn the various defensive formations and you can design a feature for your evaluation function based on giving bonus points for having your own king well protected by the correct piece.

Gaining material in a game of shogi is useful for two reasons, and some method must be found to reflect this fact in your evaluation function. When you capture an enemy piece you deprive his king of a certain measure of protection – if the captured piece was near to the king this protection will be much greater than if the piece was many squares away from the king. You also have an extra piece 'in hand' which may be used later in the game to achieve some strategic aim or to expose the enemy king still further during the blistering attack which you launch prior to checkmate. One way in which your program can measure the value of a captured piece lies in the loss of mobility experienced by your opponent when you capture one of his pieces. Another way is simply to add a certain number of points for every piece that you hold in hand.

So far we have discussed only a very small proportion of the total number of shogi principles, but these are among the most important. A computer program which takes into consideration mobility, king attack, king safety and the number of pieces held 'in hand' would be able to play a game better than the novice who has just learned the rules of the game. One very important aspect of shogi is the mating attack, and this is one area in which your program will be able to play better than many humans, because it requires pure calculation.

The mating attack

In shogi there is no endgame in the same sense as there is in chess. Because captured pieces can reappear on the board, it is rare for a shogi game to end when the board is almost devoid of material. To win at shogi you must launch a successful mating attack. We have already discussed two of the evaluation features which can help a program set up and develop an attack against the enemy king. The tactical phase that ends the game will often contain a long, forcing sequence of moves that is difficult for many human players to spot. A computer program should have no such problems, provided that it is looking along the correct path of the tree.

The answer lies in knowing where to search for a mating continuation, and in ignoring all other factors when looking for a mate. It is normally sufficient to have four of your own pieces attacking the enemy king area, so your mating routine can be triggered by a test which counts the number of your own pieces which impinge on any of the squares which are within (say) three squares of the enemy king. If this test provides a positive result, the program can then look along all variations in which its own moves are checking moves. During this phase of the game all other moves may be ignored, on the assumption that if he is given a single move's respite, your opponent will be able to bring another piece to the defence of his king, or will move his king to a safer square. The routine which searches for mate should therefore be single-minded, and by ignoring all moves other than checks, it ought to be able to search 7 or 9-ply deep, or even further. If no mate is found within some predetermined horizon, the program simply reverts to the middle game search algorithm and looks for a move which improves its strategic control of the position.

How to deal with drops

As I mentioned earlier, one of the most serious problems in writing a strong shogi program is the very large branching factor caused by being able to drop a captured piece on to almost any vacant square on the board. (In fact you may drop on to any vacant square provided that (a) you are not dropping a pawn, lance or knight on to a square from which it will never be able to move; (b) you will not have two unpromoted pawns on the same file at the same time; (c) you do not drop a pawn in such a way as to give checkmate on the move.) How can we reduce the branching factor without ignoring most of the better drops?

The answer lies in identifying a number of key vacant squares (say ten) and examining drops only on to those key squares. This can be accomplished by using the evaluation function to measure the improvement in score that could be achieved by dropping a hypothetical piece (a 'genie') on to each vacant square. The genie has the power of all the other pieces combined, and by estimating its effect on the mobility, king safety, king attack and other features of the evaluation function, when placed on each of the vacant squares, it is possible to produce a ranking order for the vacant squares which indicates which squares are the best candidates for drops. By reducing the number of such squares from (at least) 42 to ten, we can reduce the total number of moves which the program needs to consider. This is especially important when more than one type of piece is to be held in hand.

If a shogi-playing program is too difficult

It is, perhaps, daunting enough to the reader for me to suggest that you learn a new game as complex as shogi without my adding to this suggestion with the thought that you should also write a shogi-playing program. You may feel that the game itself requires enough of your time, and that a shogi-playing program might be beyond you, especially in view of the paucity of literature on shogi heuristics. In that case, there is still one programming exercise which you will definitely find worth your while, as it will test your understanding of many of the tree-searching ideas that we have discussed in this book, and it will stretch your ability to write code that executes efficiently.

Just as there are many people who are interested in chess problems ('White to Play and Mate in Two Moves'), so there is even greater interest in shogi problems. An extremely interesting programming exercise can be found in writing a program which will search for checkmates. In the composition of a chess problem it is part of the composer's task that he must not allow a checking move to be the key to the solution. In shogi, the opposite is true – all moves in a shogi problem must be checks or replies to check.

A program which solves shogi problems must therefore employ an efficient test to determine whether or not a move is legal (ie, whether a reply to check achieves the aim of moving out of check), and whether or not a move gives check. These two tests are sufficient, since a move which fails both tests is inadmissible in the tree search. Your problem-solving program has only a very small number of branches at each node, and so a deep search is possible without the program consuming enormous amounts of time. There is not too much scope within a problem-solving program for speeding up the search without the use of heuristics, but one or two notions do suggest themselves. Prefer a checking move that is near to the enemy king to one which is further away (reason – a far away move allows more interposing possibilities). Prefer a 'safe' checking move to a move which allows the free capture of material (reason – with more pieces of your own side on the board, you have greater chances of forcing mate). Prefer to evade check by moving the king than by interposing a piece (reason – an interposing move may allow a free capture). Prefer to evade check by capturing the checking piece than by moving the king (reason – the less material your opponent has on the board, the harder it will be for him to force checkmate).

Of course, these rules of thumb all have very many

exceptions, but other things being equal (which they never are) all of them have some value in ordering the search.

Bibliography

Fairbairn, J.: *How to Play Shogi.* Shogi Association: *Shogi* (magazine).

The reader is strongly warned against all other shogi literature published prior to 1983 in any language other than Japanese.

CHAPTER 18
Dominoes

At first sight, dominoes is not a particularly demanding game, but to play really well requires a combination of deep calculation and a certain measure of memory. In one respect the game is very similar to backgammon – luck plays a big part, but the skilled player can play with the odds and come out on top in a long series of encounters.

How to play a simple version of dominoes

A set of dominoes may be compared to a deck of cards, with 'suits' and 'denominations'. In most countries the domino set comprises 28 dominoes, each of which has two numbers painted on it. The numbers lie in the range 0 through 6, and no two dominoes have the same two numbers. Thus, the complete set comprises:

6-6	6-5	6-4	6-3	6-2	6-1	6-0
	5-5	5-4	5-3	5-2	5-1	5-0
		4-4	4-3	4-2	4-1	4-0
			3-3	3-2	3-1	3-0
				2-2	2-1	2-0
					1-1	1-0
						0-0

The concept of a suit is somewhat strange in dominoes: we may refer to all the dominoes containing a 6 as the 6-suit, but of course this suit will also contain a domino which may be found in the 5-suit, one which may be found in the 4-suit, etc.

Countless games may be played with the set of dominoes. Here I shall describe a very simple game which I used to play as a child.

All dominoes are turned face down and shuffled, and each player picks seven dominoes at random, which he then looks at. The game may be played with two, three or four players, but I always found the game with two players was the most challenging and the most enjoyable. There is some method for deciding who goes first – this may be done by the toss of a coin, or it may alternate from one game to the next, or it can be the player who holds the highest double (in which case this double must be played on the first move). Once a domino has been placed on the table, face up, the players take it in turns to move.

In order to make a move a player must put down a domino which has, as one of its numbers, the same number as one of the ends of the chain of dominoes already on the table. The new domino is put on the table in such a way that the matching parts of the two dominoes are next to each other. The other end of the new domino then forms a new end to the chain. Whenever a double domino is placed on the table it is put at right-angles to the end of the chain whose number matches the double. The example given in Figure 56 illustrates the first few moves of a game.

Thus the game progresses, until the player whose turn it is to move cannot put a domino from his own hand at either end of the chain. He must then pick up dominoes from the shuffled set one at a time until he gets one which may legally be played at one end of the chain. The first player to get rid of all his dominoes wins the hand, and his opponent is debited by the number of points showing on all the dominoes remaining in his hand. It is customary to play until one player's total reaches a certain threshold, say 101, and he loses the game.

The first player (who won the toss) puts down the 5-4:

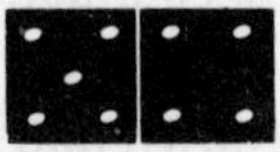

The second player puts the 4-2:

The first player puts the 2-2:

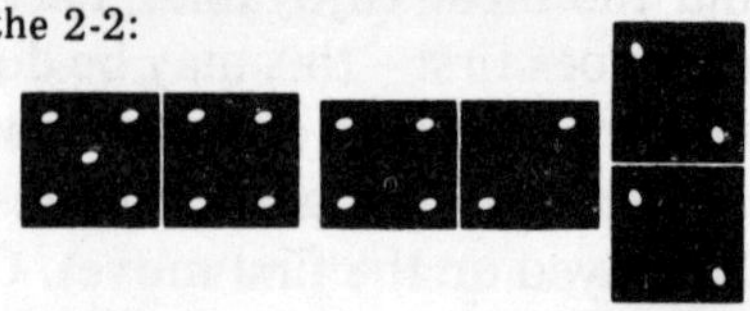

The second player adds the 5-1:

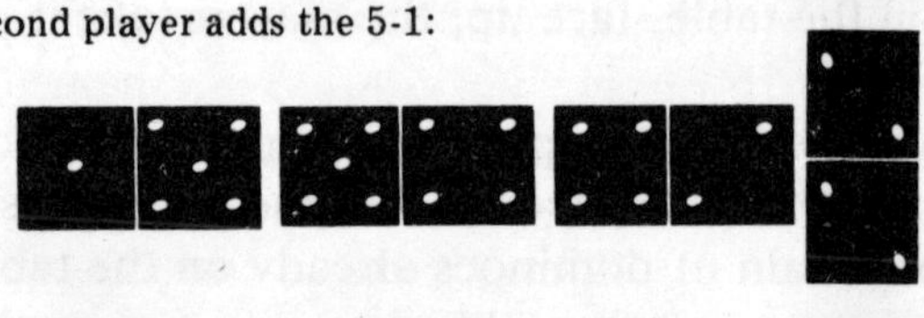

The first player places the 2-6:

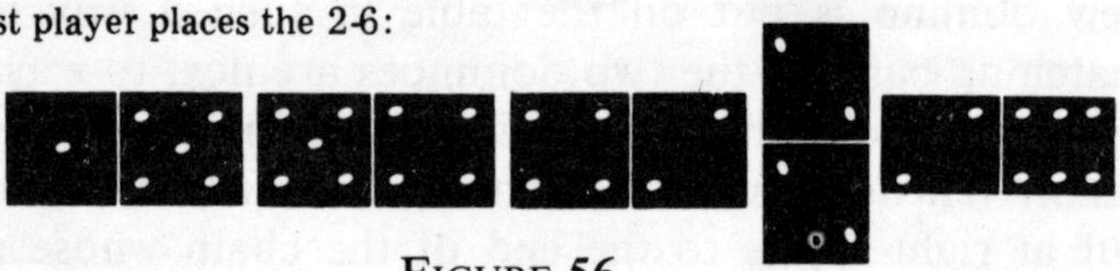

FIGURE 56

Playing strategy

The game may conveniently be split up into two distinct phases and we shall briefly consider the second phase first. Once all the dominoes from the shuffled set have been taken into the players' hands, it is easy for the players to determine exactly which dominoes are held by his opponent. (Of course, in a three- or four-handed game it is usually not possible to determine where the remaining dominoes lie until later in the game, when each player has only two or three dominoes left. Then it will usually be possible to deduce which players have which dominoes from a knowledge of which players 'passed', ie indicated that they had no legal move.)

In a two-handed game, once you know which dominoes remain in your opponent's hand, it is relatively easy to search the game tree that includes every possible way in which the remaining dominoes can be played by each side. Since the average number of legal moves at the closing stage of the game is roughly two, the size of the whole of the game tree will be roughly 2^{14} terminal nodes, and so using the alpha-beta algorithm will enable the program to search this tree while examining only 100–200 terminal nodes. The evaluation function should reflect the method of scoring by assigning to each terminal node the number of pips on the remaining dominoes in the hand of the player who loses. Thus pips in the user's hand will be measured on the scale of positive integers, those in the computer's hand will be negative integers. Since your computer will be able to calculate and search the game tree more quickly and more accurately than human players, there is considerable scope for your program to defeat a human from a theoretically losing position, since the program will always play the endgame perfectly, whereas a human will sometimes miscalculate.

The program can increase its advantage in the endgame in certain situations where it has more than one move which will, with best play, lead to the same result. It can choose the move which, in some sense maximises the probability that its opponent will make a mistake. The simplest way to do this is to choose whichever move will lead to the best score if the user makes the smallest mistake possible during the remainder of the game. If the moves still appear to be of equal merit, assume that the user will make the second smallest mistake possible, and so on. This optimistic modification to the traditional method of searching the game tree is not dissimilar to Donald Michie's technique for assuming imperfect play on the part of the opponent, which was mentioned in an earlier chapter.

A more difficult problem to solve is how to decide what

move to make in a pre-endgame situation, when the program does not know exactly which dominoes are held by its opponent. The strategy here is similar to the one employed in some of the card games discussed earlier. The program begins the game with the knowledge that each unseen domino has the same probability of being in the user's hand and then these probabilities are adjusted in the light of experience (ie which dominoes are played by the user and in which situations the user is forced to take dominoes from the shuffled set). Let us see how this method works by examining the first few moves of a sample game. We shall assume that we are playing the version in which the player holding the highest double makes the first move.

The program is dealt the following seven dominoes:

6-4 6-1 5-3 5-0 3-3 3-0 2-1

The user does not have the double 6, and so asks the program 'Do you have the 6-6?' When the program replies 'No', the user puts down the 5-5. Immediately the program assigns a probability of zero to the 6-6, since it is certain that the 6-6 is not in the user's hand, and all the remaining unseen dominoes have a probability of 0.3 (6/20), since the user now has six dominoes and there are 20 unseen dominoes, excluding the 6-6 which the program knows is not in the user's hand.

The program must now decide between playing the 5-3 and the 5-0, and it is here that we must employ some sort of evaluation function. What are the features that we should consider for such a function?

It is clear that one important aspect of dominoes lies in trying to prevent your opponent from putting down one of the dominoes in his hand, thereby forcing him to pick up from the shuffled set and putting off the time when he will have got rid of all his dominoes. So one feature must relate to the probability that the user will be able to put down a domino from his hand on the next turn. If the program now plays the 5-3, the user will have to play a 5 or a 3. The program can calculate the expected number of 5s and 3s in the user's hand simply by adding together the probabilities for the 5s and 3s. Similarly, the program can calculate the expected number of 5s and 0s (in case the program decides to play the 5-0). We shall call the expected number of moves by the opponent E.

Another important feature is the probability that after the user has moved the computer will have a legal move at its disposal and this feature should reflect the fact that the program would like to have as wide a choice as possible. This feature can also take advantage of the probabilities, albeit in a more complicated manner, as can be seen from the following discussion.

If the program plays a 5-3, the user has a number of theoretically feasible plays at his disposal. If we denote the dominoes assumed to be playable by D_a D_b D_c D_d . . . etc., and the probability of the user having each of these dominoes in his hand is denoted by $P(D_a)$, $P(D_b)$, $P(D_c)$, $P(D_d)$ . . . etc., then by making the approximation that the user is equally likely to make any of the legal moves at his disposal, we can derive the following measure for the expected number of legal moves at the program's disposal after the user's next move if the program chooses 5-3 at this move:

$$P(D_a) \times N_a + P(D_b) \times N_b + P(D_c) \times N_c + P(D_d) \times N_d + \ldots \text{etc.},$$

where N_a, N_b . . . etc., are the number of moves at the program's disposal should the user choose to play domino a, b . . . etc. (Note that in certain circumstances one domino can be played at either end of the chain, for example if the ends of the chain are a 6 and a 1, then the 6-1 domino can be played either way round. Each of these plays should be counted as a separate play for the purpose of counting the values of the N_a, N_b . . . etc.) We shall call this expected number of legal moves for the program EP.

One other feature which is useful to take into consideration is the number of pips on each of the dominoes that the program can play in a given situation. Since the losing player in a hand is penalised to the extent of the pips on his remaining dominoes, it is obviously a useful generalisation to play the domino with the highest pip count, all other factors being equal. But since this heuristic would result in very predictable play on the part of the program, in a way which an intelligent human opponent could use to his advantage, it would be wise to vary the play of the computer slightly by ensuring that a measure of randomness was used in the decision-making process. I would suggest that when the computer was ahead in the hand, ie when the user had picked up more dominoes from the shuffled set than had the computer, then weighting for this pip feature should be small, so that the program might play less predictably. When the program was doing badly, the weighting for this feature should be relatively large, so that if the user won the hand (as might seem likely) the program's loss on that hand would be minimised. When neither side seemed to have any advantage in a hand, the weighting should be somewhere between the two. We shall call the number of pips played PP.

Our evaluation function now looks like this: ($W_1 \times$ opponent's expected number of legal moves) + ($W_2 \times$ computer's expected number of legal replies) + ($W_3 \times$ number of pips played on this move) or, more symbolically:

$$W_1 \times E + W_2 \times EP + W_3 \times PP$$

Adjusting the probability table

After each play by the user it will be necessary to adjust the table of probabilities for all the remaining unseen dominoes. Obviously we gain the greatest amount of information when the user cannot make a move without picking up from the shuffled set, because at that time we know that he does not hold any of the dominoes which can legally be played. We therefore set the probability for each of these legal dominoes to zero, and normalise the probabilities for the remaining dominoes. We also learn a certain amount when the user actually plays a domino – he no longer has any likelihood of holding that domino in his hand since it is now on the table, so its probability is set to zero and again the remaining probabilities are normalised. In addition to these rather obvious situations, there are occasions when the program can derive useful information from the user's choice of which domino to play.

Let us assume, for example, that the ends of the chain show a 3 and 1, and that the program has previously shown itself to be out of 1s (having picked up from the shuffled set at a time when both ends of the chain showed a 1). Then, if the user does not play the 3-1 on the 3, which would be sure to deprive the program of a move and compel it to pick up dominoes ad nauseam, then it is safe to assume that the user does not hold the 3-1 (unless he is foolish). The probability for the 3-1 can therefore be set at zero and the remaining probabilities normalised. When considering such situations, the program should ensure that a play such as the 3-1 will not deprive the user of any legal moves, unless the user would then have many fewer dominoes than the program, in which case, with neither side being able to move, the computer would lose the hand.

For those readers who feel that the strategy described so far is lacking in real sophistication, there is one further refinement which would make the program outstandingly strong, but for the move execution time to be realistic your program would need to be written in assembler language. When the user has made a move, if the program has a choice of reply it should perform the following calculations.

For each and every possible combination of dominoes in its opponent's hand (of which there will never be more than about 39,000), the program should compute the scores which it will assign to each of the user's legal moves, and convert these scores into probabilities, by normalising them. It will then have, for each possible user holding, the probability with which each move would be made. The program then looks at the move actually made by the user, and uses Baysian probability to determine the probability that the move actually came from each of the possible holdings. Finally, knowing the probability that the user actually holds each of the possible holdings, the program can calculate a much more accurate estimate for the user holding each of the unseen dominoes that could be in his hand. This series of calculations can be done when the user makes his first free choice of play (ie ignoring situations in which the user moves first), and can retain this information throughout the hand. After the user's second free choice move, the program can combine the results of the two sets of calculations by determining the mean probability for each domino from the two calculations. The third time the program would weight the old and new calculations in the ratio of 2:1, to take into account the fact that the old calculations were made on the basis of two moves, while the new ones were made solely on the basis of the last move. The fourth time would see weightings of 3:1 and so on. This level of sophistication would probably produce a program of World Championship calibre!